You Can't Do It Alone

You Can't Do It Alone

A Communications and Engagement Manual for School Leaders Committed to Reform

Jean Johnson

Written in cooperation with Public Agenda
Foreword by Daniel Yankelovich
With special thanks to Jonathan Rochkind

ROWMAN & LITTLEFIELD EDUCATION

A division of

ROWMAN & LITTLEFIELD PUBLISHERS, INC.
Lanham • New York • Toronto • Plymouth, UK

Published by Rowman & Littlefield Education
A division of Rowman & Littlefield Publishers, Inc.
A wholly owned subsidiary of The Rowman & Littlefield Publishing Group, Inc.
4501 Forbes Boulevard, Suite 200, Lanham, Maryland 20706
http://www.rowmaneducation.com

Estover Road, Plymouth PL6 7PY, United Kingdom

British Library Cataloguing in Publication Information Available

Library of Congress Cataloging-in-Publication Data

Johnson, Jean, 1949–
    You can't do it alone : a communications and engagement manual for school leaders
committed to reform/Jean Johnson.
        p. cm.
    Summary: "You Can't Do It Alone provides school leaders with a crisp summary of
opinion research among teachers, parents, and the public conducted by Public Agenda,
Education Sector and other respected analysts. It offers tips on what leaders can do to
more successfully engage these groups in areas such as reforming teacher evaluation,
turning around low-performing schools, and building support for world-class
standards" —Provided by publisher.
    Summary: "Today, having good ideas for improving schools is not enough.
Superintendents and principals need to build a consensus for change in their
communities and within the schools themselves. Reform simply won't work unless
teachers, students, parents, and community members grasp the need for change and
begin to see themselves as part of the solution. You Can't Do It Alone explains what it
will take to engage these crucial groups in the mission of reform and offers practical,
down-to-earth advice on how to do it" —Provided by publisher.
    ISBN 978-1-61048-300-1 (cloth : alk. paper)—ISBN 978-1-61048-301-8 (pbk. : alk.
paper)—ISBN 978-1-61048-302-5 (ebook)
    1. School principals—Professional relationships.   2. Educational leadership.
3. School improvement programs.   4. Communication in education.   I. Title.
    LB2831.9.J64 2012
    371.2—dc23   2011039055

Printed in the United States of America

For Daniel Yankelovich, Deborah Wadsworth, and Ruth Wooden

Contents

Foreword by Daniel Yankelovich

Jean Johnson has written a wise and important book (as well as a mercifully short one). *You Can't Do It Alone* tackles head-on one of our nation's "must-solve" problems—the deeply flawed condition of our education system. As the world's economies grow more integrated and competitive, the education systems of other nations are improving, while ours—once the envy of the world—is falling behind.

This problem threatens our future standard of living and the promise of social mobility that lies at the heart of the American dream. The nation's implicit social contract is that Americans can improve their lot in life through their own hard work and education. This is the promise that holds us together. To the extent that our education system ceases to be competitive in world markets, we violate our nation's core belief system.

This threat to our way of life is no secret. It is the reason that so much frenetic energy is devoted to education reform. Everyone knows how high the stakes are. Through advancing a strategy for successful education reform that is fresh and original, Johnson offers the nation a strong dose of hope.

It would have been easy to criticize the key players—the teachers, unions, principals, superintendents, local school boards, parents, students and the public at large. Instead, Johnson brings a compassionate understanding to the struggles that all participants undergo as they attempt to navigate the system.

Johnson modestly calls her book "a manual" for leaders in the education reform movement. And it *is* a manual—chock full of research findings, guiding principles, and practical results. But it is far more than that. There are two features of the book that, when integrated with each other, make it an important contribution to how to think about education reform. One is the book's extraordinary amount of data on how the various participants in the world of education see themselves and their role in bringing about reform. These data place its reform strategy on a firm foundation of fact rather than opinion or ideology.

From the book's vast inventory of research findings, I've listed below those that strike me as particularly important—and surprising. They constitute a useful overview of the current state of our education system.

- **Importance of reform.** Unlike issues that evoke public ambivalence such as global warming, the public knows how vitally important this issue is. Seven out of ten Americans believe that it is urgent to improve our nation's schools.
- **Importance of college.** A generation ago, fewer than two out of five Americans (36 percent) regarded a college education as very important. That number has now more than doubled—to a whopping seventy-five percent majority.
- **New jobs demand higher education skills.** Government estimates are that nearly eight out of ten new jobs will require higher education.
- **Upgrading the quality of teaching.** Three out of four of the nation's school superintendents believe that improving the quality of teaching is job #1 in the school reform effort.
- **Teachers believe that discipline problems undermine their teaching.** Almost eight out of ten teachers cite problems with disruptive students as a major factor in preventing their teaching from being as effective as it should be. The current method—suspending disruptive students—is seen as highly ineffective and even counterproductive. Not surprisingly, a large number of teachers—four out of ten—state that they are disheartened and discouraged. The same proportion feels that their schools lack an "orderly, safe, and respectful school environment." And the vast majority of the public (75 percent) regards lack of respect for teachers as a serious problem.
- **A significant number of schools are dropout factories.** Fully half of the nation's high school dropouts come from twelve percent of the nation's schools. Dropout rates in these schools can be as high as fifty, sixty or seventy percent. Only about fifteen percent of schools in minority/poverty districts have teachers with significant experience, self-confidence, and effective methods of instruction.
- **Teachers feel left out of the reform movement.** Teachers experience the reform movement as something that is happening to them, rather than as a mission they are part of: seventy percent feel excluded from the decision process. And only seven percent of teachers rate standardized test scores as a sound measure of teacher performance. While teachers embrace some versions of pay for performance, they reject the assumption that student test scores are the right metric for judging performance.

- **The school principal—a key player.** Many facts converge on agreement that the school principal is the "secret sauce" either of school success or failure. Yet, only four percent of principals cite their academic preparation as being important in preparing them for their jobs.
- **Lack of student motivation.** Johnson refers to the widespread lack of student interest, motivation and engagement as the "elephant in the room"—a presence that can hardly be ignored but usually is. In my own view, unless this issue is addressed, the best-designed reform plans are likely to fail.

The other striking feature of *You Can't Do It Alone* is its emphasis on a few inescapable truths. These must be taken into account if education reform is to succeed.

As long as the American economy was producing an abundance of high-paying/low-skill jobs, our education system could afford to be highly selective, favoring the self-motivated and comfortable-with-school echelons of our nation's youth. But in recent years the United States has exported these kinds of jobs to low-wage nations, and they have just about disappeared from our economy. Our education system is now required to provide high-level skills to a far wider range of students—a task for which it is ill prepared.

As if this weren't difficult enough, many of our schools in low-income communities lack adequate community support. In these communities, parents and schools are uncomfortable strangers to one another. Most parents are too heavily burdened to be effectively involved with the schools. Johnson argues that without fullhearted community support and agreement on educational goals, it is difficult to see how the problems of overloaded principals, demoralized and undertrained teachers, and disruptive and unmotivated students can be fixed.

There are enough schools (mainly in middle- and upper-income communities) that do enjoy full community support to demonstrate that, under the right conditions, success is possible. When parents and the community do give their indispensable support, schools can and do carry out their educational mission. Johnson points out that the public doesn't place all the blame for failure on the schools. Average Americans acknowledge that they must share responsibility.

What I value most about Johnson's strategy is that it is developed within a fresh framework. It starts with listening. Her strategy is to listen attentively and respectfully to all the players—students, parents, and teachers, as well as leaders. She lauds the power of listening as the best way to turn critics into positive participants.

Inviting those who are most deeply affected to participate in shaping policies that directly impact their lives has always been important. But in today's culture it is indispensable. It is impossible to conceive of successful school reform without the active support of the community. Knowing how to bring the stakeholders into the tent, rather than leaving them outside, is also best practice for democracy. One of Johnson's most useful contributions is to draw upon the toolkit that the Public Agenda has developed over its 35-year history to bring creative listening, dialogue, and engagement into reasonably simple everyday practice in the interest of successful school reform.

Many of the prevailing reform ideas have been developed within the same stale elitist framework that currently dominates all forms of problem solving in American policy circles. This framework remains popular despite the fact that it doesn't work very well on issues that deeply engage the feelings and values of the American people. It is profoundly "elitist" because it depends so heavily on expertise and top-down solutions. Its dominant assumption is that, since the experts know best, they should shape policies and everyone else should dutifully fall in line.

Recognizing the need for public support, the elitist framework puts a lot of emphasis on PR, spin, and top-down communication. It doesn't see the need for serious listening to those who aren't experts, since it assumes that they cannot contribute substantively to policy. It favors "accountability" in the sense of precise measurement of outcomes, however remote from peoples' concerns these may be—as long as they are measurable. It is rife with specialization, since our culture of expertise is based on ever-narrower domains of specialized knowledge. Among one subgroup of experts—business leaders and economists—there is a tendency to want to import business and/or economic models whether or not they are genuinely suitable. For example, the insistence on pay for performance is based on the crude assumption that money transcends all other motivations—a gross distortion of reality in many domains, particularly in teaching. Pay for performance based on standardized test scores is a product of this distorted elitist framework.

This framework has become so prevalent that we have forgotten a simpler, more traditional American framework that puts emphasis on listening and engaging. The elitist framework with which we have grown all too familiar violates both democratic principles and common sense. It surely defies common sense to think that anyone would conduct teacher training without consulting the best and most experienced teachers. Or that the schools could gain an understanding of student motivation without talking to the students. Or that the vast majority of parents who want their children to do better at school need not be consulted about things they might do, even with limited means, to help their children.

This means that everybody needs to be confident they are listened to. Jean Johnson gives us the tools to make this happen.

—Daniel Yankelovich, Co-Founder, Public Agenda

Chapter 1

It's Enough to Make Your Head Spin

In my job at Public Agenda (a nonprofit research and engagement organization[1]), I have spent nearly 20 years exploring how different groups—parents, students, teachers, employers, and others—think about the challenges facing America's public schools. Public Agenda has conducted dozens of surveys, hundreds of focus groups, and scores of community forums talking to people across the country—individuals from all walks of life—about what's good, bad, and in-between in public education today.

When we conduct focus groups with principals and superintendents, something quite remarkable happens. Just as we begin to wrap up the session, after a good two hours or so of discussion, the participants often start trading business cards and e-mail addresses. Nearly every one of them wants to talk more. My sense is that principals, superintendents, and administrators nationwide are thirsty for meaty, down-to-earth discussions about the common challenges they face.

It's easy to see why. Being a school leader has never been more complicated. The job requires juggling a myriad of complex educational, managerial, regulatory, and financial responsibilities. School leaders are facing higher expectations and, in most cases, they're working with fewer resources. On top of it all, they are operating in an era of sweeping, almost head-spinning change.

Today, it's not enough to effectively manage the schools we have. Leaders need to stay abreast of scores of new ideas about teaching and learning. They need to absorb and sort through the new theories, models, and policies that seem to hurtle toward them daily. As leaders, it's just part of the job to "keep up" on new thinking. But here's the bottom line for me—and it's the rationale for writing this book:

1

If school leaders want to create long-lasting, sustainable improvement in public schools, they simply have to help teachers, parents, taxpayers, and others grasp the need for change and participate in it. They need to engage these groups much more effectively in the mission of reform.

ADDRESSING THE HUMAN FACTOR

You Can't Do It Alone focuses directly on this undertaking—how leaders can help key education stakeholders cope with change and engage them more effectively in improving public schools. Given everything school leaders have on their plates, it's easy to understand why this work often falls to the bottom of the list. But engaging these pivotal groups in meaningful dialogue about schools is much more than "good politics" or "good public relations."

In the most fundamental sense, genuine reform rests on the human factor—how teachers, students, parents, and the broader community think about and respond to change. People's ideas, assumptions, fears, motivations, concerns, even their passions can either drive change or derail it. In the end, it will be almost impossible for school leaders to spur long-lasting reform without an evolution in the attitudes, expectations, and habits of the human beings involved. Unless we address the human factor in education, even the best plans and strategies will unravel.

It goes without saying that school leaders need to have sound, well-thought-out ideas on how to improve schools and enhance learning. They need to weigh priorities and develop sensible ideas on how to get from here to there. Principals in particular need to analyze their own school's problems and identify practical ways to address them. But school leaders also need effective strategies for helping teachers, parents, students, and community members become allies and partners in reform, not just passive audiences, or constituencies to be managed.

Look at what's been happening in education in the last few years and consider the communications and engagement challenges that have emerged in the wake of change.

- The goals for K–12 education have undergone a seismic shift in the last generation. A whole cast of government, corporate, foundation, and community leaders is calling for higher high-school graduation rates, higher college completion rates, higher student achievement across all demographic groups, and significantly more emphasis on economically important subjects like science and math. According to U.S. government projections, "nearly 8 out of 10 new jobs will require higher education and work force training" over the next decade.[2] President Obama, for one, wants every student to complete at least one year of college-level study beyond high school, a step up that will allow the United States to regain its position of having the world's best-educated work force.[3] How do school leaders help families understand and prepare for this new environment?

- In states and districts nationwide, policymakers and education leaders are reimagining decades-old policies on teacher pay and evaluation and how teachers and principals work together. The new thinking here is tantalizing, and the laser-like focus on teacher effectiveness is long overdue. But change at this pace can be unnerving and threatening to teachers. How can principals and district leaders bring teachers into these discussions? How can leaders and teachers find common ground on policies that are fair and respectful to teachers and good for students as well?

- A new generation of teachers is coming into the profession—young adults with distinctive motivations and expectations. Meanwhile, school leaders need to attract and retain the very best teachers, and increasingly, principals are working side-by-side with their teachers to improve instruction. Principals are no longer just *school* leaders, they are *instructional* leaders as well. How can they be most effective in this new role? How can they build a common vision and sense of purpose among their teachers—especially the younger ones just coming into the field?

- Competing demands on state and local education funding have walloped school budgets, and most principals and superintendents are being asked to do more with fewer resources. In some cases, there's almost no room to maneuver. How can school leaders work with the community to do the most with what they have? How can they protect themselves and their schools against short-sighted decision making based solely on the need to quickly cut costs?

- The U.S. Department of Education has called on state and local school leaders to act boldly on persistently failing schools—the small percentage of schools often tagged as "dropout factories." The impetus for groundbreaking, even radical change is stronger than ever, and principals and superintendents are on the front lines. Unfortunately, rather than offering hope, calls for bold action often generate hostility and fear in the broader community. How can school leaders change this dynamic? How can they convert resistance to change into a genuine partnership for better schools?

- Finally, there's a new mindset about school leadership itself. To use the image that has emerged from Public Agenda research, principals and superintendents are increasingly expected to be "transformers" not just "copers."[4] Being a good manager and coping well with daily emergencies isn't enough anymore. To transform a school means changing the assumptions and customary habits of teachers and students and, in many cases, the broader community as well. How can school leaders push this new mindset forward?

In the following chapters, I present much more information on why outreach and engagement are so crucial to supporting and sustaining reform. *You Can't Do It Alone* also lays out new thinking on how to build "an informed public" for education (and other issues) stemming from the ground-breaking work of Public Agenda founder Daniel Yankelovich. A pioneer in the field of public opinion, Yankelovich argues that long-lasting change simply isn't sustainable without broad public buy-in. He believes that much of what leaders do today trying to get that buy-in is counterproductive at best.[5]

Using Yankelovich's work as a foundation, the book describes basic principles and strategies for engaging teachers, parents, voters, colleagues, and others to play constructive roles in the pervasive change sweeping public education today. This is a book about creating dialogue, finding consensus, and building the will to transform American schools into true centers of opportunity and learning.

In preparing the book, I have gathered and synthesized several different kinds of information that I hope school leaders will find thought-provoking and useful:

First, the book crystallizes Public Agenda's extensive body of opinion research on how different groups—teachers, parents, students, employers, the general public, and others—see public schools today and the degree to which each understands the need to move away from the status quo and embrace new ideas and ways of doing things. I have also incorporated useful insights coming from many other organizations and researchers. There is plenty of good information out there. Essentially, Chapters 3 through 10 are a guided tour to the attitudes and perceptions different stakeholders bring to the field's most important dilemmas and controversies. Since teachers are a crucial audience (and potential partner) for reform-minded leaders, I devote several chapters to their views, looking in particular at how younger and more-seasoned teachers see a whole range of professional and curricular issues. To me, understanding where people start is the precondition to establishing dialogue and more open and candid communications.

Second, the book presents the Yankelovich/Public Agenda model of how people typically learn about complex issues, adapt to new situations, absorb new information and realities, and come to reconcile their own sometimes conflicting values and priorities. After introducing the model, the book then offers more specific guidance on how school leaders in K–12 education can help key stakeholders cope with the extraordinary level of change we see in education today.

Last, the book explores how some school leaders have found new ways to bolster and cement reform by reaching out to their colleagues and communities, and it profiles some of the innovative work being done by my colleagues Will Friedman and Alison Kadlec through Public Agenda's public engagement initiatives. There are new models being developed and tested, and the track record so far is impressive. Superintendents, principals, and other district leaders are in a unique position to propel change by engaging teachers, families, and communities in meaningful dialogue about improving schools. There are practical, effective, proven strategies for bringing diverse groups to the table. There is no reason school leaders have to go it alone.

Based on what I have seen in our research at Public Agenda, being a school leader is gratifying, absorbing, and hardly ever boring. It can also be exhausting and isolating. One participant in a Public Agenda study put it this way: "You're the only principal. You make the decisions. . . . It can be very lonely." But principals and other school leaders are also powerful agents of change.

My goal here is to offer down-to-earth advice on ways to address the deeply human issues that can enhance or stall educational change. My hope is that this book, growing out of what I have learned in my work at Public Agenda, can spur school leaders to tackle this new mission with enthusiasm and self-assurance and forearm them to do it well.

NOTES

1. You can find out more about Public Agenda at www.publicagenda.org. The website houses Public Agenda's extensive opinion research on education and other issues and offers advice and materials on both community and leadership engagement.

2. White House Fact Sheet, *Building American Skills by Strengthening Community Colleges,* 2010, http://www.whitehouse.gov/sites/default/files/White_House_Summit_on_Community_Colleges_Fact_Sheet.pdf.

3. "College for All," Inside Higher Education, February 25, 2010. http://www.insidehighered.com/news/2009/02/25/obama.

4. Public Agenda, *A Mission of the Heart: What Does It Take to Transform a School?* Conducted for The Wallace Foundation, 2008, http://www.publicagenda.org/files/pdf/missionheart.pdf.

5. See for example, *Don't Count Us Out,* Public Agenda and the Kettering Foundation, 2011, http://publicagenda.org/dont-count-us-out.

Chapter 2

Mind the Gap

When the Alliance for Education, a respected advocate for world-class standards in U.S. public schools, surveyed Americans in 2009, the results showed a broad appetite for reform. About two-thirds of the public said that it was "urgent" or "extremely urgent" to improve elementary (64%) and middle schools (67%). Nearly three-quarters (73%) said the same about U.S. high schools.[1]

Moreover, nearly 8 in 10 Americans said that they were either "extremely" or "very concerned" about the number of minority students who don't graduate from high school, along with the number of high school students who get diplomas, but still aren't ready for college-level work. The survey takers included statistics on high school dropouts and college readiness in the questions in order to get a more accurate picture of the public's views.[2]

Looking at these numbers, you could be forgiven for assuming that Americans across the country are impatient for change and receptive to groundbreaking new ideas on how to improve education. And in part, they are. But as we'll discuss in subsequent chapters, public and parental ideas about public education are more complex than these survey results suggest, and to some extent ambivalent. Americans' views on schools are traditional in some areas and more innovative in others. They are looking for reform in some spheres, even as they resist it elsewhere.

If this seems like a confusing and unpredictable public opinion environment, education leaders should be reassured—they are actually in a better situation than leaders in many other sectors. Americans do believe that education is important to the country's future and crucial to their own children's chances in life.[3] Even Americans without school-age children are interested in schools and want good ones in their communities.[4] The public is arguably better informed about public education than they are about issues like energy and foreign policy.

However, there is still a huge gap in perspective between how school leaders think about improving schools and what's on the minds of much of the public. Most Americans know very little about how schools are regulated and funded. The disputes and tensions that preoccupy education professionals—accountability standards, federal mandates, and the like—are often barely on the public's radar. At the same time, the public has some major concerns about public education that get comparatively little attention in the expert domain.

Most seriously perhaps, far too many parents are not adequately informed about what their children need to learn in order to succeed in a far more competitive international economy. In some 20 years of observing public-school parents in focus groups, I can honestly say that I have never seen a mom or dad who didn't care whether their child succeeded or failed in school. Yet it is also clear to me that some families have very little grasp of how to help their children thrive in school, and many currently lack the ability to do so.

David Mathews, who served as secretary of health, education, and welfare for President Ford and now leads the Kettering Foundation, has written about an even more troubling gap. Mathews worries that the once-strong bond between schools and communities has frayed over the years. "Kettering Foundation research," Mathews writes, "found a number of people who don't equivocate in saying that the public schools are not *their* schools. . . . Some without children enrolled may argue that schools are the parents' responsibility. Parents, on the other hand, may see the schools as tax-paid utilities. . . . As consumers, their job is to watch educators the way they would watch a cashier counting change."[5]

That could be a problem. If parents see education as something schools provide and they consume and pay for, they may not fully recognize their own responsibilities in helping children thrive in school. If parents and citizens fail to see local schools as *their* schools—as valued institutions that belong to them and exist for them—they will be less likely to give schools and the children attending them the support they need and deserve.

TWO WRONG WAYS TO REACT TO PUBLIC OPINION

Given the iffy state of public opinion on education and other issues, it's not uncommon for leaders, experts, and the media to wring their hands and bemoan the country's future. Some see the public's lack of knowledge and sophistication as an unmovable barrier. They dismiss public thinking because it's not "informed," and they try to work around it. Some take matters into their own hands and push solutions forward without extensive public discussion or support. This kind of top-down approach can work for a while, and it may be successful (and even warranted) in some discrete areas that aren't especially important to the public. But it is extremely difficult to sustain long-lasting reforms in schools if they involve fundamental changes that go against the grain of what most people expect and want. In the long run, a top-down approach undercuts democratic government which rests at least in part on the idea that citizens should have a say in how problems get solved.

At the opposite end of the spectrum, some leaders pander, seemingly willing to comply with existing public opinion regardless of the long-term consequences. Their policy is "go with the flow." In the worst instances, they avoid addressing genuinely urgent issues because the public is not focused on them—or because addressing them forthrightly might arouse public opposition.

The way national elected officials have handled the federal budget over the years is an exceptionally dispiriting example. For decades, they increased spending on popular programs like Social Security and Medicare and cut taxes because that's popular too. Now that the country's debt has exploded to treacherous levels, elected officials are in a political vise. Much of the public isn't realistic about what it will take to solve the problem. Postponing the hard decisions puts the country's economy and standard of living at risk. It's not a good place to be.

WHAT'S A SCHOOL LEADER TO DO?

For education leaders, responding to public opinion sometimes poses a keen dilemma. On one hand, education leaders need to take the public's views seriously. After all, public education relies on taxpayer dollars, and it provides services to people's children. It would be arrogant and irresponsible to dismiss Americans' values and priorities entirely.

On the other, some of the most historic reforms in education were pushed forward before they had broad public support. This country would be a poorer place—ethically, spiritually, and economically—if leadership had stood by waiting for public majorities to support desegregation or equal education opportunities for minorities, women, and other underserved groups.

So the question is how to bridge the gaps in understanding and perspective that often surface between school leaders and parents and the broader public. Of course, these aren't the only critically important groups involved. Reaching out to teachers is paramount, and much of this book is specifically devoted to engaging teachers in school reform.

UNDERSTANDING WHERE PEOPLE START

To me, bridging these gaps involves several basic tasks. One is for leaders themselves to develop a more nuanced, accurate picture of the attitudes and concerns that parents, teachers, and other important groups bring to school reform. Another is to become more familiar with some of the new thinking about how people learn about issues and how they adapt and adjust when faced with new problems and challenges. A third is taking a look at some very practical strategies for engaging more Americans in more thoughtful discussions about specific issues in education.

There's also the problem of deciding when engagement is needed and when it's probably not worth the time it would take to do it. School leaders can't possibly mount outreach and engagement initiatives on every issue or dispute that crops up. Trying to take every controversy in education "out to the public" would be monumentally counterproductive. That's not what leadership is about. The better path is to target outreach and engagement to the issues where they are likely to do the most good.

What would those be? When there are huge, potentially troublesome gaps between the way leaders see an issue and the way other groups are thinking about it. In these instances, better outreach and engagement can be enormously helpful. There are also areas where forming partnerships with parents, teachers, and the broader community can contribute to stronger, more lasting solutions.

School leaders already have a very long "to do" list. But here are four reasons why putting more effective outreach and engagement on that list could move reform forward.

1. **Schools can't do it alone.**
   Most Americans—both within and outside of education—can identify problems in the schools that need to be solved. If nothing else, the country can no longer live with inadequate levels of learning among so many young Americans, given the intensity of worldwide economic competition. But the truth is that schools and teachers will be hard-pressed to succeed with nation's most disadvantaged children— those who most need and deserve society's help—if they act alone. Problems like truancy and dropping out are quintessentially problems schools can't solve by themselves. They require action from the community as a whole—parents, grandparents, mentors, community and religious groups, businesses, and local agencies. To tackle problems like these, schools need a community-wide resolve to act, and that means school leaders need to find effective ways to generate and support it.

2. Schools and school leaders are pulled in too many directions.

Much of the hope and responsibility for transforming schools falls to super-intendents and principals, and there is strong research showing that they are the pivotal players.[6] But Public Agenda's surveys also show that they are constantly pulled in many directions, and that they are typically surrounded by individuals and groups, all of whom think their own particular issue is the most important one. What can school leaders do to help people coalesce around some broadly backed, well-chosen goals so that real progress is possible? How *do* you get people singing off the same song sheet?

3. Teachers are rattled.

Public Agenda's surveys show many teachers are troubled by the pace of reform and worried about what is expected of them and how new policies will work. Even teachers who are lukewarm about traditional teacher evaluation and compensation policies have questions about whether new policies will be respectful of the important work they do. The research also shows definitively that when teachers admire and trust their school leaders, they are far more open to and sometimes even enthusiastic about change. How do principals and superintendents reach out to teachers to bring them into these discussions? How do they help teachers understand what lies ahead and reassure them that change will be fair-minded and carefully thought through?

4. Too much of the public is naïve about the challenge.

Whether it's coming from elected officials like President Obama or entrepreneurs like Bill Gates, there is an extraordinary leadership consensus that the American workforce will need much higher levels of learning to compete in the new knowledge-based global economy. But much of the public hasn't yet focused on what it will take to meet this challenge. There are also warning signs that many may be taken aback when the drive to ratchet up learning really hits home—when, perhaps, a local high school ups the ante on math and science requirements or when schools transfer resources away from long-standing, popular programs to beef up academic courses and attract the best teachers. When people are caught unprepared, they sometimes react in counterproductive ways. When they understand the challenge and why it matters, they can be part of the solution.

THERE ARE LIMITS TO "MESSAGING"

The changes facing schools today involve fundamental shifts in the way teachers, students, and parents conduct their daily lives. To succeed, new policies and reforms require authentic support in the community and confidence and purposefulness in classrooms.

Building this support is not easy. Standard public relations strategies, even if most districts could actually afford them, generally don't work well for changes of this scope. Even the most carefully developed message or beautiful set of public service advertisements can't build the relationships required to address problems like truancy or lack of parental support for learning. Messaging doesn't reassure teachers who are worried that new evaluation, compensation, and tenure policies will be unreasonable or poorly executed.

MIND THE GAP AND REACH OUT

Building consensus, improving communications, and seeking out feedback have always been elements of strong leadership in the schools and elsewhere. To my mind, they have become even more essential for leaders committed to pushing change forward.

If you happen to be from New York City, or you visit the city and ride the subway, you know that the title of this chapter, "Mind the Gap," is the transit authority's helpful advice on exiting the train. In stations where the train stops right beside the platform, you can bound right off and be on your way. But in some stations, there is a gap between where the train door opens and the platform surface some inches away. If you "mind the gap," you'll take an extra large step, and you'll be fine. If you don't know about the gap, or you ignore it, you can break your ankle or worse. (Don't even think about it, which is another good New York expression.)

For school leaders, minding the gap means knowing how the concerns of other key stakeholders in education may differ from yours (at least initially). And it means developing the skills to create the kind of authentic dialogue that will help resolve these differences. And whether you're riding the subway or dealing with your fellow humans, "minding the gap" takes some effort and persistence, but it is definitely better than getting tripped up by it.

NOTES

1. Alliance for Education, June 2010, Pages 1–2, http://www.all4ed.org/files/071410PollReleasePublicQuestionnaire.pdf.

2. Alliance for Education, Page 8, http://www.all4ed.org/files/071410PollReleasePublicQuestionnaire.pdf.

3. See, for example, Public Agenda, *Are We Beginning to See the Light?* Prepared for the GE Foundation, Full Survey Results, December, 2009, http://www.publicagenda.org/pages/math-and-science-ed-2010#Methodology.

4. See, for example, Phi Delta Kappa/Gallup Poll, *Highlights of the 2010 Phi Delta Kappa/Gallup Poll,* September, 2010, http://www.pdkintl.org/kappan/docs/2010_Poll_Report.pdf.

5. David Mathews, *Why Public Schools, Whose Public Schools,* NewSouth Books, 2003, Page 11.

6. See the extensive work of The Wallace Foundation on educational leadership at http://www.wallacefoundation.org/KnowledgeCenter/KnowledgeTopics/CurrentAreasofFocus/EducationLeadership/Pages/default.aspx.

Chapter 3

The Indispensable Compact—Why Engaging Teachers Is Job No. 1

Most school leaders aren't in much doubt about what leads to better schools and higher levels of student learning. For three out of four superintendents, improving the quality of teaching is job number one.[1] When members of the American Association of School Administrators were asked to rank nearly a dozen different ideas for developing good schools, more than three-quarters put the spotlight on teaching. In comparison, only about a quarter chose ideas such as improving parent participation or using more technology."[2]

The next few chapters take an in-depth look at how teachers nationwide are thinking about the top issues in public education today. Chapter 4 focuses on teachers' views about reforms in teacher evaluation and compensation. Chapter 5 explores the degree to which younger teachers think differently about their jobs than their older colleagues. Chapter 6 examines how teachers are responding as principals around the country take more active roles as instructional leaders and classroom coaches.

This chapter, however, takes a step back from the specifics and focuses on teacher morale and the prevailing concerns many teachers bring to their jobs. For superintendents, principals, and administrators, understanding and anticipating the mindset teachers bring to current education debates can help anticipate some of the adverse reactions to reform—reactions that often delay or derail needed change.

LIVING ON THE SAME PLANET

Many principals and superintendents were teachers before moving into their current positions, and most have a good grasp of how teachers see things. But school leaders are also charged with improving schools, while most teachers are focused primarily on their own students and classrooms. What's more, the pace of change in education is hitting the two groups in very different ways. As much as school leaders fret about mandates and regulations, they play a dominant role in determining what will and will not happen in their districts and schools. Most are in fact propelling change, pushing forward on a list of reforms and improvements aimed at ramping up student learning.

Teachers, in contrast, often see "school reform" as something that is happening to them—not as a mission they're part of. Even though most teachers say they love teaching itself,[3] and the vast majority support higher standards and expectations in public schools, many are also unnerved and demoralized by much of the "reform movement." Moreover, research and analysis by Public Agenda, among others, shows persuasively that teachers' views on key reform issues varies dramatically depending on whether they respect and admire their principals.

It is important to understand the concerns and sense of disillusionment that affects so many teachers today. It is also important to know that teachers' views can change with good leadership.

ARE TEACHERS THE PROBLEM?

When *Time Magazine* reviewed the documentary film, *Waiting for "Superman,"* its headline read "Are Teachers the Problem?"[4] For those who haven't seen the film, it chronicles the experiences of several low-income families struggling to get their children out of low-performing public schools and into more effective charters. Reviewer Richard Corliss called it "edifying and heartbreaking" and applauded it for spotlighting "the coddling of bad teachers by their powerful unions [which] virtually ensures mediocrity, at best, in both teachers and the students in their care."[5]

Many in public education, and teachers especially, perhaps, considered the film a slap in the face, a compelling, but manipulative assault on teachers and public schools overall. The American Federation of Teachers, for one, said that it relied on "a few highly sensational and isolated examples in an attempt to paint all public school teachers as bad."[6]

But perhaps the most important point to make here is that many teachers felt beleaguered and under attack long before *Waiting for "Superman."* In

2003, a Public Agenda survey found that 76 percent of teachers agreed that teachers were being made the "scapegoats for all the problems facing education."[7] This question was included in the survey because the idea—that teachers are being blamed for failures in public education that are beyond their control—emerged repeatedly in focus groups conducted earlier.

The teaching profession can't be immune to criticism, and teachers shouldn't be praised or rewarded just for showing up or just because they "try hard." The students have to come first. But if large numbers of teachers sense that they are under assault or misunderstood or disrespected, that's not conducive to good schools either.

THE KEY MESSAGES FROM THE OPINION RESEARCH

Here are some of the broad perceptions and concerns among teachers that leap out of the research, both from Public Agenda and other groups such as Education Sector and the FDR Group:

Finding No. 1: Most teachers believe they have been left out of conversations on improving schools and enhancing learning, even though they have vital, firsthand knowledge to offer.
When Public Agenda conducts focus groups with teachers on reform plans in their own districts, we are often surprised by how little teachers know about the new policies and how often their reactions reflect rumors or piecemeal information rather than what school leaders have actually proposed. With so little clarity and so much confusion, it's probably not surprising that many teachers are unsettled by the prospect of change. For example:

- Seventy percent of teachers nationwide say they feel they are often "left out of the loop" in their district's decision-making process.[8] Fully 8 in 10 agree that "although they are on the front lines, teachers are rarely consulted about what happens in their schools."[9]
- Seventy percent say that when district leaders talk with them about school policy, it's only to win their support for "what the district leadership wants to accomplish." Fewer than a quarter (23%) say it's "to gain a better understanding of the issues and concerns" of teachers.[10]
- Many teachers question whether their own union genuinely seeks their input: only 31 percent say that a large number of teachers are involved in union decisions; 51 percent say most are made by a "small group of deeply engaged veteran teachers and staff."[11]

Finding No. 2: Most teachers believe lack of student effort and parental support are undermining their ability to raise achievement for all students.
In the minds of many teachers, one of their chief worries gets considerably less attention than it deserves. While the education debate swirls about common standards and differential pay, most teachers see lack of student effort and parental support as one of the preeminent obstacles to effective teaching. The problems run the gamut from students who disrupt classes to those who text in class to those who cheat or are repeatedly truant. Then there are the parents who insist that their little darlings can do no wrong. The specifics vary, but there is a strong prevailing sense among teachers that they need better student cooperation and effort—and they need the parents to back them up—to do an effective job. They alone cannot deliver strong academic results.

- More than three-quarters of secondary teachers (76%) say that if it "weren't for discipline problems" they could be "teaching a lot more effectively."[12]
- Eighty-five percent of secondary teachers say the school experience of most students suffers because of "a few persistent troublemakers."[13]
- Nearly 7 in 10 teachers (68%) say that removing "students who are severe discipline problems" from regular classes and placing them into alternative programs would be a "very effective way" to improve teacher effectiveness.[14] For comparison's sake, just 8 percent think that tying teacher pay to student performance would be a "very effective way" to increase teacher effectiveness.[15]
- Half of high school teachers (49%) say that "lack of student effort" is the main reason some of their students won't be ready for college. Another 15 percent say it's "lack of encouragement from family and friends."[16]
- Asked to choose between working at "a school where student behavior and parental support were significantly better," or a "school that paid a significantly higher salary," more than 8 in 10 teachers of all ages chose the school with the better environment over the one that offered more money.[17]

Results like these (and there are plenty more in teacher surveys) show that concerns about motivating students and insuring that classes are orderly enough for the teacher to teach and the kids to learn aren't confined to a subset of teachers who lack good classroom management skills. This is an issue that troubles great swaths of the field. In fact, teachers who aren't worried about it at all are the exception rather than the rule.

Finding No. 3: Two out of five teachers are "disheartened" about their jobs.
In 2009, Public Agenda joined with Learning Point Associates, now part of American Institutes for Research (AIR), to conduct a national, in-depth survey of 890 public school teachers nationwide.[18] This lengthy survey included questions on how teachers view their schools, their leaders, their students, and the

field as a whole. The overall results are interesting (and quoted liberally in this book), but the most intriguing part of the study was an analysis of how teachers break out into three distinct groups: the "Disheartened," the "Contented," and the "Idealists." Each group has distinctive priorities and concerns:

Disheartened teachers: "It's a wonder more teachers don't burn out." About 40 percent of teachers were considered "disheartened" in their jobs based on their responses to a number of questions.

- Disheartened teachers were twice as likely as other teachers to "strongly agree" that teaching is "so demanding, it's a wonder that more people don't burn out." More than 7 in 10 said they "strongly" agreed with this statement and another 24 percent agreed "somewhat."
- More than 7 in 10 said that "too many kids with discipline and behavior issues" is a major drawback of teaching—at least 30 points higher than the other groups.
- Seven in 10 saw testing as a major drawback to teaching.

ARE YOUR TEACHERS REALLY ON BOARD? SIX SIGNS OF A DISHEARTENED TEACHER

One of the most troubling findings from the Public Agenda/AIR national survey of classroom teachers a few years ago is that some 4 in 10 teachers across the country are disheartened and frustrated in their current jobs. The researchers used a "cluster analysis" to sort and group the teachers' answers to more than 100 separate questions, and then divided the teachers into three groups based on their responses: the Idealists (23%), the Contented (37%) and the Disheartened (40%).[1]

Table 3.1 lists some of the questions where the responses of the Disheartened teachers differed dramatically from the responses of the Idealist and Contented teachers. For school leaders, attitudes like this are warning signs that something is wrong. It may be that an experienced teacher is burnt out or that a new teacher is not really suited to the field. Answers like these can also be a strong indicator that there may be administrative or management problems at a school—that teachers aren't getting the support they need and deserve. Whatever the cause, answers like these should prompt school leaders to sit up and take notice.

1. All findings concerning "Contented," "Idealist," and "Disheartened" teachers are from Jean Johnson, Andrew Yarrow, Jonathan Rochkind, and Amber Ott, *Teaching for a Living: How Teachers See the Profession Today,* http://www.publicagenda.org/pages/teaching-for-a-living-full-survey-results.

Table 3.1.   Disheartened Teachers: The Six Questions That Tell the Story

	How Disheartened Teachers See It	*How Other Teachers See It*
1. Teaching is so demanding, it's a wonder that more people don't burn out. Do you strongly agree, somewhat agree, somewhat disagree, or strongly disagree with this statement?	73% "strongly agree."	Fewer than 4 in 10 Idealist or Contented teachers say the same.
2. There's a lack of support from administrators. Is this a major drawback to teaching, a minor drawback, or not a drawback at all?	61% see this as a major drawback of teaching.	Fewer than 1 in 10 Idealist or Contented teachers see this as a major problem.
3. There are too many kids with behavior and discipline issues. Is this a major drawback to teaching, a minor drawback, or not a drawback at all?	72% saw this as a major drawback of teaching.	Only 24% of Idealists and 41% of Contented teachers see this as a major drawback.
4. There's too much testing. Is this a major drawback to teaching, a minor drawback, or not a drawback at all?	70% say this is a major drawback of the field.	About half of Idealist and Contented teachers see testing as a major drawback.
5. When it comes to having an orderly, safe, and respectful school atmosphere, are the working conditions at your school very good, manageable, or a serious problem?	Fewer than 3 in 10 say their schools are very good in this respect.	Nearly 7 in 10 Idealists and 76% of Contented teachers give their schools "very good" ratings here.
6. Overall, how would you rate your current principal? Making decisions that improve your school? Excellent, good, fair, or poor?	Just 8 percent give their principals "excellent" ratings in this area.	Over half of Idealist and Contented teachers say their principals are "excellent" in this area.

Source: Public Agenda

- More than 6 in 10 said lack of administrative support is another major drawback at their schools.
- More than half of disheartened teachers taught in low-income schools.

Idealists: "Helping underprivileged kids is why I choose to teach."
About 1 in 4 public school teachers (23% of the sample) counts as an idealist. Nearly 8 in 10 teachers in this group (78%) said that helping underprivileged students was one of the main reasons they became a teacher. Among this group:

- Eighty-eight percent believed that "good teachers can lead all students to learn, even those from poor families or who have uninvolved parents"—the highest percentage of any group.
- Three-quarters said student effort is "mainly determined by what teachers do" rather than preexisting student motivation—again a higher percentage than any other group.
- More than half were younger teachers (32 or younger) and nearly 6 in 10 taught in elementary school.
- Forty-five percent taught in low-income schools.
- Thirty-six percent said that, although they intended to stay in education, they plan to leave classroom teaching for other jobs in the field.

Contented teachers: "Teaching is exactly what I wanted."
The remaining teachers, about 37 percent of the teachers surveyed, are quite satisfied and comfortable in their jobs, and most seem to be in a school that supports and values them.

- Sixty-three percent of contented teachers said they "strongly agree" that "teaching is exactly what I wanted," a higher percentage than the other groups.
- Seventy-six percent said they have very good working conditions when it comes to an "orderly, safe, and respectful school atmosphere"—the highest percentage of any group studied.
- More than 7 in 10 said they have enough planning time to create high quality lesson plans—again, the highest percentage of the three groups.
- Only 26 percent considered low pay a major drawback of teaching.
- Nearly two-thirds (64%) taught in a middle-income or affluent school, and nearly everyone in this group (94%) had been a public school teacher for more than 10 years.

These findings of course don't indicate how well these different categories of teachers actually perform in the classroom. The "idealistic" or "contented" teachers may not be effective in improving student learning even though their outlook is upbeat. Some "disheartened teachers" may do a good job teaching despite their low morale. The problem in this case is that effective teachers who are disheartened may leave the field because their work lives are so stressful.

Finding No. 4: A good principal makes all the difference.

The majority of teachers feel that they have been overlooked in the movement to redesign and reform schools and improve student learning. Similarly large numbers believe that promoting better student and parent cooperation should be a centerpiece of the reform. And clearly a large group of teachers is struggling. But one of the major differences between teachers who are thriving in today's reform climate and those who are at sea is whether they see their principals as helpful and supportive.[19] Take a look at Table 3.2. The differences can be striking:

Table 3.2.   Teachers Who Admire and Respect Their Principals Versus Those Who Don't

	% Among Teachers who Give their Principals "Fair" or "Poor" Ratings for Supporting them as Teachers	% Among Teachers who Give their Principals "Good" or "Excellent" Ratings for Supporting them as Teachers
Agree strongly that "teaching so demanding that it's a wonder more teachers don't burn out."	68%	44 %
Consider "kids with discipline and behavior issues" a major drawback of teaching.	64%	45%
Consider "too much testing" a major drawback of teaching.	70%	54%
Worry that principals might use performance-based pay to "play favorites."	87%	50%. Ideally, this figure should be lower. See Chapter 4 for more.
Say teachers facing "unfair charges from students or parents," have no place to turn but the union.	64%	44%. Again, it would be better if more teachers believed that they could count on their principals' support.

Source: Public Agenda

IS IT JUST VENTING?

Some level of carping and second-guessing is to be expected in any field, and most of us view a little grousing on the job as a basic human right. The question is whether and how school leaders should address these concerns and complaints from teachers. Based on everything I have seen looking at opinion studies in education over the years, these findings are strong. The numbers are large—70, 80, almost 90 percent of teachers in some cases. Surveys also show a remarkable consistency. Different questions worded in different ways get similar results. And these are findings that have been strong for years. They didn't just pop up suddenly when Race to the Top was launched or when *Waiting for Superman* was released.

THE TAKEAWAYS

School leaders can mull over these results and think about the degree to which they apply to the teachers they work with. They can also evaluate the degree to which concerns like these can be addressed without undercutting reforms to improve student learning that simply have to go forward. But given the overall teacher mindset laid out here, here are some key takeaways as I see them.

Takeaway No. 1: We need to invite teachers to the table on reform. They need to understand and take responsibility for change alongside leadership and administration.
School leaders can't assume that their teachers understand the whys and wherefores of major reforms as well as they do, especially those stemming from federal and state initiatives. The research shows this time and time again. These issues may dominate school leaders' discussions and plans, but teachers are often much less clear on the details and much less knowledgeable about how changes will affect their jobs and schools. For most teachers, the focus of their work is on their own students and classes, not on system-wide reforms. Even those who are following the debates may feel that their views don't matter and wouldn't be welcome even if they sought out greater involvement.

What's more, considering teachers' insights about how changes will play out in the classroom and getting the benefit of their experiences working directly with students and parents is essential. Teachers have ideas that can improve schools, enhance student learning, and help make reform stick.

If we want teachers to enlist in the movement to advance education's power and impact for all students, we simply have to do a better job here. Reform is going to be very tough sledding as long as teachers see it as something that is happening to them, rather than something they are a part of.

Takeaway No. 2: If 40 percent of teachers are disillusioned and disheartened about teaching, that can't be good for kids.
If studies showed that 40 percent of U.S. soldiers were disillusioned or disheartened about their mission, we would have hearings in Congress and the Joint Chiefs would be organizing task forces to remedy the situation. Public education will be hard put to fulfill its goals if the "troops on the ground" are so demoralized.

The answers aren't easy, and they certainly demand solutions tailored to different districts and schools. Some of these teachers probably shouldn't be teaching. If they don't yet have tenure, school leaders should be on the lookout for this sense of disillusionment. It would be better for these particular teachers if they found more suitable careers sooner rather than later—teaching doesn't always work out. Some more experienced teachers may need to be eased out of the profession or perhaps moved out of the classroom into other areas in education. Some of these teachers may be in schools where they are not getting the leadership and support they deserve. In different circumstances, they may flourish. The chief message for me, though, is that this situation can't be ignored. It demands a leadership response.

Takeaway No. 3: Is it time to talk about the elephant in the room?
Responsible and compassionate adults don't blame students for poor educational outcomes. In the end, as adults, this is our responsibility. And, in fact, three-quarters of teachers believe that "good teachers can lead all students to learn, even those from poor families or who have uninvolved parents." But that doesn't mean that teachers always have the time, resources, and support they need to reach all of their students. Nor does it mean that lack of student effort and lack of parental support are trivial obstacles that any teacher can easily overcome. And by the way, based on what we see in the survey research, problems of poor student effort and uninvolved parents are not confined to low-income schools—not by any means.

Today, there is a concerted attempt to learn more precisely what makes some teachers more effective than others. (It's about time. Most people outside education probably assume that research like this was conducted long ago.) Maybe it's time for a similarly concerted effort to learn more about what motivates and engages students so that teachers can tap into this powerful force. Meanwhile, school leaders need to talk more with their own teachers, parents, and students about alternatives for improving student behavior and enhancing student cooperation and effort. There are some specific ideas about how to launch this conversation later in the book.

Takeaway No. 4: Never underestimate the power of a good principal—or the damage unleashed by an incompetent one.
In Public Agenda's school leadership study, *A Mission of the Heart,* we distinguished between principals who are "transformers" and principals who are "copers." To some degree, coper principals share the mindset of disheartened teachers—a feeling of being overwhelmed and barely able to cope with existing circumstances. And like disheartened teachers, their potential to lead schools effectively should be evaluated on a case-by-case basis. Some may not have the potential to be transformative principals. Some may need more training to take on the job. Some may not have the autonomy and support they need to be effective. It's hard to be a transformer with your hands tied behind your back. What's not in doubt is that the quality of school leadership has a major impact on whether teachers fear and resent reform or whether they accept and grow with it.

Education Secretary Arne Duncan has said that Americans should "dramatically improve respect and admiration for teachers,"[20] and publicly recognizing good teachers and finding ways to reward them financially and otherwise should certainly play a role in that. But all the prizes and bonuses in the world may not produce the results we want unless teachers feel included in the reform movement and believe that they will get the support they need to be effective in the classroom.

NOTES

1. *In Education, Change Is the Status Quo: An AASA Survey of School Superintendents,* American Association of School Administrators, 2010, Page 4, http://www.aasa.org/uploadedFiles/Policy_and_Advocacy/files/AASAPDK-Gallup PollFINAL083010.pdf.

2. Ibid.

3. See, for example, Jean Johnson, Andrew Yarrow, Jonathan Rochkind, and Amber Ott, *Teaching for a Living: How Teachers See the Profession Today,* Survey by Public Agenda and Learning Point Associates/AIR, Originally published in *Education Week,* October 21, 2009, http://www.publicagenda.org/pages/teaching-for-a-living-full-survey-results.

4. Richard Corliss, "Are Teachers the Problem?" *Time Magazine,* September 29, 2010, http://www.time.com/time/arts/article/0,8599,2021951,00.html#ixzz1AFZkCNtq.

5. Ibid.

6. "Not Waiting for Superman," American Federation of Teachers, http://www.aft.org/notwaiting/.

7. Steve Farkas, Jean Johnson, and Ann Duffett with Leslie Moye and Jackie Vine, *Stand by Me: What Teachers Really Think About Unions, Merit Pay and Other Professional Matters,* Public Agenda, 2003, Page 12, http://www.publicagenda.org/files/pdf/stand_by_me.pdf.

8. Steve Farkas, Patrick Foley, and Ann Duffett, with Tony Foleno and Jean Johnson, *Just Waiting to Be Asked? A Fresh Look at Attitudes on Public Engagement,* Public Agenda, 2001, Page 31, http://www.publicagenda.org/files/pdf/just_waiting_to_be_asked.pdf.

9. Ann Duffett, Steve Farkas, Andrew J. Rotherham, and Elena Silva, Waiting To Be Won Over, Education Sector, May 2008, Page 18, http://www.educationsector.org/usr_doc/WaitingToBeWonOver.pdf.

10. Steve Farkas, Patrick Foley, and Ann Duffett, with Tony Foleno and Jean Johnson, *Just Waiting to Be Asked?,* Page 18, http://www.publicagenda.org/files/pdf/just_waiting_to_be_asked.pdf.

11. Steve Farkas, Jean Johnson, and Ann Duffett with Leslie Moye and Jackie Vine, *Stand by Me,* Page 48, http://www.publicagenda.org/files/pdf/stand_by_me.pdf.

12. Public Agenda, *Teaching Interrupted: Do Discipline Policies in Today's Public Schools Foster the Common Good?* Public Agenda and Common Good, 2004, Page 45, http://www.publicagenda.org/files/pdf/teaching_interrupted.pdf.

13. Ibid.

14. Jean Johnson, Andrew Yarrow, Jonathan Rochkind, and Amber Ott, *Teaching for a Living: How Teachers See the Profession Today,* Survey by Public Agenda and Learning Point Associates/AIR, Originally published in *Education Week,* October 21, 2009, http://www.publicagenda.org/pages/teaching-for-a-living-full-survey-results.

15. Ibid.

16. Scholastic and the Bill & Melinda Gates Foundation, *Primary Sources, America's Teachers on America's Schools,* 2010, Page 56, http://www.scholastic.com/primarysources/pdfs/Scholastic_Gates_0310.pdf.

17. Jane G. Coggshall, Ph.D., Amber Ott, Ellen Behrstock, and Molly Lasagna, *Supporting Teacher Talent: The View From Generation Y,* Full Survey Results, Public Agenda and Learning Point Associates/AIR, 2010, http://www.publicagenda.org/pages/supporting-teacher-talent-view-from-Generation-Y-topline.

18. All findings concerning "Contented," "Idealist," and "Disheartened" teachers are from Jean Johnson, Andrew Yarrow, Jonathan Rochkind, and Amber Ott, *Teaching for a Living: How Teachers See the Profession Today,* http://www.publicagenda.org/pages/teaching-for-a-living-full-survey-results.

19. Public Agenda and Learning Point Associates/AIR, *Retaining Teaching Talent,* Full Survey Results Analyzed by Principal Ratings, 2009. Contact info@publicagenda.org for additional details.

20. "Secretary Duncan on Supporting Teachers, Ed.Gov Blog, November 2010, http://www.ed.gov/blog/2010/11/secretary-duncan-on-supporting-teachers/.

Chapter 4

Change the Rules and People Are Bound to Get Upset

It's had a lot of different names over the years—merit pay, incentive pay, performance pay, differential pay. But whatever you call it, the idea of rewarding teachers financially, based on how effective they are in the classroom, has taken center stage among school leaders at the national, state, and local levels.

For superintendents, principals, and school administrators, decisions to introduce performance pay (we'll use that name here) suggest a series of other changes as well. If you're going to reward teachers based on their classroom effectiveness, you need a way to judge it. If you identify especially effective teachers, you probably want to find ways to get other teachers to adopt their most successful techniques. If you identify teachers who are routinely ineffective in helping students learn, then you need to figure out how to ramp up their effectiveness or, in some cases, persuade them to leave the classroom.

On paper at least, devising a plan to tie teachers' pay to their impact on student learning seems reasonably straightforward. You devise a way to judge each teacher's performance, set up a system for adjusting teacher pay on the basis of that performance, get the powers that be to approve it, and then tell the teachers about the new policy so that they'll be motivated to do their best. But in real life, everything is different:

- **Right now, there is no definitive answer on how to determine which teachers are the most effective and which are less so.** There's a grab bag of tools—student test scores, classroom observations, and peer review are the main ones—but no one system has been fully vetted and proved superior. Researchers are working on this[1] and coming up with some fascinating and potentially important results. But for leaders in public schools, it can

27

seem like the entire public education system is in the midst of a nation-wide professional development experiment. After decades of perfunctory or nonexistent teacher evaluation, the fact that researchers, reformers, district leaders, and teachers themselves are taking a closer look at what works and what doesn't is welcome news. But it also presents a challenge for school leaders. You need a system, and there's no foolproof recipe for creating one.

- **Figuring out the best way of tying teacher pay to performance is tricky.**[2] There's a whole series of questions here. Is it better to set up a system designed to reward and retain the very best teachers, or should you shoot for a system that ties compensation for all teachers to their performance? How do you organize a system that's fair to teachers who are working with students who are struggling? How do you organize a system that's fair to teachers who teach different subjects—some of which have clear standards and specific testing protocols and some of which don't? How do you transition from a system that barely even collected information on each teacher's impact on his or her students to one where a paycheck is based on it?

- **Many teachers are doubtful and resentful.** For many teachers, the national push to revamp long-standing policies on teacher evaluation and pay is just another piece of evidence that reformers 1) don't care what teachers think, and 2) have no idea how hard teaching is. Surveys show that teachers have decidedly mixed feelings about how these reforms will work in practice if they are implemented. Nearly three-quarters of teachers worry that performance-pay plans will create "unhealthy competition and jealousy" among teachers; 6 in 10 say principals might use it to play favorites or reward teachers who "don't rock the boat."[3]

  In focus groups, teachers often see these kinds of reforms as an implied criticism that they don't work hard enough (when most teachers think they work pretty hard already, thank you very much). Many teachers seem perplexed by the implication that they could conjure up improved student test scores if they just put in a little extra effort. This may not be the message that performance-pay advocates want to send, but it is often how teachers see it. That puts a real onus on school leaders to change this dynamic.

- **You can tell people what to do, but the top-down approach may not produce the results you want.** Almost all of us have to do things we don't want to do and live with circumstances that we didn't choose—we pay taxes and put money in parking meters and try to behave nicely in airport security lines. Even the president has to follow the Secret Service's rules. But when leaders are aiming to change people's ideas about how to do their jobs, just spelling out the rules and expecting everyone to follow them can backfire. First of all, you can end up with people fighting you every step of the way, which eats up time you need for other educational missions that are crucial too. Second, you can end up with a demoralized, resentful, and distrustful workforce—if you need their support for other reforms down the road, it will be much harder to get them on board. And finally, you may miss something important if you don't consult the people who are actually doing the teaching every day in the classroom. A cornerstone of good management in just about every field is conferring with employees who are actually doing a job before making major decisions on how to improve the way it's done. It's true for corporate CEOs and military generals, and for school leaders too.

SCHOOL LEADERS HAVE TO IMPLEMENT THE CHANGES

In the past decade, much of the impetus for retooling how teachers are evaluated and compensated has come from national reformers and/or state-level decision makers—not as much from district leaders directly. Even so, it will be superintendents and principals who have to make the plans work in real life.

Since many school leaders have been classroom teachers, and since many are themselves subject to new evaluation and performance-pay policies, most aren't tone deaf to the teacher perspective. In fact, many school leaders themselves have questions about whether performance pay and related changes on evaluation and tenure belong right at the top of the school reform agenda. When Public Agenda surveyed superintendents and principals about the idea of tying teacher pay to performance several years ago, only 1 in 10 saw it as a "very effective" way to make schools better. The change preferred by most school leaders was making it easier to remove the very worst teachers in their schools—most saw this as potentially more effective than performance-pay plans.[4]

But most school leaders aren't in a position to design their own change agendas or create their own preferred policies on teacher evaluation and pay, or dismissal for that matter. Despite these limitations, however, superintendents and principals are playing powerful roles as implementers and communicators. What can school leaders do to carry out these reforms in ways that are fair and respectful of teachers, but also fair to students, families, and the tax-paying public? How can they take advantage of these changes and use them to build trust and common cause with their teachers?

THE KEY MESSAGES FROM THE OPINION RESEARCH

Working with our partner AIR, Public Agenda has conducted extensive research on teachers' views on evaluation and compensation issues over the last few years, as have other researchers. Here are some important wrinkles to consider:

Finding No. 1: Despite their overall doubts about the performance-pay movement, most teachers support rewarding teachers who excel in specific areas.
In fact, strong majorities of teachers say that giving extra financial rewards to teachers who work in low-performing schools, with struggling students, and who consistently work harder and are more effectively advancing student learning is something that they support.[5] Take a look at Table 4.1 showing how teachers rank various ideas for financially rewarding teachers who excel in various ways:[6]

Finding No. 2: Opposition to performance pay centers mainly on the idea of basing it on student test scores.
As a group, teachers make some sharp distinctions between some forms of performance pay and others, and, as Table 4.1 clearly shows, the idea of basing it on standardized test scores comes out dead last. In the Public Agenda/ AIR research, fewer than half of the teachers supported it, and in part this reflects broader reservations teachers have on testing overall. Only about 1 teacher in 10 sees student scores on state tests are an excellent way to judge student learning. In contrast, about four times as many (46%) think student engagement in class is an excellent measure.[7] A survey of teachers by the Gates Foundation asked a similar question and got similar results. While 60 percent of the teachers surveyed said that student engagement is a "very accurate" measure of the teacher's performance, just 7 percent said the same about "student grades on standardized tests."[8]

Most teachers have learned to live with standardized tests as a part of education, even if they haven't come to love them. Most teachers consider "too much testing" one of the major drawbacks of teaching, and 7 in 10 say that "student test scores are less important than a lot of other measures" when it comes to judging student progress.[9] In the end, though, most accept standardized testing as a "necessary evil," acknowledging that "ultimately, the schools need some kind of standardized assessment.[10]

For most teachers, the pushback comes when they fear that student test scores will be used as the sole or primary arbiter of how well they teach or how much they earn. Both major teachers' unions have endorsed using test

Table 4.1.   Majorities of Teachers Favor Many Forms of Performance Pay

How Much do you Favor or Oppose Giving Financial Incentives or Merit Pay to Each of the Following Groups of Teachers?	% of Teachers Saying they Strongly Favor	% of Teachers Saying they Somewhat Favor	Total % in Favor
Teachers who work in tough neighborhoods with low-performing schools	31%	40%	71%
Teachers who teach classes with hard-to-reach students	27%	41%	68%
Teachers whose kids consistently show academic growth during the school year	29%	37%	66%
Teachers who consistently work harder, putting in more time and effort than other teachers	32%	33%	65%
Teachers who receive certification from the National Board for Professional Teaching Standards	22%	38%	60%
All the teachers in the school if the students routinely score higher than similar students on standardized tests	21%	35%	56%
Teachers who consistently receive excellent evaluations by their principals	16%	37%	53%
Teachers who specialize in hard-to-fill subjects such as science or mathematics	16%	33%	49%
Teachers whose students routinely score higher than similar students on standardized tests	11%	35%	46%

Source: Public Agenda

scores as one of several elements in teacher evaluation, but to stake everything on test scores, well, most teachers just don't think that's fair. In fact, 77 percent say that it's "not fair" to attach teachers' paychecks to student outcomes because "so many things that affect student learning are beyond their control."[11]

Finding No. 3: When it comes to motivating teachers, performance pay is only one consideration among many.
Nearly all of us are motivated to some extent by the possibility of earning more money, but teachers seem less motivated by it than many other professionals. It's obvious in some ways, isn't it? No one enters public education hoping

to make a bundle. Salary and the chance for advancement are not deciding factors when most teachers choose the field. The top reasons, according to the Public Agenda/AIR work, are being able to teach a subject they love and having a teacher who inspired them when they were in school.[12]

Public Agenda has repeatedly asked teachers questions that offer them a choice between a school with higher pay versus one with better parent involvement or administrative support, and, every time, the results are not even close. Most teachers want a better working atmosphere where they can be effective and flourish in their work, and in surveys they routinely pick these qualities over the chance to increase their salaries.[13]

Most teachers also seem entirely comfortable with the way they have been paid for decades. Asked to choose between a school where they can get bonuses "based on the principal's evaluation and their students' progress" versus one that has "tenure and a guaranteed raise of three percent each year, but no opportunity for bonuses or merit pay, nearly three-quarters of teachers say they're willing to forego the bonuses.[14]

This doesn't mean that money is irrelevant to teachers—that's only true for people with trust funds. Being able to reward teachers who do excellent work in high-needs schools with students who struggle with academics could have an impact—most teachers themselves support this approach, and research by Frank Adamson and Linda Darling Hammond for the Center for American Progress suggests that extra pay targeted to effective young teachers could be useful in persuading them to stay in teaching and work in the most challenging schools.[15]

If performance pay helps here, it will be a welcome breakthrough. But teachers' reasons for staying in the field and choosing to work at some schools over others reflect a complex set of considerations. Performance pay may play a positive role, but teachers will also need good leadership, training, and support to thrive. Money alone may not turn out to be the "killer app" some reformers hope.

Finding No. 4: Teachers want other changes much more. Public Agenda has been asking teachers what kinds of reforms would improve their effectiveness in the classroom for nearly a decade, and, over time, the answers haven't changed much. Proposals to institute some form of performance pay come out at or near the bottom in survey after survey. Proposals to reduce class size, improve discipline policies, and give better professional support routinely come out on top. Most teachers simply don't believe performance pay will do much to change what happens in the classroom or in their schools. In focus groups, teachers often point out that they are motivated mainly because they enjoy teaching and want to do a good job for their students—not because of money.

So what does all this mean? That most teachers are afraid of being judged? Some may be, but most aren't. In fact, surveys show that the majority of teachers would like more feedback on their teaching from principals and colleagues. Does it mean that most teachers don't think there's any way to determine which teachers are sensational and which are less so? Nope. That's not it either. The vast majority of teachers (about 8 in 10) say most of the teachers in their own building could pretty much agree on who the really great teachers are.[16]

Nor does it mean that performance pay is doomed to be unpopular, and that school leaders are going to have to hunker down and just shove it through. What it does mean is that school leaders need to find ways to bring teachers into discussions about teacher evaluation and performance pay. Schools don't have to (and probably can't) give teachers a veto over these policies, but they do need to include them in dialogue on how the plans will work in their own schools. In this chapter, that's really the one and only takeaway.

Takeaway No. 1: Talk to your teachers about these issues.
In 2010 and 2011, Public Agenda and AIR began an experiment called "Everybody at the Table" which tested different ways to engage classroom teachers in discussions about how to evaluate and reward excellent teaching in their own districts. At first blush, maybe this seems like a naïve, goody-two-shoes endeavor, but, in fact, the results so far have been remarkable. What happened in this experiment should wipe away the assumption that teachers reject any and all changes to the status quo and want no part of this discussion. Here's what we saw and what it means for school leaders implementing new-teacher evaluation and performance-pay plans:

- **Don't assume they know.** Teachers are much less familiar with the various options for evaluating teachers and incorporating performance pay than many experts and leaders presume. In fact, one important takeaway is that some of the resistance and skittishness among teachers stems from the fact that school leaders haven't clearly explained what may happen and how it will work. Yes, there may be a memo or press release somewhere outlining the plan, but based on what I've seen in the research, most teachers just don't really know what's in the works in their districts—and that makes them nervous.
- **Don't assume they don't care.** When Public Agenda researchers asked teachers in different district and working in different circumstances to think through some different approaches to teacher evaluation and pay, nearly every one of the dozens of typical teachers who participated dove right into the discussion. They plunged in with eagerness and interest. The

vast majority did so with noteworthy good will, motivated by the idea of improving results for kids and making themselves into the best teachers possible. School leaders need to find ways to tap into this mindset. The vast majority of teachers really do want to be effective and successful in their jobs—that should be the rationale for improving teacher evaluation. It's one that just about every teacher Public Agenda has interviewed would respond to.

- **Don't assume their minds are shut.** The quick research recap in this chapter reveals several areas where teachers are ambivalent—that is, they have some conflicted thinking in their own minds that they need to work through. Here's how one young Chicago teacher interviewed for the Public Agenda/AIR project talked about the upside and the downside of performance pay: "As a teacher, I think the bonus is a motivation, but it's not our end-all motivation. I think we'd be motivated period." Not unlike many other teachers we interviewed, she values the idea of being financially rewarded for her hard work, talent, and initiative. Yet she also wonders why other people don't understand that she also brings a lot of innate pride, idealism, and professionalism to her work. Giving teachers (and their local school leaders) the chance to talk about and think about these mixed feelings can change conversations about performance pay from vitriolic and threatening to inclusive and productive.

- **Dialogue moves the needle.** For a lot of school leaders the idea of sitting down to talk with teachers about teacher evaluation and pay for performance probably sounds about as enjoyable as a root canal. But the effect of dialogue—having the chance to look at different options and talk about them with other teachers and with principals, administrators, or superintendents—can be "magical." It's an odd word to bring into a discussion of public schools and performance pay, but "magic" is the word Public Agenda founder Dan Yankelovich uses in the title of his book on using dialogue to solve problems in corporate and public policy settings—it's called *The Magic of Dialogue: Transforming Conflict into Cooperation.*[17] As Yankelovich spells out, dialogue is not just any conversation. It's a special technique that has been tested and proven in his work and the work of others. It's a technique that I describe in considerably more detail in Chapter 10. For now, though, let's just say that dialogue reduces anxiety and helps people feel less like victims and more like colleagues. It helps people, including teachers, work through their own ambivalences and conflicted feelings. It can help dissolve some of the mistrust and resentment teachers feel at the changes "being forced on them." And dialogue conveys one extraordinarily crucial message—that teachers' views are important and that school leaders want to hear and consider them.

- **There is help available.** Developing better ways to evaluate teachers and reward the best ones is a national educational mission, and this is one place where superintendents and principals really do not have to go it alone. The "Everyone at the Table" project resulted in some practical, well-tested video and print materials that school leaders can use to open a conversation with teachers locally. There is complete information about the project at www.everyoneatthetable.org.

WHEN IT'S TIME FOR THEM TO GO

Across the country, school leaders are working to develop new policies on teacher evaluation and pay as part of a national drive to enhance teaching quality. To the degree that better evaluation systems can be marshalled to help teachers teach more effectively, both students and teachers will benefit. To the degree that new compensation policies help districts hold on to talented teachers and help attract more of them to low-performing schools, the nation will win as well.

In the interim, however, most school leaders say there's another policy change that would help them even more—streamline the process for getting inferior, substandard teachers out of the classroom.

Unless they do something that's absolutely off the wall.
In Public Agenda surveys, more than 7 in 10 superintendents and principals say that "making it much easier" for them to remove ineffective teachers—even those with tenure—would be a "very effective way" to improve school leadership.[1] Add in the school leaders who think this idea would be at least somewhat effective, and you have a supermajority in favor of going this route. In fact, it's pretty hard to find a school leader who doesn't think streamling this process would be helpful.

For most school leaders, removing teachers who are clearly incompetent is an uphill battle. More than 9 in 10 school leaders say that it would be very or somewhat difficult for them to get a tenured teacher out of their schools within a year, even if they were "extremely dissatisfied" with said teacher's performance.[2] As one principal complained in a Public Agenda focus group, "It takes one year and one-half to get rid of a tenured teacher unless they do something that's just absolutely off the wall."[3]

There's evidence that the broader public is concerned too. According to a 2011 Rasmussen Reports poll, 63% of Americans say it is too hard to get rid of poor teachers. Among those with children currently going to school, the concern is even higher: 73 percent say it's too difficult now to remove teachers who aren't doing a good job.[4]

Nearly half of teachers say they know someone who should go.
It may come as something of a surprise to those who don't actually talk to teachers much that most also see problems in the process. Research by the FDR Group and Education Sector shows that more than half of teachers (55%) say that, in their own district, "the process for removing teachers who are clearly ineffective and shouldn't be in the classroom—but who are past the probationary period—is very difficult and time-consuming." Just 13 percent of teachers gave their own district's process a thumbs up, although about a third of teachers (32%) admitted that they didn't really know.[5] What's more, nearly half of the teachers (46%) said that they personally know a teacher who is "clearly ineffective and shouldn't be in the classroom.[6] About the same number (49%) said that the teachers' union "sometimes fights to protect teachers who really should be out of the classroom."[7]

Politicians and pundits sometimes paint a picture of school leaders battling for change while teachers cling resolutely to the details of union contracts—even to the point of protecting teachers who aren't doing their jobs. The reality is more subtle and more reassuring. Most teachers do value the unions' role in defending teachers accused of wrongdoing or being ineffective. They want to make sure that teachers get a fair hearing rather than being summarily fired.[8]

1. Jean Johnson, Ana Maria Arumi, and Amber Ott, *Reality Check 2006, Issue No. 4: The Insiders: How Principals and Superintendents See Public Education Today,* Public Agenda, 2006, Page 17, http://www.publicagenda.org/reports/reality-check-2006-issue-no-4.

2. Public Agenda, *Reality Check 2006, Issue No. 4: The Insiders: How Principals and Superintendents See Public Education Today.* Contact info@publicagenda.org for additional information.

3. Steve Farkas, Jean Johnson, and Ann Duffett with Beth Syat and Jackie Vine, *Rolling Up Their Sleeves: Superintendents and Principals Talk About What Is Needed to Fix Public Schools,* Public Agenda, 2003, Page 32, http://www.publicagenda.org/reports/rolling-their-sleeves.

4. Rasmussen Reports, "63% Say It's Too Hard To Get Rid of Bad Teachers," February 7, 2011, http://www.rasmussenreports.com/public_content/lifestyle/general_lifestyle/february_2011/63_say_it_s_too_hard_to_get_rid_of_bad_teachers.

5. Ann Duffett, Steve Farkas, Andrew J. Rotherham, and Elena Silva, *Waiting To Be Won Over,* Education Sector, May 2008, Page 23, http://www.educationsector.org/usr_doc/WaitingToBeWonOver.pdf.

6. Ibid.

7. Ibid., Page 21.

8. See for example Jean Johnson, Andrew Yarrow, Jonathan Rochkind, and Amber Ott, *Teaching for a Living: How Teachers See the Profession Today,* Survey by Public Agenda and Learning Point Associates/AIR, Originally published in *Education Week,* October 21, 2009, http://www.publicagenda.org/pages/teaching-for-a-living-full-survey-results.

NOTES

1. The Gates Foundation, for example, is supporting the work of a number of researchers through its Measures of Effective Teaching (MET) project. The multi-year initiative "seeks to uncover and develop a set of measures that work together to form a more complete indicator of a teacher's impact on student achievement." The work, in the Foundation's words, may eventually "transform how teachers are recruited, developed, rewarded, and retained." http://www.gatesfoundation.org/united-states/Pages/measures-of-effective-teaching-fact-sheet.aspx.

2. Again, a number of different groups are developing guidelines for plans that districts can use as a starting point. The Center for Teaching Quality has one developed by "a team of accomplished American teachers." For more, see Performance-Pay for Teachers: Designing a System that Students Deserve at http://www.teachingquality.org/legacy/TSP4P2008.pdf.

3. Public Agenda and Learning Point Associates/AIR, *Retaining Teaching Talent,* 2009, http://www.publicagenda.org/pages/supporting-teacher-talent-view-from-Generation-Y-topline.

4. Jean Johnson, Ana Maria Arumi, and Amber Ott, *Reality Check 2006, Issue No. 4: The Insiders: How Principals and Superintendents See Public Education Today,* Public Agenda, 2006, Pages 17–18, http://www.publicagenda.org/reports/reality-check-2006-issue-no-4.

5. Public Agenda has included questions about "merit pay," and "financial incentives" in a number of studies using different wording to describe the concept. Question wording does not seem to affect the results to any substantial degree.

6. Public Agenda and Learning Point Associates/AIR, *Retaining Teaching Talent,* http://www.publicagenda.org/pages/supporting-teacher-talent-view-from-Generation-Y-topline.

7. Ibid.

8. Scholastic and the Bill and Melinda Gates Foundation, Primary Sources: America's Teachers on America's Schools, Scholastic, 2010, Page 41. http://www.scholastic.com/primarysources/pdfs/Scholastic_Gates_0310.pdf.

9. Public Agenda and Learning Point Associates/AIR, *Retaining Teaching Talent,* http://www.learningpt.org/expertise/educatorquality/genY/FullSurveyData.pdf.

10. Ibid.

11. Ibid.

12. Ibid.

13. Ibid.

14. Ibid.

15. Frank Adamson and Linda Darling-Hammond, "Speaking of Salaries: What It Will Take to Get Qualified, Effective Teachers in All Communities," Center for American Progress, May 2011, http://www.americanprogress.org/issues/2011/05/pdf/teacher_salary.pdf.

16. Public Agenda and Learning Point Associates/AIR, *Retaining Teaching Talent,* http://www.learningpt.org/expertise/educatorquality/genY/FullSurveyData.pdf.

17. Daniel Yankelovich, *The Magic of Dialogue,* Touchstone, 2001.

Chapter 5

Are Younger Teachers Different, and What Can School Leaders Do to Keep the Best Ones in the Classroom?

Roberta Flack, Bill O'Reilly, comedians Andy Griffith and Billy Crystal, not to mention Gene Simmons, the KISS guitarist.[1] There are quite a few of the rich and famous who were teachers when they were younger. A widely reported story is that Simmons lost his teaching job in Harlem when he replaced the Shakespeare play in the curriculum with Spiderman comics, thinking the comics would be more likely to entice his students to read.[2]

It's hard to say whether the teaching profession and the students of America are better or worse off because these people left education for other endeavors. But the fact is that a lot of people "used to teach," and that brings up a set of tough interconnected issues facing school leaders today:

- Many of today's teachers will be retiring over the next decade. According to a 2009 report from the National Commission on Teaching and America's Future (NCTAF), over half of the current teaching corps are baby boomers. In 18 states and the District of Columbia, more than half of the teachers are over 50.[3]
- Replacing teachers, and hiring and cultivating new ones is expensive and challenging to any principal or superintendent.
- Many teachers leave the field in the first few years. According to NCTAF, "half of new hires are replaced every five years" in some districts.[4]
- Between 2004 and 2008, the number of Gen Y teachers (those born after 1977) doubled.[5]

School leaders need to figure out how to attract top teaching talent and how to work effectively with a new generation of teachers. Engaging these younger teachers in improving their schools and enhancing student success is crucial if the United States is going to build the public education system we need for the future. Luckily, the question of how younger teachers think about the profession and the challenge of teaching—and whether school leaders need to develop new and different strategies for working with them—is a topic that has interested a number of researchers and experts.

A couple of years ago, Public Agenda, working with AIR,[6] surveyed nearly 900 public school teachers nationwide and compared the views of those under age 32—so-called Gen Y teachers—with the views of older colleagues. The study included questions about the teachers' motivations for entering the field, their ideal work environment, their views on improving schools and teaching, and how they think about the "hard factors" of the job, such as pay and the chances for advancement.[7] Education Sector and the FDR Group have examined teachers' views on pay and performance, unions, and career development, again taking a special look at younger teachers' attitudes.[8] And AIR joined with the American Federation of Teachers to explore what kind of professional development and administrative support would enable younger teachers to do their best and persuade them to remain in the field.[9]

THE KEY MESSAGES FROM THE OPINION RESEARCH

So what do younger teachers want and expect from teaching? What do they hope to contribute to it? Are they sufficiently different from older teachers so that school leaders need to rethink their ways of working with and managing these younger members of the teaching corps?

Here's where the classic teenager's response, "sort of," is right on the money.

Finding No. 1: Younger teachers are less likely to see teaching as a lifelong career.
Just over half of younger teachers (56%) say they see teaching as a lifelong career compared to about three-quarters of teachers 33 and older.[10] Part of this difference is undoubtedly due to the fact that younger teachers are just that—younger—and just starting out in their adult work lives. Many people in many professions test out different careers before settling on one. Older teachers have been teaching long enough to know whether it's a field that suits them; many younger teachers may still be searching for the right career fit for them.

A fair number of younger teachers (42%) say they might leave the classroom for another kind of education career, while just 15 percent of the older teachers say this.[11] One young teacher interviewed in a Public Agenda/AIR focus group summed up her take this way: "I just think . . . people who are always classroom teachers and never branch out into other parts of education . . . start to get a little wacky after a while."

As a group, younger teachers are more likely than older colleagues to say that they chose to teach specifically to help youngsters from poor families have a better chance in life.[12] Some may see this as something they want to do "for a while." Others may gauge their interest in staying in the profession by the degree to which they believe they are successful in accomplishing this goal.

Finding No. 2: Younger teachers are somewhat more interested in performance pay.

This finding emerges in both the Public Agenda/AIR and the Education Sector/FDR research, and several factors seem to be at work. Some experts have speculated that younger teachers—in the Gen Y generation—have a different mindset about work and reward. Clearly some do, but in the research I have reviewed, the appeal of performance pay seems to be more practical than ideological. Since younger teachers, unlike their older colleagues, haven't gotten "used to" a system based on seniority, many don't find the idea of a change particularly threatening or noteworthy. And in most circumstances, younger teachers are at the low end of the pay scale, so performance-pay plans offer them an avenue for augmenting what they earn.

But there is an important caveat here. Even though younger teachers tend to be more open to performance-pay proposals, fewer than half support proposals to tie an individual teacher's pay to his or her own students' test scores.[13] In fact, younger teachers' judgments about performance pay follow precisely the same pattern as the judgments of older teachers. They are most likely to support it for teachers who invest extra effort and excel in working in challenging schools and with struggling students.[14] Like their older colleagues, most younger teachers worry that performance-pay plans may create rivalry among teachers or result in principals playing favorites.[15]

Finding No. 3: Younger teachers may also be more interested in nontraditional approaches to pensions and tenure and less supportive of unions.

Younger teachers are more likely to prefer a 401K-type retirement plan rather than a traditional pension—39 percent of younger teachers veer toward private accounts versus 29 percent of older teachers.[16] And nontenured teachers (who are typically younger) are more likely to voice interest in trading tenure for a $5000 pay increase—about 4 in 10 would make the trade compared to about 25 percent of tenured (and typically older) teachers.[17] Fewer than a quarter of teaching newcomers say that "being in the union provides feelings of pride and solidarity."[18]

But despite these differences, most younger teachers are not calling for a radical break with traditional professional arrangements. Younger teachers may be less attached to unions, but most also say that without them teachers might be vulnerable to school politics and that their salaries and working conditions might be "much worse."[19] And only 30 percent of those who have been teaching for less than five years think that offering new teachers higher salaries in exchange for smaller pensions is a good or excellent way to improve the profession.[20]

Finding No. 4: Younger teachers know that teaching is hard. Most are looking for help.
According to the Public Agenda/AIR work, more than 9 in 10 Gen Y teachers strongly (41%) or somewhat (53%) agree that teaching is "so demanding that it's a wonder that more people don't burn out."[21] Not surprisingly, then, most younger teachers are eager for advice and counsel from both principals and other teachers on how to improve their effectiveness and comfort level in the classroom. This is a key dimension of working with younger teachers—one that's examined in more detail in Chapter 6.

HOW MUCH CAN SCHOOL LEADERS DO?

For school leaders, getting younger teachers off on the right foot and taking steps to reduce the churn among teachers in their districts is a major challenge. What's more, principals and superintendents don't control all the factors, nor do they write all the rules on pay and promotion. At first glance, it might appear that school leaders have relatively little impact on whether talented young teachers stay in the field or whether they leave for careers that pay more—and often pay considerably more—for jobs that aren't nearly as hard.

But principals especially can have an enormous impact on young teachers' decisions about whether to stay or go. Equally important, school leaders also play a central role in determining whether younger teachers develop the skills and confidence they need to be effective in the classroom if they do stay in the field.

THE TAKEAWAYS

Based on what younger teachers say when they are asked about what would help them become better teachers and get more satisfaction out of their jobs, here are some major themes.

Takeaway No. 1: Don't assume that all younger teachers have radically different views about pay, retirement, tenure, and other professional factors.

The research shows that many younger teachers are interested in nontraditional professional arrangements, but at this point, most still aren't. In the Public Agenda/AIR study, one question gave teachers (younger and older teachers) a choice: Would you rather work in a "school that has tenure and a guaranteed raise of three percent each year, but no opportunity for bonuses or merit pay," or one "that does not offer tenure and set raises, but [where] teachers can receive extra pay based on the principal's evaluation and their students' progress"? Robust majorities of both groups chose the traditional arrangements—67 percent of the younger teachers and 75 percent of the older ones.[22]

In focus groups for the project, very few younger teachers even brought up the topic of pay for performance, tenure, or pension arrangements. Most were far more interested in talking about their classes, colleagues, administratrators, the parents, and the students. For experts and reformers, professional and pay arrangements are a hot topic, but there's little evidence that most younger teachers are strongly pushing for change here. Many are somewhat dispirited by the idea that some of their college classmates are earning substantially more than they earn as teachers, and academic researchers have found, for example, that increasing teacher salaries overall can increase the number of college graduates willing to enter the profession.[23] But in Public Agenda/AIR research, even the idea of raising teacher salaries to the level of salaries for doctors and lawyers (something most districts couldn't even begin to consider) wasn't especially tempting; fewer than half of younger teachers (47%) throught it would be a very effective way to improve the field.[24] Most young people who choose to teach know that they're not going to rake in the cash. Nearly 7 in 10 first-year teachers say that it is possible for a teacher to make a reasonable living.[25]

As a group, younger teachers may be more open to and somewhat more interested in innovative plans on compensation, promotion, tenure, and such, but there's no evidence (at least so far) that these issues are pivotal factors in whether individuals become teachers, whether they become effective, and/or whether they leave the field after a few years.

Takeaway No. 2: Don't assume that younger teachers have radically different views about what would improve teaching and schools.

Based on multiple studies of teachers' views on how to improve the profession and help more children achieve in school, teachers have a lot in common regardless of age.

Look at Table 5.1 listing a dozen different ideas for improving teaching, along with the rankings of younger and older teachers.[26] The same four items occur at the top of each list—better training to teach in diverse classrooms, help with students who have discipline issues, smaller classes, and better technology. And the same four ideas are at the bottom—tying pay to student performance, eliminating tenure, testing teachers on their subjects, and grouping students by ability. And the gap in level of support is huge. More than half of all teachers say the top four ideas would be "very effective;" fewer than 1 in 4 see the bottom four items as especially useful.

The takeaway here is that most teachers, regardless of age, are looking for changes that affect how their classrooms work, not changes in compensation and promotion policies. That doesn't mean salary, tenure, and related issues aren't important, but it does suggest that school leaders can play an enormous role in helping teachers be (and feel) more effective, even though they don't set all the rules.

Takeaway No. 3: Do assume that younger teachers want and need advice about becoming more effective teachers.

If school leaders put in the effort to attract and hire gifted young teachers, and they give them the guidance and counsel they need to be genuinely effective in the classroom, how can they reduce the likelihood that the best ones will leave for more lucrative opportunities? After all, teaching doesn't pay as much as business or finance or the law, and in tough economic times, most states probably aren't going to be offering substantial raises for even stellar teachers. Pay-for-performance bonuses will always look puny compared to Wall Street.

So what can school leaders do to keep their best young teachers when they don't really hold all the cards? The answer is: quite a bit. Most teachers of all ages show a remarkable preference for working in schools with supportive administrators as opposed to schools where they could earn more. Furthermore, opinion research among teachers shows strongly that one of the best predictors of how they view their jobs is how they rate their principals.

Principals can help teachers feel supported rather than isolated. They can encourage collaboration, or they can undercut it. They can make young teachers feel comfortable asking for advice, or they can imply that they should be working things out on their own. Everything I see in Public Agenda's research—and in the research of other organizations—suggests that young teachers can thrive when principals pursue the former course in each instance. The research also shows indisputably that they can founder if their principals pursue the latter.

Table 5.1. Teachers' Priorities for Improving Teaching

Percent Saying Item Would be "Very Effective Would you Say [Item] Would be Very Effective, Somewhat Effective, not too Effective, or not Effective at all (in Terms of Improving Teacher Effectiveness)?	*Gen Y*		*Teachers Age 33 and Older*
Better preparation to teach in a diverse classroom	65%	Remove students with severe discipline problems from the classroom	70%
Reduce class size by 5 students	63%	Reduce class size by 5 students	67%
Remove students with severe discipline problems from the classroom	56%	Better preparation to teach in a diverse classroom	61%
Make the latest technology available in the classroom	52%	Make the latest technology available in the classroom	55%
Improve professional development opportunities for teachers	50%	Improve professional development opportunities for teachers	52%
Increase salaries comparable to doctors or lawyers	47%	Increase salaries comparable to doctors or lawyers	50%
Make it easier to terminate ineffective teachers	30%	Requiring new teachers to spend much more time teaching under the supervision of experienced teachers	38%
Requiring new teachers to spend much more time teaching under the supervision of experienced teachers	25%	Make it easier to terminate ineffective teachers	35%
Making sure that students in the classroom have roughly the same ability	23%	Requiring teachers to pass tough tests of their knowledge of the subjects they are teaching	16%
Eliminating teacher tenure	12%	Making sure that students in the classroom have roughly the same ability	16%
Requiring teachers to pass tough tests of their knowledge of the subjects they are teaching	10%	Tying teacher pay to performance	8%
Tying teacher pay to performance	10%	Eliminating teacher tenure	7%

Source: Public Agenda

Takeaway No. 4: A chance to grow and do new things could be as important as money.

There is one last element that could make a difference in retaining gifted young teachers in K–12 schools: The chance to take a break, explore new territory, or take on new challenges could be a powerful incentive to stay in teaching.

A number of years ago, Public Agenda conducted focus groups with students at top colleges, exploring their ideas on the pros and cons of teaching as a career. One concern that emerged strongly is that young people in their twenties have a hard time envisioning (and being excited about) doing the same job in the same way in the same place for several decades. As one student told us, "teaching can be very stationery in what you teach . . . like world history for sophomores in high school, year after year after year. . . ."[27]

What's more, the idea of being able to do something different for a while has an indisputable appeal to teachers, both veterans and those who are new to the field: 77 percent of teachers say that making it "far easier to leave and return to teaching without losing retirement benefits" would be a good or excellent idea for attracting and keeping more talented people in the field.[28]

There's also the option of tackling new challenges within education itself. According to the Public Agenda/AIR study, only about half of younger teachers are confident that they want to stay in teaching, but roughly 4 in 10 say that they would like to stay in education, perhaps in another position. That's an intriguing finding, and there is a lot of work being done to develop new career ladders and other policies that provide more diverse experiences and opportunites for growth for teachers as they progress through their careers.

The idea is to develop a more flexible "educator career continuum," and the Public Agenda/AIR report, *Retaining Teaching Talent: The View From Gen Y,* describes some specific steps policy makers and school leaders could take.[29] One option comes from the Teach Plus, a program "incubated" by the Rennie Center for Education Research and Policy in Cambridge, Massachusetts. Its work focuses "on demonstrably effective teachers in the second stage of their careers (years 3 through 10) who want to continue classroom teaching while also expanding their impact as leaders in their schools and in national, state, and district policy."[30] Teach Plus teachers don't just teach; they become advocates for the profession and for improvements designed to strengthen teacher effectiveness.

Another source of ideas is *Teaching 2030* by Barnett Berry and the "Teaching 2030 Team" at the Center for Teaching Quality (www.teachingquality .org).[31] Berry wants to build a group of 600,000 "teacherpreneurs"—teachers who are "teacher educators, policy researchers, community organizers, and trustees of their profession," in addition to being in-the-classroom teachers. Berry's idea is to give teachers new avenues for professional growth while staying in the classroom. He also wants to harness young teachers' voices as advocates for better schools and improved teaching nationwide.

And of course, for any school leader who sees part of his or her mission as identifying and mentoring the principals and superintendents for the next few decades, the Gen Y teaching corps could be fertile hunting ground. Boomer teachers will be retiring in big numbers, but so will boomer principals and superintendents, so building for the future is essential.

The bottom line is that most younger teachers are seeking collaboration and feedback, and they may fail to flourish if they feel isolated or if they're left trying to solve the challenges of teaching on their own. Perhaps it's a generational difference—some studies of Gen Y workers in other fields suggest that this generation tends to value collaboration more than earlier generations.[32] Perhaps it's that they're still learning on the job and looking for help. Whatever the source, it is an assignment that falls squarely in the laps of school leaders, and it's the next topic we take up.

NOTES

1. Ethan Trex, "15 Famous People Who Used to Teach," September 1, 2009, https://www.mentalfloss.com/blogs/archives/33288, and "Famous Celebrities Who Used to Be Teachers," Associated Content from Yahoo, October 28, 2007, http://www.associatedcontent.com/article/424740/famous_celebrities_who_used_to_be_teachers_pg2.html?cat=4.

2. Daniel Willingham, "LBJ & Gene Simmons of Kiss? Ten Teachers Who Made a Mark in Another Field," *Encyclopedia Britannica Blog,* February 16, 2009, http://www.britannica.com/blogs/2009/02/lbj-gene-simmons-of-kiss-ten-teachers-who-made-a-mark-in-another-field/.

3. Thomas G. Carroll and Elizabeth Foster, *Learning Teams: Creating What's Next,* National Commission on the Future of Teaching, April 2008, Page 3, http://www.nctaf.org/resources/research_and_reports/nctaf_research_reports/documents/NCTAFLearningTeamsPolicyBriefFINAL.pdf.

4. Ibid., Page 2.

5. Jane Coggshall, Ellen Behrstock-Sherratt, and Karen Drill, *Workplaces That Support High Performing Teaching and Learning,* American Federation of Teachers and American Institutes for Research, April 2011, Page 4, http://www.aft.org/pdfs/teachers/genyreport0411.pdf.

6. In 2010, Learning Point Associates joined with American Institutes for Research (AIR) and is now included under their umbrella. Find out more about their work at http://www.air.org/.

7. Jane Cogshall, Amber Ott, Ellen Behrstock, and Molly Lasagna, *Retaining Teaching Talent: The View From Gen Y,* Public Agenda and Learning Point Associates/AIR, November 2009, http://www.learningpt.org/expertise/educatorquality/genY/SupportingTeacherEffectiveness/index.php.

8. Ann Duffett, Steve Farkas, Andrew J. Rotherham, and Elena Silva, *Waiting To Be Won Over,* Education Sector, May 2008, http://www.educationsector.org/usr_doc/WaitingToBeWonOver.pdf.

9. Jane Coggshall, Ellen Behrstock-Sherratt, and Karen Drill, *Workplaces That Support High Performing Teaching and Learning,* http://www.aft.org/pdfs/teachers/genyreport0411.pdf.

10. Public Agenda and Learning Point Associates/AIR *Retaining Teaching Talent,* 2009, http://www.learningpt.org/expertise/educatorquality/genY/FullSurveyData.pdf.

11. Ibid.

12. Ibid.

13. Public Agenda and Learning Point Associates/AIR, *Retaining Teaching Talent,* http://www.learningpt.org/expertise/educatorquality/genY/FullSurveyData.pdf, and Ann Duffett, Steve Farkas, Andrew J. Rotherham, and Elena Silva, *Waiting To Be Won Over,* Page 14, http://www.educationsector.org/sites/default/files/publications/WaitingToBeWonOver_0.pdf.

14. Ibid.

15. Public Agenda and Learning Point Associates/AIR, *Retaining Teaching Talent,* http://www.learningpt.org/expertise/educatorquality/genY/FullSurveyData.pdf.

16. Ibid.

17. Ann Duffett, Steve Farkas, Andrew J. Rotherham, and Elena Silva, *Waiting To Be Won Over,* Page 5, http://www.educationsector.org/sites/default/files/publications/WaitingToBeWonOver_0.pdf.

18. Ibid., Page 14.

19. Public Agenda and Learning Point Associates/AIR, *Retaining Teaching Talent,* http://www.learningpt.org/expertise/educatorquality/genY/FullSurveyData.pdf.

20. Ann Duffett, Steve Farkas, Andrew J. Rotherham, and Elena Silva, *Waiting To Be Won Over,* Page 15, http://www.educationsector.org/sites/default/files/publications/WaitingToBeWonOver_0.pdf.

21. Public Agenda and Learning Point Associates/AIR, *Retaining Teaching Talent,* http://www.learningpt.org/expertise/educatorquality/genY/FullSurveyData.pdf.

22. Ibid.

23. There is a helpful review of the academic research on teacher salaries in Frank Adamson and Linda Darling-Hammond, *Speaking of Salaries: What It Will Take to Get Qualified, Effective Teachers in All Communities,* Center for American Progress, May, 2011, http://www.americanprogress.org/issues/2011/05/pdf/teacher_salary.pdf.

24. Public Agenda and Learning Point Associates/AIR, *Retaining Teaching Talent,* http://www.learningpt.org/expertise/educatorquality/genY/FullSurveyData.pdf.

25. Jonathan Rochkind, Amber Ott, John Immerwahr, John Doble, and Jean Johnson, *Lessons Learned, Issue No. 3: Teaching in Changing Times,* National Comprehensive Center for Teacher Quality and Public Agenda, 2008, Page 26, http://www.publicagenda.org/files/pdf/lessons_learned_3.pdf.

26. Public Agenda and Learning Point Associates/AIR, *Retaining Teaching Talent,* http://www.learningpt.org/expertise/educatorquality/genY/FullSurveyData.pdf.

27. Public Agenda, "What Would It Take To Attract More Talented, Accomplished Americans To Teaching?" A Pilot Study Conducted by Public Agenda for the Woodrow Wilson Foundation, 2007.

28. Ann Duffett, Steve Farkas, Andrew J. Rotherham, and Elena Silva, *Waiting To Be Won Over,* Page 15, http://www.educationsector.org/usr_doc/WaitingToBe WonOver.pdf.

29. Jane Cogshall, Amber Ott, Ellen Behrstock, and Molly Lasagna, *Retaining Teaching Talent: The View From Gen Y,* http://www.learningpt.org/expertise/ educatorquality/genY/SupportingTeacherEffectiveness/mod1F6–20.php.

30. Teach Plus, "Why We Exist," Accessed July 1, 2011, http://www.teachplus .org/page/history-and-mission-62.html.

31. See Barnett Berry, *Teaching 2030*, Teachers College Press, 2011. For more information, visit http://www.teachingquality.org/publications/teaching-2030-book.

32. See Jane Cogshall, Amber Ott, Ellen Behrstock, and Molly Lasagna, *Retaining Teaching Talent: The View From Gen Y,* Page 19, http://www.learningpt.org/ expertise/educatorquality/genY/SupportingTeacherEffectiveness/index.php.

Chapter 6

Being an Instructional Leader—Getting the Results the Kids Deserve

Everyone probably has his or her own favorite principal from literature or the movies or TV. Mine happens to be the wonderful Eve Arden who played the principal of Rydell High School in the movie *Grease*. She doesn't spend too much time on academics or mentoring teachers. She seems to be more than fully occupied rounding up misbehaving students, sorting out schedules, chaperoning school dances, and making announcements over the PA.

That's probably what many Americans assume principals do today, but, in recent years, the job has become much more substantive and much more challenging. Principals are supposed to lead the school of course, but they're also supposed to be instructional leaders—the persons who select, manage, motivate, coach, and evaluate a team of teachers.

It's a big job. Hiring, motivating, and evaluating are tasks that managers take on in most fields, but in education, there's an added dimension. It's more than just finding good people and letting them do their thing. Instructional leaders are principals who communicate an explicit, comprehensive vision of how children learn. They visit classrooms regularly, assess teaching strengths and weaknesses, and offer feedback and advice. They actively assist teachers to become more effective at helping students learn.

The Institute for Educational Leadership sees this role as perhaps the major challenge for principals in the future. "Schools of the twenty-first century will require a new kind of principal . . . [one whose main responsibility will be] instructional leadership that focuses on strengthening teaching and learning."[1] Given the vibrancy of this vision and the emphasis national, state, and districts leaders have put on it, how is it really working out in schools? What obstacles do principals face in carrying out this facet of their work? And what do teachers think about having principals much more deeply involved in advising them about the best ways to teach?

THE BOTTOM LINE—"WE'RE HERE TO IMPROVE INSTRUCTION SO KIDS CAN LEARN."

Public Agenda's surveys of principals suggest that almost all readily accept this challenge. In fact, more than 9 in 10 principals (92%) say that "ensuring that all teachers use the most effective instructional methods" is an essential part of being a school leader today.[2] And the vast majority of principals agree that "creating a teacher-selection process that ensures the best teachers are recruited to the school" and "providing professional development opportunities to enhance the skills of new or struggling teachers" are also key components of school leadership. As one elementary school principal interviewed by Public Agenda put it: "It's the instructional leadership that makes a difference. The bottom line is we're there to improve instruction so the kids can learn."

What's more, most principals believe that the quality of teaching has been improving. Despite considerable hand-wringing in the press about the qualifications of young people entering teaching today, one-half of principals (51%) say they believe the quality of new teachers has improved, whereas 37 percent say it has stayed the same. Fewer than 1 in 10 principals (7%) believe the quality of new teachers is getting worse.[3]

Unfortunately, the surveys also show that not all principals voice the same high levels of satisfaction with their teachers. Public Agenda's research shows a sharp divide between principals' views on teachers, depending on the schools and districts where they work. Although 65 percent of principals in mainly white schools said they were "very satisfied" with their teachers, just 44 percent of principals in mainly minority schools said the same thing.[4] Multiple assessments of how teachers are distributed among high-poverty and low-poverty districts confirm the principals' troubling judgment.

Researchers Frank Adamson and Linda Darling-Hammond reviewed a raft of studies for their report, *Speaking of Salaries.* They put it this way: "By every measure of qualifications—certification, subject matter background, pedagogical training, selectivity of college attended, test scores or experience—less-qualified teachers tend to be found in schools serving greater numbers of low-income and minority students.[5] According to research reviewed by the Center for Public Education, an organization that advises school board members, "only about 15 percent of expert teachers (experienced teachers who have proven they can produce above-average gains in student achievement) teach in high-poverty, underachieving schools."[6]

In Public Agenda studies, principals working to transform schools in mainly minority, low-income settings often talk about the challenge of helping teachers be successful with students who often come to class with multiple educational challenges. One elementary principal, for example, worried about finding teachers who have the needed skills to "diagnose reading problems [and help] struggling readers." Another high-needs principal said that "knowledgeable and competent staff" was his top priority. "A lot of time, in high-needs schools, you . . . have less experienced teachers, which is difficult," he said. "Those types of schools need the expertise of more experienced teachers."[7]

Principals generally are focused on the need to improve teachers' impact in the classroom, as opposed to having concerns about the teachers' knowledge of their subject area. For example, fewer than 10 percent of principals say that "quite a large number of teachers" need greater help in content knowledge. In contrast, discipline issues and techniques for helping struggling students seem to be major stumbling blocks. More than one-third of principals (38%) say that "quite a large number" of new teachers need "a lot more training on effective ways to handle students who are discipline problems." More than one-half (53%) say that large numbers of new teachers need "a lot more training on effective ways to reach struggling students."[8]

And most principals bring considerable personal experience to the table in this area. According to the Department of Education's National Center for Education Statistics, the country's 90,470 public school principals bring on average a good dozen years of teaching experience to the job.[9]

THE KEY MESSAGES FROM THE OPINION RESEARCH

So, most principals accept the challenge of being instructional leaders. They see areas for improvement, and they have personal experience and insights that could be valuable. What's more, in their roles, they see a lot of teachers in action and can judge their impact on their students. But what's the situation from the teachers' perspective? Are most teachers receptive and eager for feedback, or are large numbers likely to be resistant and even insulted? Here's the good news:

Finding No. 1: Most teachers would appreciate their principals' advice. Most teachers clearly prefer working with principals who help them improve their teaching. More than 6 in 10 teachers say that they would rather have a "principal who frequently observes my classroom and gives me detailed feedback on how I am doing" rather than one "who conducts formal observations of my teaching only once a year or so and gives me only general feedback" (36%). Among Gen Y teachers, 70 percent say they prefer a principal who gives detailed feedback.[10]

Finding No. 2: Both teachers and principals know that being certified is not enough.

Most teachers and principals agree that formal teacher certification, although important, guarantees only a minimum of skills. Both groups think there's plenty left to learn once teachers actually have their own classrooms. Neither group sees poor content preparation as the major problem. Most new secondary teachers are confident in their knowledge of their subject area. Most new elementary teachers are confident about their ability to teach reading and math, although the confidence levels are somewhat lower for science.[11]

Finding No. 3: Most teachers need help making sure students master needed skills—especially students who struggle.

About 9 in 10 teachers say they feel reasonably confident that can help most of their pupils master the skills and knowledge they are expected to know by the end of the year, but a deeper look at the findings isn't nearly as reassuring. In fact, most teachers voice at least some level of doubt about meeting standards. Just 36 percent say they are "very confident" that most of their students will reach expected levels of learning by the end of the year.[12] Even more worrying, teachers' confidence levels sink dramatically when they are asked about what they can accomplish with their "hardest-to-reach" students. Only 11 percent say they are very confident about helping students who struggle reach expected learning levels. Nearly 4 in 10 (39%) say they are not too confident or not confident at all in this area.[13]

Finding No. 4: Newbies crave advice.

Among new teachers, the desire for feedback and good advice from principals and more experienced colleagues is almost palpable. In focus groups for the Public Agenda/AIR project, younger teachers repeatedly talked about how crucial feedback and advice are to them. "I would prefer my principal to walk in," one elementary teacher reported. "In fact, he does all the time. He walks in and observes all of us. I have no problem with my teaching, and I would like people to come in and observe me because I want to hear constructive feedback."[14]

Another teacher explained that she was looking for genuine feedback, not the perfunctory visit and pat on the back: "Don't just come in and give me a 'satisfactory'—I appreciate [when] principals actually take the time to care for the child's education and make sure that the teachers in there are really doing their job." The researchers involved in the study emphasized that "in general, those who participated in the focus groups were quick to point out that the [principals'] comments do not necessarily have to be positive or celebratory."[15] The call is for help, not just adulation or boosterism.

Finding No. 5: Two challenges are especially daunting—learning to teach in diverse classrooms and working with students with special needs.
When new teachers look back on their teacher preparation, they hone in on two areas where their training came up short: dealing with diverse classes and working with children with special needs. Although majorities of new teachers say that working with ethnically diverse classrooms was covered in their training, only 39 percent say the training actually helped them once they were on the job.[16] As one teacher explained in a focus group conducted for the study: "I was completely unprepared for dealing with the poverty issues and social issues that occur at our school."[17] The pattern is very similar for working with students with special needs—most new teachers say their training covered it, but less than half say the training actually helped them a lot once they were on the job.[18] Notably, nearly all new teachers surveyed in this 2008 study reported having at least some special needs students in their classes, so helping them learn effective ways to work with special needs students has to be a priority for school leaders.

THE TAKEAWAYS

The bottom line is that most teachers say they are eager for their principals' feedback. Most principals see helping teachers improve their teaching as a key part of their jobs. Principals and teachers do seem to share similar views on what the priorities and goals for instructional leadership should be. Even so, the research offers some specific guidance on where school leaders should focus their efforts, and it carries one major warning for all those committed to and charged with making instructional leadership work.

Takeaway No. 1: Instructional leadership—finding the time to do it is job one.
Let's start with the biggest challenge for principals—and it's the area where principals need support from district administrators and superintendents. Principals need to have the time to invest in observing and working with teachers on improving their impact.

Surveys of both principals and teachers strongly suggest that, despite good intentions, principals are spread too thin to be able to give all of their teachers the kind of regular support and advice they are seeking. Here's the dilemma. Three in 10 principals (31) say they are observing classroom teachers and providing feedback every day or almost every day, and another 38 percent do this once or twice a week.[19] But the typical principal is working with dozens of teachers and, of course, principals have a long list of responsibilities and tasks to complete in addition to providing help on instruction.

Meanwhile, most teachers just aren't getting that much help—at least based on what they report in surveys. One in 10 teachers (11%) say their principals never observe them to offer feedback, and about 7 in 10 say that this happens at most a few times a year.[20] Principals may be putting extensive effort into the instructional leadership mission, but, for most teachers, getting their principals' feedback and advice is still fairly infrequent.

This is a challenge for the field overall. Instructional leadership is a crucial role—and it's the centerpiece of the new vision of school leaders as transformers, not just copers. But principals need to have enough time to actually do the job and/or they need the help of coaches, administrators, and senior teachers who can join them in the effort.

Takeaway No. 2: Find ways to encourage teachers to help each other.
Research among teachers strongly indicates that good advice doesn't have to come from principals alone, which, given all that principals have on their plates, counts as good news. Many teachers regularly seek out advice from their colleagues, and school leaders who reinforce and enable this kind of collaboration among teachers will find a receptive audience. In fact, teacher surveys suggest that many principals are already doing a good job in promoting teamwork in their schools. More than two-thirds of teachers (67) strongly agree that their school "encourages teamwork among teachers and other professional staff."[21] What's more, both younger (68%) and older teachers (67%) say they prefer a school where there is a lot of collaboration among the teachers and where they get help from instructional administrators on lesson plans over a school with "less collaboration, but where teachers are freer to design their own lesson plans."[22]

Not surprisingly perhaps, new teachers especially seem to crave and value advice from their colleagues, and they are more likely to see collaboration with other teachers as an element that contributes to their success.[23] As I noted earlier, one of the areas of greatest uncertainty for new teachers is how to work with special needs students. Even though less than half of new teachers say their preservice training helped them a lot in this area, nearly 7 in 10 say they get good or excellent advice from other teachers on how to help children with special needs.[24]

In focus groups conducted for the Public Agenda/AIR report, Gen Y teachers who worked in environments where they received help and advice from other teachers gave them thumbs-up endorsements. A Chicago teacher said: "I've been extremely lucky. Ever since the school has been founded, we have things like teacher talk . . . where we meet every week, and we either develop our curriculum, or we see each other teaching, and help each other with problems. [We work on] how to target students better and what things we can apply to improve ourselves in our school. That has been vital to our school."

Takeway No. 2: Secondary school principals face added challenges as instructional leaders.
Experts and reformers frequently talk about teachers as if all teachers faced the same challenges and difficulties—a rose is a rose is a rose seems to be a common assumption. But teachers, especially new ones, encounter different kinds of problems and hurdles depending on where they teach. One major consideration—and one that probably doesn't get as much attention as it deserves—is the difference between trying to get little kids excited about reading and spelling and trying to get teenagers excited and focused on polynomials and Spanish verbs. Compared to elementary school teachers, middle school and high school teachers are:[25]

• More likely to be frustrated about lack of student motivation
• Less likely to believe that good teachers can lead all students to learn
• More concerned about lack of administrative support in their schools
• And less likely to be confident that their students are learning

And beyond all this, new secondary school teachers are more likely than elementary teachers to see a major gap between what they learned during their training and what really happens once you have a class full of teenagers in front of you.

Secondary teachers are more likely to say that their training placed too much emphasis on theory and too little on the practical aspects of running a classroom. And for some, the struggle to be effective in the classroom undermines their morale and confidence. Secondary teachers are twice as likely as elementary teachers to say that a major drawback of teaching is that too many students are unmotivated and just going through the motions."[26]

This is a call for help, especially for teachers just starting out. Principals can take the initiative to organize mentoring and collaboration between more experienced and successful teachers and the newbies. Principals themselves may need to put on their "instructional leadership" hats a little more often for their teachers who are in their first year in a middle school or high school classroom.

Takeaway No. 3: As instructional leaders, principals in high-needs schools face a special challenge.

In the last chapter, I mentioned a Public Agenda study which analyzed teachers' views and grouped the nation's teaching corps into three groups—contented, disheartened, and idealistic teachers. Nearly a quarter of America's teachers are idealists. They tend to be younger (although not exclusively so) and more than three-quarters have been teaching for less than 10 years. Maybe that's an indicator that teaching takes a toll over time, but it also suggests that many young teachers have aspirations that school leaders in high-needs schools may want to tap into.

I often think of this as the "Teach for America" effect. The spirit of that organization—that teaching is a way to make our society fairer and give every child a true chance at success—has extended far beyond that one group. Idealistic teachers are more likely than other teachers to believe that "good teachers can lead all students to learn, even those from poor families or who have uninvolved parents." They are more likely to believe that student effort is "mainly determined by what teachers do," not just their innate motivation. The vast majority of this group says that "the idea of putting underprivileged kids on the path to success" was a major reason they chose to teach. Younger teachers—that Gen Y group that is just starting out in the profession—say this is one of their main motivations for becoming a teacher, by a healthy 15-point margin over older colleagues.

But there is a dilemma here—idealism doesn't necessarily translate into effectiveness in the classroom. It's up to school leaders to insure that teachers have the skills to follow through. One somewhat disappointing result from the research is that many new teachers believe (rightly or wrongly) that they have been assigned classes with the hardest-to-reach students. What's more, nearly all new teachers believe that giving less-experienced teachers the most challenging classes is simply "wrong."[27] Less than half of new teachers strongly agree that they are "very confident" that their students are learning and responding to their teaching on "most days."[28]

This is a warning sign for school leaders, especially those who are working in low-income neighborhoods and/or trying to turn persistently failing schools around. The teachers may be idealistic and well intentioned, but many, by their own admission, are not fully confident that they are having an impact. It's an opening for school leaders to offer help, and it's an indication that they may need to step in to help their teachers if all students are to receive the education they deserve.

A WELCOME DEVELOPMENT FOR PRINCIPALS AND TEACHERS

The vast majority of principals seem to relish the idea of being an instructional leader, and I suspect that for many, being able to sink their teeth into the real heart of education is a welcome relief from negotiating the bus schedule and making sure that all the required paperwork gets to the central office on time.

One heartening sign of the strength and viability of the idea is that principals and teachers share a common definition of where teachers need help. The overlap is quite notable. If principals were focused on one set of challenges while teachers were focused on something else, the prospects for working together would be considerably less promising. But everything that I have seen in the multiple studies that Public Agenda has done, and the serious work being done by others, is that principals have an open invitation from their teachers to offer advice and counsel. The principal who doesn't accept the invitation is missing an extraordinary chance to boost student learning and enhance teacher morale simultaneously.

For principals, superintendents, and administrators who would like some specific advice on programs and ideas to help teachers improve their impact and on keeping good teachers motivated and in the classroom, here are some good places to start:

A Better System for Schools: Developing, Supporting and Retaining Effective Teachers by Barnett Berry, Alesha Daughtrey, and Alan Wieder, Center for Teaching Quality, 2010, http://teachersnetwork.org/effectiveteachers/images/CTQ_FULLResearchReport__021810.pdf.

Designing Support for Beginning Teachers by Kendyll Stansbury and Joy Zimmerman, WestEd Knowledge Brief, 2000, http://www.wested.org/online_pubs/tchrbrief.pdf.

Developing and Retaining Effective Teachers and Principals by Harry K. Wong and Rosemary T. Wong, Effectiveteaching.com, November 2010, http://www.newteacher.com/pdf/Developing.pdf.

Fifteen Ideas for Promoting Effective Teaching in MCS with Master Teachers, Teaching Plus, Spring 2011, http://www.teachplus.org/uploads/Documents/1307040587_FifteenIdeasForPromotingEffectiveTeachingInMCS.pdf.

Improving Teacher Quality by Sabrina Laine with Ellen Behrstock-Sherratt and Molly Lasagna, Jossey-Bass, 2011.

Moving Beyond the Obvious: Examining Our Thinking about Linguistically Diverse Students by Robert T. Jiménez, Learning Point Assoicates, 2005, http://www.learningpt.org/pdfs/literacy/diverse.pdf.

Workplaces That Support High Performing Teaching and Learning by Jane Coggshall, Ellen Behrstock-Sherratt, and Karen Drill, American Federation of Teachers and American Institutes for Research, April 2011, http://www.aft.org/pdfs/teachers/genyreport0411.pdf.

NOTES

1. Quoted in National Governors' Association, *Issue Brief: Improving Teaching and Learning by Improving School Leadership,* September 12, 2003, http://www.avs.nl/esha/Documents/Improving+Teaching+and+Learning+by+Improving+School+Leadership.pdf

2. Jean Johnson, Ana Maria Arumi and Amber Ott, *Reality Check 2006, Issue No. 4: The Insiders: How Principals and Superintendents See Public Education Today*, Public Agenda, 2006, Page 2, http://www.publicagenda.org/reports/reality-check-2006-issue-no-4.

3. MetLife, Inc., *The MetLife Study of the American Teacher: Past, Present and Future,* 2008, Page 179. http://www.eric.ed.gov/PDFS/ED504457.pdf.

4. Jean Johnson, Ana Maria Arumi, and Amber Ott, *Reality Check 2006. Issue No. 4: How Principals and Superintendents See Public Education Today,* Public Agenda, 2006, Page 13, http://www.publicagenda.org/reports/reality-check-2006-issue-no-4.

5. Frank Adamson and Linda Darling-Hammond, *Speaking of Salaries: What It Will Take to Get Qualified, Effective Teachers in All Communities,* Center for American Progress, May 2011, http://www.americanprogress.org/issues/2011/05/pdf/teacher_salary.pdf.

6. Center for Public Education, "Wanted: Good Teachers," October 8, 2008, http://www.centerforpubliceducation.org/Main-Menu/Staffingstudents/Wanted-Good-teachers-/default.aspx.

7. Public Agenda, Focus groups conducted for *A Mission of the Heart: What Does It Take to Transform a School?* Conducted for The Wallace Foundation, 2008, http://www.publicagenda.org/files/pdf/missionheart.pdf.

8. Steve Farkas, Jean Johnson, and Ann Duffett with Beth Syat and Jackie Vine, *Rolling Up Their Sleeves,* Page 29, http://www.publicagenda.org/reports/rolling-their-sleeves.

9. National Center for Education Statistics, "Number, highest degree, experience, and salaries of principals in public and private elementary and secondary schools, by selected characteristics: 1993–94, 2003–04, and 2007–08," Accessed July 3, 2011, http://nces.ed.gov/programs/digest/d10/tables/dt10_089.asp.

10. Jane Cogshall, Amber Ott, Ellen Behrstock, and Molly Lasagna, *Retaining Teaching Talent: The View From Gen Y,* Public Agenda and Learning Point Associates/AIR, November 2009, Page 13, http://www.learningpt.org/expertise/educatorquality/genY/SupportingTeacherEffectiveness/index.php.

11. Jonathan Rochkind, Amber Ott, John Immerwahr, John Doble, and Jean Johnson, *Lessons Learned, Issue No. 3: Teaching in Changing Times,* National Comprehensive Center for Teacher Quality and Public Agenda, 2008, Page 10, http://www.publicagenda.org/files/pdf/lessons_learned_3.pdf.

12. Steve Farkas, Jean Johnson, and Ann Duffett, *Stand by Me*, Public Agenda, 2003, Page 41, http://www.publicagenda.org/files/pdf/stand_by_me.pdf.

13. Ibid., Page 42.

14. Jane Cogshall, Amber Ott, Ellen Behrstock, and Molly Lasagna, *Retaining Teaching Talent: The View From Gen Y*, Page 13, http://www.learningpt.org/ expertise/educatorquality/genY/SupportingTeacherEffectiveness/index.php.

15. Ibid., Page 14.

16. Jonathan Rochkind, Amber Ott, John Immerwahr, John Doble, and Jean Johnson, *Lessons Learned: New Teachers Talk about Their Jobs, Challenges, and Long-Range Plans, Issue No. 3: Teaching in Changing Times*, Page 9, http://www .publicagenda.org/reports/lessons-learned-issue-no-3-new-teachers-talk-about-their-jobs-challenges-and-long-range-plans.

17. Ibid., Page 11.

18. Ibid., Page 9.

19. MetLife, Inc., *The MetLife Study of the American Teacher: Past, Present and Future*, 2008, Page 180. http://www.eric.ed.gov/PDFS/ED504457.pdf.

20. Ibid., Page 171.

21. Ibid., Page 172.

22. Jane Coggshall, Ellen Behrstock-Sherratt, and Karen Drill, *Workplaces That Support High Performing Teaching and Learning*, American Federation of Teachers and American Institutes for Research, April 2011, Page 15, http://www.aft.org/pdfs/ teachers/genyreport0411.pdf.

23. Ibid., Page 13.

24. Jonathan Rochkind, Amber Ott, John Immerwahr, John Doble, and Jean Johnson, *Lessons Learned: New Teachers Talk about Their Jobs, Challenges, and Long-Range Plans, Issue No. 3*, Page 14. http://www.publicagenda.org/reports/lessons-learned-issue-no-3-new-teachers-talk-about-their-jobs-challenges-and-long-range-plans.

25. For detailed findings and discussion, see Jonathan Rochkind, Amber Ott, John Immerwahr, John Doble, and Jean Johnson, *Lessons Learned: New Teachers Talk about Their Jobs, Challenges, and Long-Range Plans, Issue No. 1: They're Not Little Kids Anymore*, National Comprehensive Center for Teaching Quality and Public Agenda, 2007, http://www.publicagenda.org/files/pdf/lessons_learned_1.pdf.

26. Jonathan Rochkind, Amber Ott, John Immerwahr, John Doble and Jean Johnson, *Lessons Learned: New Teachers Talk about Their Jobs, Challenges, and Long-Range Plans, Issue No. 1:* Page 13.

27. Jonathan Rochkind, Amber Ott, John Immerwahr, John Doble, and Jean Johnson, *Lessons Learned: New Teachers Talk about Their Jobs, Challenges, and Long-Range Plans, Issue No. 2: Working Without a Net*, National Comprehensive Center for Teaching Quality and Public Agenda, 2008, Page 39, http://www.publicagenda.org/files/pdf/ lessons_learned_2.pdf.

28. Jonathan Rochkind, Amber Ott, John Immerwahr, John Doble and Jean Johnson, *Lessons Learned: New Teachers Talk about Their Jobs, Challenges, and Long-Range Plans, Issue No. 1: They're Not Little Kids Anymore*, National Comprehensive Center for Teaching Quality and Public Agenda, 2008, Page 38, http:// www.publicagenda.org/files/pdf/lessons_learned_1.pdf.

Chapter 7

The Knowledge Sweepstakes

For one of his last novels, Charles Dickens penned the wonderful title *Great Expectations*. It refers to Pip's aspirations as he grows to adulthood and makes his way in Victorian England. Today the phrase could easily be applied to the aspirations Americans place on the schools. At the national level, leaders in government and business see good schools and higher student achievement as essential to maintaining the country's toehold in a competitive global economy. Locally, good schools and a well-educated workforce attract employers and home buyers. Parents look to the schools to put their children on a path to economic security in an era when getting and keeping a good job depends on having knowledge and skills. Being willing to work hard just isn't enough anymore.

COLLEGE OR BUST

For both leaders and the public, that increasingly means that schools are expected to prepare all students for college or some other postsecondary training. Based on U.S. government projections, "nearly 8 out of 10 new jobs will require higher education and workforce training" over the next decade.[1] Major foundations such as the Bill & Melinda Gates Foundation and the Lumina Foundation have launched multiyear initiatives to increase college entry and degree completion. The College Board, for one, has set a goal of having 55 percent of young Americans with at least a two-year degree by 2025.[2] (We're currently at just under 40%.[3]) President Obama has recommended that all students complete at least one year of education beyond high school.[4]

In this case, leaders and the broader public are on exactly the same page. As recently as 2000, just 31 percent of Americans believed that a college education was essential to succeed in the American workplace. By 2009, a 55 percent majority had come to believe it—a stunning increase in a relatively short period of time. More and more Americans see getting a college degree as an economic necessity. Unfortunately, the United States still has a road to travel in insuring that all students leave high school prepared for postsecondary work. According to the ACT College Readiness Standards, 78 percent of students entering higher education are not adequately prepared for college-level reading, English, math, or science.[5]

A related problem is that even though more young Americans are starting college, many of them fail to finish. According to the U.S. Department of Education, only 20 percent of young people who begin their higher education at two-year institutions graduate within three years.[6] There is a similar pattern in four-year institutions, where about 4 in 10 students receive a degree within six years.[7]

CALLING MR. WIZARD

But getting more students into and completing college isn't the only mission for many government, business, and education leaders. They contend that the country needs to dramatically ramp up K–12 and college achievement in science and math, or to use the common reform jargon, "STEM" (for Science, Technology, Engineering, and Math), to insure the country's economic future. Students who don't master these subjects won't be eligible for the growing number of jobs requiring this kind of training. If the United States doesn't produce enough students who excel in these areas, we may not have enough scientists, engineers, and inventors to create the innovations that propel job growth and economic vitality.

So basically, American schools face a three-pronged challenge—1) to educate more students to higher levels of learning, 2) to prepare more of them to succeed in college, and 3) to significantly improve American student achievement in science and math.[8] The capsule version is that schools need to arm students with world-class skills and knowledge.

Over the past decade, states and districts nationwide have responded by designing more rigorous courses, increasing graduation requirements, including more students in advanced placement courses, and other steps. As of June 2010, the United States has, for the first time ever, voluntary "Common Core State Standards" in math and reading developed by the National Governors Association and the Council of Chief State School Officers.[9] Most states have already adopted the standards, and beginning in the 2014–2015 school year, students will be tested on them.[10]

School leaders not only have to implement all these changes—which is challenging enough by itself—they have to help the people they work with understand these changes and related ones coming down the road. According to Achieve, a leading advocate for world-class learning standards, "communications about why a rigorous curriculum matters for students' futures is critical."[11]

And that's where school leaders come in. Some states have organized formal public relations efforts and/or set up websites for students and their parents explaining and promoting world-class learning standards,[12] but there is still a huge communications gap. Working on the front lines with teachers, parents, and students, school leaders, almost by default, are the ones who will communicate what the changes are and why they are necessary. Moreover, unless teachers, parents, and students genuinely understand, believe in, and enlist in this new mission of making sure American students achieve world-class levels of knowledge, achieving it is going to be difficult.

THE KEY MESSAGES FROM THE OPINION RESEARCH

For many economists and business and government leaders, substantially increasing student learning in K–12 schools is a national priority. Are teachers, parents, and students ready to join in this undertaking? Do they understand what it means and why it is so important? Here's where most people start:

Finding No. 1: Most Americans say that getting a college education is crucial for success in the work place today, but not everyone is convinced that "college is for everyone."
Americans' views about the importance of going to college have changed dramatically in recent years. According to the 2010 Phi Delta Kappa/Gallup Poll survey on education, 75 percent of the public says that today a college education is "very important," compared to just 36 percent in 1978.[13] And today, more than 8 in 10 Americans believe that all high school students should be prepared for "college and a career. More than 9 in 10 public school parents believe their children will go to college.[14] And 95 percent of students agree that "it is important that I go to school or college after high school in order to be prepared for work or a career."[15]

But beneath the surface, there are questions, especially among teachers. Just 4 in 10 teachers strongly agree that "all my students, given the right support, can go to college if they choose," although another 34 percent agree somewhat.[16] Even among "idealist" teachers—the group that is most committed to education as a path to success for their students, just over half say that all of their students could attend college with the right support.[17]

There are also doubts among young people who have started college, which may offer a partial explanation for why the country's college dropout rates are so high. Most of today's young adults say they had encouragement from parents, teachers, and others to attend college,[18] and nearly two-thirds strongly agree that people make more money if they have a college degree.[19] But like their teachers, not all are convinced that college is for everyone. A solid 50 percent of young people aged 22 to 30 who have started college strongly agree that it "is not for everyone—some people just don't like school."[20]

Finding No. 2: Most Americans like the idea of improving STEM education, but there is a gap between endorsing the vision and understanding what it really means in local schools.

Most Americans believe that students benefit from studying more math and science, and even though relatively few see significant demand right now, more than 8 in 10 say there will be a lot more jobs requiring math and science savvy in the future.[21] What's more, 9 in 10 Americans say that studying advanced math and science is useful even for students who don't pursue STEM careers, and 88 percent agree that students with advanced math and science skills have an advantage in getting into college.[22]

Despite the broad enthusiasm for the general idea of having more students study "advanced" math and science, much of the public hasn't really focused on what this actually means for the schools, teachers, and students in their communities. For example, just over a quarter of the public sees courses like calculus (26%) or physics (28%) as absolutely essential. Asked about their own children's schooling, less than half of parents want more emphasis on advanced courses like physics (42%) or calculus (42%). Nearly 7 in 10 Americans say that science can wait until middle school and high school—which is definitely not an approach most working scientists would recommend.[23]

Finding No. 3: Many students aren't that enthusiastic either.

Just because there are good job prospects down the line for people who excel in math and science doesn't mean that most students are drawn to that kind of work. In a 2006 Public Agenda survey, more than 4 in 10 high school students said they would be "very unhappy" in a career that required a lot of math and science.[24] This certainly raises the question of whether students and their parents recognize the changes that are taking place in the labor market and understand what kinds of skills and training will benefit them in the future. It also raises questions about the quality of science and math teaching, and whether, as instructional leaders, principals need to emphasize teaching that more successfully engages students with hands-on and project-based learning.

THE TAKEAWAYS

In many respects, the broader public and parents are open to the idea of world-class learning, but superintendents and principals clearly have a job to do engaging them on the specific agenda items. What can superintendents and principals do to help build broader support for world-class learning?

Takeaway No. 1: Educators have to take the lead.
The research suggests that although most parents aren't pushing for tougher courses and graduation requirements in math and science (and that some may feel threatened initially by them), there is broad support for proposals aimed at improving student achievement in this area. School leaders need to have the confidence to move ahead and look for ways to help parents, teachers, and students through the rough patches. There is majority support for more rigorous approaches. For example, 8 in 10 Americans say establishing a national curriculum in math would improve STEM education, with more than half (53%) saying it would improve it "a lot." More than three-quarters (78%) say the same about a national curriculum in science. A plurality of parents with children in grades 6 through 12 say they want to see more emphasis in their children's schools on STEM topics such as computer programming (65%), basic engineering principles (52%), and statistics and probability (49%). Parents would also like to see their local schools spend more money on well-equipped science labs (70%), more equipment for hands-on learning (69%) and more equipment to help students learn computer and technology skills (68%), although in tough economic times, support for the concept doesn't necessarily translate into a vote to pay higher taxes to achieve it. (This is a topic I take up in the next chapter.) Still, having such large numbers of citizens and parents buying into the vision is an enormous asset—one school leaders can use to motivate people as they move forward.

Takeaway No. 2: It's time to get specific. School leaders need to help teachers, parents, and students gain a more concrete vision of the opportunities and how rich and diverse they are.
Several years ago when Bill Gates testified before Congress on science and technology issues, he pointed out that there are roughly 100,000 new jobs in computer science and engineering every year, but only about 15,000 new

graduates with degrees in that field.[25] It's a surprising stat for most of us, and one problem for educators is that most parents and students don't have specifics like that in their heads. When Public Agenda organizes focus groups or citizens' meetings where parents discuss science and math education, the conversations—and the interest and engagement level—often change dramatically when participants who work in these fields begin to talk about their jobs and what they involve.[26]

The takeaway here is that most parents and students need help in understanding the vast career potential in fields like engineering and energy, health care, and in the corporate world, academia, and even K–12 education itself for people willing to invest what it takes to get good at math and science. The image of "having a STEM career" is much too general for most people to latch onto. It's like they know that they want to drive from New York to Los Angeles, but they haven't looked at a map or thought about the route and where they will spend the night along the way. Nor, to continue my analogy, have they considered all the fascinating alternatives for getting there.

Based on multiple Public Agenda projects on STEM education, bringing local businesses and working STEM professionals into contact with teachers, students, and their parents can be pivotal. In one regional study, 8 in 10 students indicated that they would be much more motivated to take higher-level math and science courses if they knew that "most good colleges expect you to have advanced science and math courses on your high school transcripts."[27] The vast majority also indicated they would be more motivated to ramp up their science and math coursework if they knew it could open up good job opportunities for them.[28]

It may also be helpful to spell out that there are good opportunities for those who prefer to continue their education through specialized one- or two-year certificate programs, not just for those aiming for BA and graduate degrees. As just one example, 71 percent of Americans say that having local businesses provide internships and other business partnership programs where high school students can gain practical job skills is a good way to improve math and science education.[29]

Takeaway No. 3: School leaders need to help parents understand that basics aren't enough.

If you take a look at the survey data on parents' views on science and math education, there seems to be a discrepancy—most parents endorse the idea of having their own children take advanced math and science courses in high school, but many fewer want their children's schools to put more emphasis on subjects like physics and calculus. What's going on there?

The explanation is that for many parents, "advanced" simply means making sure that all kids master basic math and science. Many parents do not understand the expert argument that their children need to master these subjects at a much higher level than in the past. In many respects, it's the same problem that's outlined above. People have absorbed the general idea, but they don't really understand the specifics. And again, here's where educators really need to lead. Most parents and students genuinely want educators (and business and higher education professionals) to help them understand what levels of knowledge their children need to go forward. Most people aren't themselves scientists or engineers or economists, nor are they labor-market planners or futurists. Most people just don't know how quickly jobs are changing. They don't realize how savvy workers are in some countries that compete with us in today's global economy.

Helping people go beyond the vision to grasp the specifics is paramount. Unfortunately, it is not at all rare in Public Agenda focus groups to encounter students with dreams of a STEM career—being a veterinarian or nurse are common examples—who simply do not understand what they need to study now to get to their goal later. To avoid yanking these young people's dreams away from them, schools and school leaders have to step up to the plate to advise families about the specifics. There's a lot to be done here. See the box entitled "Could I Get a Little Advice Here?" later in this chapter for more on this challenge.

DON'T KNOW MUCH ABOUT HISTORY . . .

There is a major push among educators and business and government leaders to bring the knowledge and skills of U.S. high school graduates up to "world-class standards." But there is a quieter rumble of concern about whether we're doing a good enough job educating students to take on their future role as citizens.

For example, according to results from the National Assessment of Educational Progress, fewer than 1 in 5 students in U.S. schools scores at a "proficient" level in U.S. history. For fourth graders, one measure of proficiency is being able to identify and say why Abraham Lincoln is an important historical figure.[1] For middle schools students, the test included a question about the advantages American troops had over the British in the Revolutionary War. For high schoolers, it might include knowing that China was an ally of the North Koreans during the Korea War.[2]

The results are equally discouraging for civics. According to the National Center for Education Statistics, "the percentage of students performing at or above the proficient level [in civics] in 2010 was 27 percent at grade four, 22 percent at grade eight, and 24 percent at grade twelve." [3] The group that designed and oversees the civics testing says that it was guided "by the conviction that the world's oldest constitutional democracy depends, in large measure, on the education of our young citizens. In each succeeding generation it is necessary to develop a firm understanding of the core documents of American liberty—the Declaration of Independence and the U.S. Constitution, including the Bill of Rights—and a reasoned commitment to their values and principles." [4]

Based on the NAEP tests, at least 3 out of 4 American students haven't even mastered the basics in civics and history, and polls routinely show that American adults don't do much better. In a 2011 poll by *Newsweek*, 3 in 10 Americans couldn't name the vice president and 44 percent couldn't define the Bill of Rights. [5]

As the *Newsweek* piece pointed out, Europeans seemed to do a little better. A study in 2009 by the *European Journal of Communications* showed that even though the United States originally declared war against Afghanistan after September 11, fewer than 6 in 10 Americans could identify the Taliban. Meanwhile, three-quarters of the Finns, Danes, and British has no problem with that. [6] Scholars who follow Americans' views in this area say the pattern of citizens not being able to identify "common knowledge" facts about history, government, and public affairs is a long-standing one. [7]

In a recent Public Agenda survey (See Table 7.1), about 4 in 10 parents of elementary school students wanted their child's school to put more emphasis on "social studies and geography," while half (50%) wanted the emphasis to stay the same. Parents tended to give similar responses about physical education and art and music. As a group, they were more likely to want the schools to put more emphasis on computer skills, reading and writing, and science and math. [8]

But it's worth noting that very few parents wanted *less emphasis* in any of these areas, even though the survey question emphasized that there is a "limited amount of time in the school day." Just 3 percent of the parents said there should be less emphasis on social studies and geography.

A Public Agenda survey of the broader public conducted shortly after the September 11 attacks found two-thirds of Americans (67%) saying it is absolutely essential for ordinary Americans to have a detailed knowledge of their constitutional rights and freedoms. Ninety percent agreed

Table 7.1. Parents' Views on What Schools Should Emphasize More

Keeping in Mind there is a Limited Amount of Time in the School Day, do you Think the Elementary School should be Teaching your Child a lot more of the following, should there be less Emphasis, or is He/She Learning Enough as is? [Base: Asked of Parents with Elementary School Children]	% Saying More Emphasis	% Saying the Same	% Saying Less Emphasis
Computer skills and technology	59%	32%	3%
Reading and writing skills	54%	41%	—
Hands-on science activities	52%	38%	4%
Handwriting and penmanship	52%	40%	3%
Learning how to cooperate, share, and work with classmates	50%	45%	1%
General math concepts like estimation and word problems	49%	40%	3%
Basic math like multiplication and long division	49%	36%	3%
Physical education	41%	49%	4%
Social studies and geography	39%	50%	3%
Art and music	34%	49%	10%

Source: Public Agenda

that "since the terrorist attacks of September 2001, it's more important than ever to know what our Constitution stands for."[9] It's a common human mindset—we often put a greater value on things like our health, our families and friends, and our democracy when we feel they might be in jeopardy.

And even though the public is often shocking haphazard in its grasp of key historical facts, the Public Agenda study showed that most people in the United States do seem to have absorbed the general principles—the freedom to express your political views, the right to vote, the need to balance the will of the majority against the rights of the minority. The survey also found "strong resistance to the notion that America's classrooms should present the nation's history in the best possible light. Nine out of 10 Americans say school children should be taught the bad and the good, warts and all."[10]

As in so many areas, opinion survey findings can initially be unnerving, but the findings here suggest that school leaders have an open door to talk with parents and communities about the need to rev up student learning in civics and history and what a top-quality education in those areas should look like.

1. Sam Dillon, "U.S.Students Remain Poor at History, Tests Show," *The New York Times,* June 14, 2011, http://www.nytimes.com/2011/06/15/education/15history.html?_r=1&emc=eta1.

2. Ibid.

3. National Center for Education Statistics, The Nation's Report Card: Civics 2010m http://nces.ed.gov/nationsreportcard/pdf/main2010/2011466.pdf.

4. National Assessment Governing Board, NAEP Civics Project, Civics Framework for the 2010 National Assessment of Educational Progress, http://www.nagb.org/publications/frameworks/civicsframework.pdf.

5. "How Ignorant Are Americans? Take the Quiz," Newsweek, March 20, 2011, http://www.newsweek.com/2011/03/20/how-dumb-are-we.html.

6. Ibid.

7. Ibid.

8. All data from Public Agenda, *Are We Beginning to See the Light?* Prepared for the GE Foundation, December 2009, Full Survey Results, http://www.publicagenda.org/pages/math-and-science-ed-2010#Methodology.

9. Public Agenda, "Americans Proud of U.S. and Constitution, but Want Children Taught the Bad with the Good," September 17, 2002, http://www.publicagenda.org/press-releases/americans-proud-us-and-constitution-want-children-taught-bad-good.

10. Ibid.

Takeaway No. 4: It's a question. Do school leaders need to find different solutions for students who are "different drummers"?

The vast majority of parents want their children to go to college, and the vast majority of high school students say college is their goal, but the truth is that not every student is an enthusiastic one. Based on Public Agenda's research among young adults who start college, as many as 1 out of every 4 may be half-hearted and ambivalent about conventional college academic work. Many say they struggle to pay attention in class and complete assignments. Some trudge through and eventually earn a diploma, but as a group, they are more likely to drop out of college, even though most clearly understand the economic penalty of entering today's workforce without a degree.

The research also shows convincingly that many of these less-than-enthusiastic collegians are "different drummers" who even in high school thought of themselves as dreamers or students who didn't like sitting in class.[30] In focus groups, they often describe themselves as people who like "to work with their hands." Sometimes people say they like to "work out-of-doors."

While policy makers and reformers are rightly focused on upping college attendance and completion, some young people are falling by the wayside, and helping them shape a rewarding future is, to me at least, one of the most important and least discussed challenges in education today. There are questions about exactly what we mean by "going to college" and whether the classic academic models centered on reading, lectures, theses, and term papers is really the right plan for everyone. Nearly everyone who has gone to college remembers classmates who were indifferent, perhaps even failing students, yet who went on to remarkable and socially useful careers. Academic knowledge is essential to our success as a nation, but as a nation, we will also need people who have other skills and interests.

Increasingly, there is a strong undercurrent of skepticism about whether just sending more students to college—at least as it has been traditionally conceived—is always the best way to help all students pursue their own distinctive talents and/or whether it is the best use of the nation's higher education resources. Some are also raising questions about whether sending more students to college will provide more Americans with the job security and economic stability most are aiming for.[31] On the other hand, the idea of discouraging high school graduates with lackluster academic records from pursuing college introduces troubling issues as well.

Compared to countries like Germany, Austria, Denmark and Switzerland, the United States does not have a robust or well-respected system of apprenticeships and certificate programs for students who are less academically inclined, so the options here are more limited. But even if we decide to develop a more "European" route, there are questions. In the American economy, the pay gap between college-educated workers and those with only a high school diploma is substantial and daunting. Are we consigning some portion of every graduating class to a lifetime of economic insecurity by encouraging them to follow a noncollege route? Would having a two-track system result in fewer children from minority and low-income families going to college? Would it deepen the racial and ethnic inequities in our country and our economy? There is also the issue of whether such a system shuts off options for any young person who is something of a late bloomer.

School leaders can't address this challenge single-handedly, especially since most have their hands full insuring that as many students as possible master the more rigorous academic material needed for more advanced study. But school leaders probably do need to ask themselves whether their schools can do more to help a greater of students develop the study habits and capacity to concentrate on academic work that leads to success in college (and later on in the workforce too). It also raises questions about whether there should be more alternative high school programs and courses designed explicitly to meet the interests and talents of this "different drummer" group.

COULD I GET A LITTLE ADVICE HERE?
WHERE HIGH SCHOOL COUNSELING FALLS SHORT

The decisions young people make about whether to go to college, where to go to college, and how to pay for it can shape the entire course of their lives. School leaders—and the public at large—hope that high school counselors are giving students good advice, especially those who are the first in their families to go on to college. But three converging trends are leaving high school counselors scrambling. As a result, many students simply are not getting the information and advice they need. It's a dilemma for school leaders, because in tough economic times, there may not be clear, easily affordable solutions. School leaders may need to innovate and get creative to get the kids the help they need.

Let's say that you're a high school counselor; here's what you face:

- **More students are going to college.** Most families want their children to go to college, and the number of young people continuing their education beyond high school is at historic highs. Nearly 7 in 10 of the 3.2 million young Americans who graduated high school in 2010 enrolled in some sort of postsecondary education.[1] That means counselors have more students that need their help in this area.
- **There are more higher-ed options than ever before.** Traditional four-year college programs and two-year community college programs have been joined by all manner of new one-year options focusing on specific skills and careers. The higher-ed system now includes a thriving for-profit sector, along with private and public institutions across the country. There are a lot of choices, and that means that counselors themselves need more expertise to be able to give students good advice.
- **College costs are going up, and the financial-aid system is no piece of cake.** There is financial aid available in all sorts of packages—scholarships, loans, work-study programs, and others. What's more, it comes from all sorts of sources—federal and state government, higher-education institutions, philanthropies, financial institutions, and others. A recent Public Agenda survey showed that most young people who successfully complete a college degree could describe FAFSA—the federal government's gateway application for Pell grants and government loans. But among young people who began working with no degree beyond high school, 7 in 10 had no idea what the term even referred to.[2] To get the help, students and their families have to know how to apply. And

many will need help completing the paperwork which can be daunting even for the savviest of parents.

From the counselor's perspective, there are more students seeking advice, and the world of higher education is becoming more complicated. And it keeps changing. Plus high school counselors have many other responsibilities in their bailiwick, and many are already coping with counselor-student ratios that are far less than optimal.[3]

Sadly, the fact that so many counselors have so much on their plates appears to be undercutting their ability to help students. According to a national sample of young adults surveyed by Public Agenda for the Bill & Melinda Gates Foundation, 48 percent said that when they were in high school, they felt like "just another face in the crowd" in dealing with their guidance counselors.[4] Roughly 6 in 10 gave their guidance counselors fair or poor ratings for helping them choose a college program, for helping them find a way to pay for it, and for helping them think about different careers.[5] In interviews conducted for the project, young people often described their interactions with high school guidance counselors as impersonal and perfunctory.

Looking at results like these, the first response can be to lash out at counselors themselves, but, in reality, most of them probably could use some help. Furthermore, findings like these raise deeper issues about how schools can best help students plan for their futures and the role counselors, teachers, and others should play in that endeavor. In an article Public Agenda prepared for *Educational Leadership*,[6] here are some questions we posed for school leaders:

- When should students begin thinking about their overall education and career goals? Is high school the best time or is it too late for some students?
- How can schools work with communities and local business and higher education partners to allow students to learn about and "road test" different ideas about their future careers?
- Should all students be encouraged to go on to college, and what do we mean by "going to college"? How can we insure that students and their families have a chance to understand and think about a diverse set of options?
- What should we do when a student's academic skills simply do not match his or her career goals?
- What do public schools owe to the young people who aren't college bound? Do schools have a responsibility for helping them navigate their

entry into the workforce? Should school leaders ask local businesses or
other institutions to step in here?
• And what about counselors and their responsibilities? Should we
  reimagine what counselors do and how they are trained? What can the
  profession do to individualize and personalize the services it offers?
• Where can school leaders and guidance counselors turn for a helping hand?

There are many potential helpers—students' families and neighbors,
higher-ed institutions, local businesses, professional associations, unions,
philanthropies, and community groups. Maybe it's time for districts and
communities to begin thinking together about who can do what and coming up with some fresher and more ingenious strategies.

1. Bureau of Labor Statistics, College Enrollment and Work Activity of 2010 High School
Graduates, April 8, 2011, http://www.bls.gov/news.release/hsgec.nr0.htm.
2. Jean Johnson, Jon Rochkind, and Amber Ott with Samantha DuPont and Jeremy Hess, *One
Degree of Separation,* Public Agenda, 2011, Page 18, http://www.publicagenda.org/reports/
one-degree-separation.
3. Jean Johnson and Jon Rochkind with Amber Ott and Samantha DuPont, *Could I Get
a Little Advice Here?* Public Agenda, 2010, Page 3, http://www.publicagenda.org/files/pdf/
can-i-get-a-little-advice-here.pdf.
4. Ibid., Page 6.
5. Ibid.
6. Jean Johnson, Jon Rochkind, and Amber Ott, "Why Guidance Counseling Needs to
Change," *Educational Leadership,* April 2010, Pages 74–79, http://www.ascd.org/publications/
educational-leadership/apr10/vol67/num07/Why-Guidance-Counseling-Needs-to-Change.aspx.

Takeaway No. 5: For school leaders working in low-income communities, the time has come.

Superintendents and principals working in low-income communities face
a distinctive challenge and a historic opportunity. Just ramping up science
and math education in the prosperous suburbs won't help the United States
measure up. Unless we do it in low-income schools, too, many children,
especially poor, minority children, will be shut out of these fields. Not only
is this deeply unfair, it means the United States will lose out on the potential
contributions of these students, and our country will be poorer for it.

Superintendents and principals in mainly minority schools certainly see
the problem—they are almost twice as likely as superintendents and principals in mainly white schools to say that their students are not taught enough
math and science.[32] And it seems that students themselves may have picked
up on the discrepancy. According to Public Agenda student surveys, black
and Hispanic students are more likely than white students to say that in their
schools students are not learning enough math and science.[33]

The challenge begins in kindergarten and goes right up through high school, and it's basically a two-parter. President Clinton summarized one part: "Unfortunately, we currently give far too many of our students a watered-down curriculum inadequate to prepare them for the challenges of the global society and information age. . . . We create a tyranny of low expectations . . . [and] low expectations are the surest way of turning a child eager to learn into an angry, high school dropout who can't read."[34]

The second part is finding and holding on to effective, well-trained science and math teachers. According to a report from the National Academy of Sciences, "schools serving minority and poor students typically have the least qualified teachers."[35] Public Agenda surveys show that superintendents and principals in mainly minority schools see the challenge here too—they're more likely to support the sometimes controversial idea of paying more to teachers in "subjects like science and math where there are severe shortages."[36]

The United States needs all of its children to advance in the STEM fields—government recognizes it, as do leading colleges and universities and major corporations, some of which have established programs specifically aimed at helping poor, minority children advance in the STEM fields.[37] There are places where school leaders can get advice on building richer, more effective STEM programs that give poor, minority students an equal shot at excellence.

Erica Walker provides a useful overview of the academic research and some thought-provoking guidance in her article "Why Aren't More Minorities Taking Advanced Math?" in the November 2007 issue of *Educational Leadership*.[38] Her conclusion? Yes, money and resources are clearly an issue, but "we are overlooking innumerable chances to develop excellence in math achievement among African American and Latino students. We know that building on students' positive perceptions of mathematics while providing rich opportunities to do mathematics in and out of school can increase the numbers of minority students demonstrating such excellence. Let us commit to doing so on a large scale."

NOTES

1. White House Fact Sheet, Building American Skills by Strengthening Community Colleges, 2010, http://www.whitehouse.gov/sites/default/files/White_House_Summit_on_Community_Colleges_Fact_Sheet.pdf.

2. The College Board, *The Complete College Agenda Report,* 2010, http://completionagenda.collegeboard.org/sites/default/files/reports_pdf/Progress_Report_2010.pdf.

3. About 4 in 10 high school graduates complete an undergraduate degree after four years, and fewer than 1 in 5 finish an associate degree or certification program after two years. U.S. Department of Education "Tracking Students to 200 Percent of Normal Time: Effect on Institutional Graduation Rates." *National Center for Education Statistics*, December 2010, http://nces.ed.gov/pubs2011/2011221.pdf.

4. White House (July 14, 2009) Press Release. Retrieved on May 2, 2011, from: http://www.whitehouse.gov/the_press_office/Excerpts-of-the-Presidents-remarks-in-Warren-Michigan-and-fact-sheet-on-the-American-Graduation-Initiative/.

5. Based on an assessment from the ACT College Readiness study reported in The National Academy of Sciences, *Rising Above the Gathering Storm, Revisited: Rapidly Approaching Category 5*, Page 11, 2010, http://www.nap.edu/catalog.php?record_id=12999#description.

6. Jean Johnson and Jon Rochkind with Amber N. Ott and Samantha Dupont, *With Their Whole Lives Ahead of Them*, Public Agenda, 2009, Page 2, http://www.publicagenda.org/theirwholelivesaheadofthem.

7. Ibid.

8. See Trends in International Mathematics and Science Study (TIMSS) at http://nces.ed.gov/timss/.

9. Tom Loveless, "How Well Are American Students Learning," Brown Center on Education Policy at Brookings, February 2011, Page 3, http://www.brookings.edu/reports/2011/0207_education_loveless.aspx.

10. Ibid.

11. Achieve, Inc., "Aligning High School Graduation Requirements with the Real World: A Road Map for States," December 2007, Page 25, http://www.achieve.org/files/Achieve_PolicyBrief_Dec18v4.pdf.

12. For some examples, see Achieve, Inc., "Aligning High School Graduation Requirements with the Real World," http://www.achieve.org/files/Achieve_PolicyBrief_Dec18v4.pdf.

13. Phi Delta Kappa/Gallup Poll, *Highlights of the 2010 Phi Delta Kappa/Gallup Poll,* September 2010, Page 21, http://www.pdkintl.org/kappan/docs/2010_Poll_Report.pdf.

14. Ibid.

15. Met Life, *The MetLife Survey of the American Teacher: Collaborating for Student Success,* April 2010, Page 105, http://www.eric.ed.gov/PDFS/ED509650.pdf.

16. Public Agenda and Learning Point Associates/AIR, *Retaining Teaching Talent,* 2009, http://www.learningpt.org/expertise/educatorquality/genY/FullSurveyData.pdf.

17. Jean Johnson, Andrew Yarrow, Jonathan Rochkind, and Amber Ott, *Teaching for a Living: How Teachers See the Profession Today,* Survey by Public Agenda and Learning Point Associates/AIR, Originally published in Education Week, October 21, 2009, http://www.publicagenda.org/pages/teaching-for-a-living-full-survey-results.

18. For detailed results, see Jean Johnson and Ann Duffett with Amber Ott, *Life After High School,* Public Agenda, 2005, http://www.publicagenda.org/files/pdf/life_after_high_school.pdf.

19. Jean Johnson and Jon Rochkind with Amber Ott and Samantha Dupont, *With Their Whole Lives Ahead of Them, Public Agenda,* 2009, Page 24, http://www.publicagenda.org/files/pdf/theirwholelivesaheadofthem.pdf.

20. Ibid.

21. Public Agenda, *Are We Beginning to See the Light?* Prepared for the GE Foundation, December 2009, Full Survey Results, http://www.publicagenda.org/pages/math-and-science-ed-2010#Methodology.

22. Ibid.

23. Ibid.

24. Jean Johnson, Ana Maria Arumi, Amber Ott, and Michael Hamill Remaley, *Reality Check 2006, Issue No. 1: Are Parents and Students Ready for More Math and Science?* Public Agenda, 2006, Page 10, http://www.publicagenda.org/files/pdf/rc0601.pdf.

25. Chairman Bill Gates, Remarks before the Committee on Science and Technology United States House of Representatives, March 12, 2008, http://www.microsoft.com/presspass/exec/billg/speeches/2008/congress.mspx.

26. Alison Kadlec and Will Friedman with Amber Ott, *Important, But Not for Me: Parents and Students in Kansas and Missouri Talk about Math, Science, and Technology Education,* Public Agenda, 2008, Page 19, http://www.publicagenda.org/files/pdf/important_but_not_for_me.pdf.

27. Ibid.

28. Ibid.

29. Public Agenda, *Are We Beginning to See the Light?* http://www.publicagenda.org/pages/math-and-science-ed-2010#Methodology.

30. Public Agenda, "Unpublished Analysis of Survey of Young Adults Aged 22 through 30 Who Started College," 2009. Additional details available by request at info@publicagenda.org.

31. Paul Krugman, "Degrees and Dollars," *The New York Times,* March 6, 2011, http://www.nytimes.com/2011/03/07/opinion/07krugman.html?_r=1.

32. Jean Johnson, Ana Maria Arumi, and Amber Ott, *Reality Check 2006, Issue No. 4: The Insiders: How Principals and Superintendents See Public Education Today,* Public Agenda, 2006, Page 12, http://www.publicagenda.org/reports/reality-check-2006-issue-no-4.

33. Jean Johnson, Ana Maria Arumi, Amber Ott, and Michael Hamill Remaley, *Reality Check 2006, Issue No. 1: Are Parents and Students Ready for More Math and Science?* Page 12, http://www.publicagenda.org/files/pdf/rc0601.pdf.

34. President Bill Clinton, *Call to Action for American Education in the 21st Century,* February 13, 1997, http://www2.ed.gov/updates/PresEDPlan/part2.html.

35. The National Academies, *Rising above the Gathering Storm—Two Years Later,* National Academies Press, 2009, Page 7, http://download.nap.edu/cart/deliver.cgi?record_id=12537.

36. Jean Johnson, Ana Maria Arumi, and Amber Ott, *Reality Check 2006, Issue No. 4: The Insiders: How Principals and Superintendents See Public Education*

Today, Pages 13–14, http://www.publicagenda.org/reports/reality-check-2006-issue-no-4.

37. Take a look at the Viva Technology program from GreatMindsinSTEM.org. The idea is to "engage inner-city and rural K–12 students, teachers and parents in activities that stimulate their interest and academic achievement in STEM subjects." It sponsors events and conversations that bring students together with "world class engineers, technologists, scientists, and mathematicians." There's more at http://www.greatmindsinstem.org/vivatechnology/.

38. Erica N. Walker, "Why Aren't More Minorities Taking Advanced Math?" *Educational Leadership,* November 2007, xhttp://www.ascd.org/publications/educational-leadership/nov07/vol65/num03/Why-Aren't-More-Minorities-Taking-Advanced-Math%C2%A2.asp.

Chapter 8

When Money Is Short

In Shakespeare's Henry VI, Dick the Butcher (who is a villain, not a hero) urges his fellow plotters to first "kill all the lawyers." School leaders trying to cope with school funding issues in today's tough economy may find themselves torn between wanting to "kill all the pollsters" and "kill all the politicians." School leaders work best when they have robust, predictable, dependable levels of funding so that they can plan on what to do. In fact, 100 percent of principals surveyed by Met Life in 2009 said that "having adequate public funding and support for education was either very or somewhat important with 96 percent saying it was "very important."[1] But given all the hoopla in politics today, that sometimes seems like too much to ask.

WILL THEY BE AXING THE DEPARTMENT OF EDUCATION?

Surveys show that even with the U.S. federal budget hemorrhaging red ink, most Americans say they want federal funding for "elementary, secondary, and higher education" either increased (63%) or kept the same (22%). Despite whatever you've heard on talk radio about axing the U.S. Department of Education, just 7 percent of the public wants federal education funding "decreased a lot" or "eliminated entirely."[2] Even with the pressure to cut spending sharply to tackle the federal deficit, funding for education will likely continue at reasonable levels. National leaders are genuinely concerned about American students' academic achievement, and they have plenty of juicier targets like agriculture subsidies and defense contractors.

However, as school leaders are the first to tell you, a good 90 percent of their funding comes from localities (about 40%) or the states (about 50%),[3] and recent cuts here have sparked teacher layoffs and school closings all around the country. The carnage may ease as the economy picks up, but maintaining taxpayer support for local schools is a major battle for most school leaders. Anyone running for elected office is loath to raise taxes, and frankly, the polls on the public's willingness to support school funding are all over the place.

The brouhaha over money and education actually presents two different dilemmas for school leaders—one is whether there is anything they can do to bolster taxpayer support for local schools, and the second is how to decide how to spend the money, especially when there is less of it available.

THE KEY MESSAGES FROM THE OPINION RESEARCH

These tough, potentially divisive questions are often suited to the more intensive public engagement efforts like the ones I describe in Chapters 10 through 12, but for now, let's take a look at the lay of the land on public attitudes on school funding, and consider some general principles.

Finding No. 1: Surveys show mixed results on whether people think more money would do any good in education.
When the Gallup/Phi Delta Kappa 2010 poll asked Americans whether money matters in terms of educational quality, about a third of the public (32%) said the amount of money schools get makes "a great deal" of difference, while another 35 percent said that money matters "quite a lot."[4] What's more, concerns about the level of school funding have been at relatively high levels over the last few years. In 1970, only about 1 in 5 Americans saw "lack of financial support" as the biggest problem facing schools in their own communities. In 2010, that number was more than a third.[5]

But a slightly different question asked in 2011 by the Rasmussen survey picked up different results, and that's nearly always a sign that people have conflicted or ambivalent views on a topic. In the Rasmussen survey, only 34 percent of voters said that they believed that "student performance would improve if more money [was] spent on funding for schools."[6] Some 4 in 10 voters said that increased funding wouldn't improve student performance, and 25 percent said they weren't sure.[7]

There are a couple of considerations here, one being that surveys of people who vote regularly (the Rasmussen survey) sometimes yield somewhat different results than surveys of the broader public like the Gallup survey cited above. And the Rasmussen researchers asked about student performance—not just the overall quality of the schools. It's a more explicit question and a higher standard. Plus a good quarter of the voters admitted that they just weren't sure, which is always a sign of some uncertainty or ambivalence among those being surveyed.

But the discrepancy between the two polls is a clear warning that public opinion is not settled and fully thought through on this issue.

Finding No. 2: People may have a wish list, but that doesn't mean they're willing to pay the bill.
It's easy to find polls showing that majorities support changes in education that would likely be very costly, such as better pay for teachers, more science labs, or universal preschool.[8] In 2006, Public Agenda asked parents to choose among four different candidates for the school board: one supporting more testing and higher standards; another supporting vouchers; another supporting more charter schools; or a candidate who "believes if the public schools finally got more money and smaller classes, they could do a better job." Parents were twice as likely to support the candidate calling for more money and smaller classes than any of the others.[9]

Yet at the national level, and in community after community and state after state, the public's appetite for services doesn't match its willingness to pay for them. This phenomenon is not unique to education. People often support costly ideas to improve health care, reduce poverty, and generally enhance the quality of life in their communities and the nation overall. The mismatch between what people say they want and what they're willing to pay for has emerged in the battle over the national debt and federal deficit. It's playing out in state capitols and city halls across the land.

What's more, even when the spirit is willing, the pocketbook may not be able. In 2010, a study by the Pew Center on the States looked at public attitudes on government finances in five states—Arizona, California, Florida, Illinois, and New York. In all five, a plurality of the public picked K–12 public education over Medicaid, higher education, and transportation, as the *one area* "that you most want to protect" from state spending cuts (Medicaid came in second).[10] In all five states, at least 6 in 10 residents said they would be willing to pay higher taxes to maintain current funding for K–12 education.[11] But as the authors of the study point out: "The size of budget shortfalls in all five states will make fully protecting K–12 education and Medicaid, the biggest recipients of state dollars, difficult. Doing so would compel deeper cuts everywhere else, and even then may not be enough."[12]

Finding No. 3: People underestimate what their districts spend, and putting the numbers in front of them *decreases*—**rather than increases—their willingness to pay.**

Unless it's part of our jobs, most of us can't recite the facts and figures on most policy issues, so there is no reason to expect that typical citizens would understand school funding issues chapter and verse. Most people do seem to know that the bulk of the money comes from state and local taxpayers. Just 1 in 5 members of the public think the federal government is "most responsible" for paying for the K–12 education system.[13]

But according to studies by *Education Next* and the Program on Education Policy and Governance at Harvard (PEPG), most people dramatically underestimate what local school districts spend on a per-pupil basis, and they're off by stunningly large margins. When the researchers asked respondents in a 2007 survey to estimate per-pupil spending in their districts, the average response was $4,231, less than half the national per-pupil average ($10,400). The actual figures, of course, vary widely from district to district,[14] but as the researchers point out, "over 90 percent of the public offered an amount less than the amount actually spent in their districts, and more than 40 percent of the sample claimed that annual spending was $1,000 per pupil or less."[15] The more recent Rasmussen voter survey in 2011 picked up the very same pattern of public thinking.[16]

There's a similar phenomenon on teacher salaries. About 45 percent of Americans say that public school teachers are underpaid, while 18 percent think they are overpaid, and about a third (32%) consider their pay "about right."[17] But again, most people aren't that clear on the details. When the *Education Next*/PEPG researchers asked people to estimate what teachers earn, the average response in 2007 was: about $33,000, while the actual average teacher pay that year was over $47, 000.[18]

The problem for school leaders of course is that people seem to be dramatically underestimating what education costs. No district in the country functions on a $1,000 per pupil, and even experts who see waste in education spending aren't suggesting cuts to that extent. But if average citizens really think that's possible, that could spell trouble.

THE TAKEAWAYS

From a communications and engagement perspective, this mix of public attitudes—wanting more services, unwillingness to pay, doubts about whether more money will help, and minimal command of the facts—is one of the most difficult issues school leaders face. Later on, I will lay out a promising long-term strategy for ensuring stable support for public schools, but for now, here are three ground rules to keep in mind. They are fairly obvious perhaps, but they are basic.

Takeaway No. 1: Take polls showing that people will pay more for schools with a Gibraltar-sized grain of salt

Having worked with surveys for decades, I believe in their value as a tool to help leaders understand public concerns and priorities, and my experience suggests that most people try to be truthful. But surveys often pick up casual top-of-the-head responses that don't reflect what people will do when they give an issue closer attention. Nowhere is the admonition against taking poll results literally more necessary than in questions about paying higher taxes for good causes. Here's why a "yes" on survey questions to up school funding doesn't necessarily mean a "yes" at the ballot box.

- People want the schools to be better, and most appear to think money matters to some extent, but they're not feeling flush. Asking people to come up with more money in these unpredictable economic times is a tough sell. Most taxpayers are middle-class, not wealthy, and even more affluent taxpayers often feel the strain of rising college costs, health care costs, and the pressure to save for retirement. It's easy to agree to higher taxes over the phone. It's much tougher to watch the money coming out of your paycheck.
- Public schools aren't the only supplicant for public funds—health care, higher education, a crumbling infrastructure, iffy retirement systems, the need to invest in green energy, and others all make a claim for public dollars.
- People don't trust government, and when push comes to shove, many don't want to give it any more of their money. The public's doubts about the federal government are well known, but state and local governments aren't exactly winning the public's praises either. Only a third of the public (33%) say they can trust their state government to do what's right all or most of the time. About half of Americans (52%) say they can trust their local government to do what's right all or most of the time.[19] Local government does better, but there's still a fairly pitiful vote of confidence.

Here's what researchers at the Pew Center and California's Public Policy Institute wrote after they looked at public attitudes on taxes and spending in five states with difficult and unsettled finances: "After years of economic and fiscal challenges, residents of these stressed states are frustrated and distrustful. New leaders will have much ground to make up."[20]

Takeaway No. 2: When it comes to school funding, all politics is local.
Many of the public's fundamental views on education don't vary much from
region to region, from city to suburb, or from low-income communities
to more affluent ones, but views on school funding can change a lot. One
reason is that the level of taxpayer support for public schools varies across the
country, from a low of $5,644 to a high of $24,939 per pupil in 2004–2005.[21]
Tax burdens vary too. Adding up what residents pay in property, sales, and
other local taxes, The Tax Foundation calculated that the totals range from
about 6.4 percent of income in Alaska to 11.8 percent in New Jersey.[22]
Clearly, those variations make a huge difference in how people see school
funding issues locally—whether they believe local schools have enough
money and whether they believe taxpayers can reasonably be asked to pay
more. This is another reason to take national poll numbers on school funding
with that giant grain of salt. And unfortunately, state and local surveys can
be misleading too.

Takeaway No. 3: Show me the money.
The research by *Education Next* and Harvard's Program on Education Policy
and Governance demonstrates convincingly that, as the researchers put it,
"whatever motivates people's concerns about school finance, it is not sound
information about what is actually being spent."[23] According to their study
(confirmed by the Rasmussen polling), people typically underestimate what
local schools spend per pupil, and, not unexpectedly perhaps, support for
additional spending drops when people learn the details.[24]

Public Agenda focus groups also pick up doubts about whether school
funds are "reaching the classroom," or whether the money is being wasted on
"administration." In a 2006 survey, fewer than half of parents (46%) surveyed
gave their local superintendents good or excellent marks for "making sure
that taxpayer dollars get to the classroom," although here again, about a
quarter of the parents admitted that they didn't know.[25]

There is ample evidence that typical citizens and leaders in government,
business, and higher education see sound K–12 education as an absolute
necessity for the country to thrive. Research suggests that good public schools
yield enormous benefits in terms of strong property values and business and
job development.[26] In most communities, people probably won't allow local
schools to deteriorate while holding tight to their wallets.

But the days of "ask and you shall receive" are gone for a good long
while. That means that school leaders need to make a solid case for why
they need additional funds. They need to explain exactly what the money
will do and assure stressed taxpayers that it will not be wasted. They need
to be prepared to demonstrate that the money is improving children's

achievement and well-being in clear, persuasive terms. And, as I discuss later, they need to be sure that there are good lines of communication open between communities and schools on what's most important and where those hard-earned tax dollars end up being spent.

The time has come for school leaders to do more to engage parents and community members, along with local business and higher education leaders, in thinking through school and funding priorities in a much more inclusive, thoughtful way. There are practical, affordable ways to do it, and some school leaders and districts are already leading the way (See Chapter 12 for some specific examples).

NOTES

1. Met Life, *The MetLife Survey of the American Teacher: Collaborating for Student Success,* April 2010, Page 98, http://www.eric.ed.gov/PDFS/ED509650.pdf.

2. CNN/Opinion Research Corporation Poll. March 11–13, 2011, at http://www.pollingreport.com/budget.htm.

3. Marc Morial, *Public School Funding: Separate and Skewed,* Common Dreams. org, December 6, 2010, http://www.commondreams.org/view/2010/12/06–2.

4. Phi Delta Kappa/Gallup Poll, *Highlights of the 2010 Phi Delta Kappa/Gallup Poll,* September 2010, Page 14, http://www.pdkintl.org/kappan/docs/2010_Poll_Report.pdf.

5. Ibid., Page 13.

6. Rasmussen Reports, "72% Say Taxpayers Not Getting Their Money's Worth from Public Schools," April 27, 2011, http://www.rasmussenreports.com/public_content/politics/general_politics/april_2011/72_say_taxpayers_not_getting_their_money_s_worth_from_public_schools.

7. Ibid.

8. See, for example, Jean Johnson, Ana Maria Arumi, and Amber Ott, *Reality Check 2006, Issue No. 3: Is Support for Standards and Testing Fading?* Public Agenda, 2006, http://www.publicagenda.org/files/pdf/rc0603.pdf; Public Agenda, *Are We Beginning to See the Light?* Prepared for the GE Foundation, December 2009, Full Survey Results, http://www.publicagenda.org/pages/math-and-science-ed-2010#Methodology; and Yeson82.com, "New PPIC Poll Shows Prop. 82 With Majority Support," at http://www.yeson82.com/rel_033006a.php.

9. Jean Johnson, Ana Maria Arumi, and Amber Ott, *Reality Check 2006, Issue No. 3: Is Support for Standards and Testing Fading?* Page 7, http://www.publicagenda.org/files/pdf/rc0603.pdf.

10. Pew Center on the States and the Public Policy Institute of California, *Facing Facts: Public Attitudes and Fiscal Realities in Five Stressed States,* June 2010, www.pewcenteronthestates.org/budgetrealities.

11. Ibid.

12. Ibid.

13. Phi Delta Kappa/Gallup Poll, *Highlights of the 2010 Phi Delta Kappa/Gallup Poll,* Page 11, http://www.pdkintl.org/kappan/docs/2010_Poll_Report.pdf.

14. William G. Howell and Martin R. West, "Is the Price Right?" *Education Next,* Summer 2008, Page 39, www.educationnext.org.

15. Ibid.

16. Rasmussen Reports, "72% Say Taxpayers Not Getting Their Money's Worth from Public Schools," April 27, 2011, http://www.rasmussenreports.com/public_content/politics/general_politics/april_2011/72_say_taxpayers_not_getting_their_money_s_worth_from_public_schools.

17. Rasmussen Reports, "46% View Unionized Teachers As a Bad Thing, 37% Disagree," February 25, 2011, http://www.rasmussenreports.com/public_content/politics/general_politics/february_2011/46_view_unionized_teachers_as_a_bad_thing_37_disagree.

18. William G. Howell and Martin R. West, "Is the Price Right?" *Education Next,* Page 39, www.educationnext.org.

19. CNN/Opinion Research Corporation Poll. February 12–15, 2010, available at http://www.pollingreport.com/institut.htm#Government.

20. Mark Baldassare, quoted re: Pew Center on the States and the Public Policy Institute of California, *Facing Facts: Public Attitudes and Fiscal Realities in Five Stressed States,* June, 2010, www.pewcenteronthestates.org/budgetrealities.

21. William G. Howell and Martin R. West, "Is the Price Right?" *Education Next,* Page 38, www.educationnext.org.

22. Based on figures from The Tax Foundation (http://www.taxfoundation.org/taxdata/show/336.html) reported in Tonya Moreno, "Where You'll Pay the Most in State and Local Taxes," About.com at http://taxes.about.com/od/statetaxes/a/Highest-State-And-Local-Taxes.htm.

23. William G. Howell and Martin R. West, "Is the Price Right?" *Education Next,* Page 41, www.educationnext.org.

24. William G. Howell, Paul E. Peterson, and Martin R. West, "The Persuadable Public," *Education Next,* Fall 2009, Page 28, www.educationnext.org.

25. Public Agenda, *Reality Check 2006,* Full Survey Results. Contact info@publicagenda.org for details.

26. See Jonathan D. Weiss, *Public Schools and Economic Development: What the Research Shows,* Knowledgeworks Foundation, 2004, http://knowledgeworks.org/sites/default/files/knowledgebase/weiss_book.pdf.

Chapter 9

It Takes Two to Tango—Ensuring That Schools Have a Good Climate for Learning

Harry Potter appears to be a reasonably well-behaved, diligent student (although he certainly has some villainous teachers), but popular culture is awash with misbehaving youngsters whom we've come to love—Tom Sawyer, Bart Simpson, Eddie Haskell, just about all the boys in *Grease,* and even a few of the girls. No one expects young people to be well-behaved and squarely focused on their school work all the time. Corralling youthful high spirits and channeling them into more productive activities is part and parcel of education. Doing that successfully is important to teachers, principals, and superintendents, and to parents and students as well.

Getting the cooperation of students and parents in the learning enterprise encompasses several different issues, and they are all almost impossible to accomplish unless families and schools each play their part. Here are the four elements I see as most important.

- **Schools need to be safe.** This is a school leader's first and foremost responsibility. When you have someone else's children under your care, that's a moral duty. But parents and students need to understand and support the rules that ensure safety, and they need to accept them as fair and fairly enforced.
- **Schools should be orderly and focused on learning.** School leaders can set expectations, but again students and parents need to understand them, and students are more likely to rise to expected standards of behavior if all of the adults in their lives—parents, teachers, and school leaders—continually reinforce what's acceptable and what's not.
- **Teachers need to be respected** and know that their principals and superintendents will support them when necessary.

- **Students need to put in the effort to learn.** By the time students get to college, we generally accept that it's the students' responsibility to apply themselves to the work. If they don't, they suffer the consequences, and we generally see that as their own fault. With younger kids, however, the situation and the responsibilities are different. Most parents—most adults in fact—view teaching children to work hard and be persistent as part of education's mission.

THE KEY MESSAGES FROM THE OPINION RESEARCH

Earlier I flagged the issue of student behavior and motivation as "the elephant in the room." It is a problem that teachers, parents, and students often talk about with concern and frustration but that receives considerably less attention in the world of education experts and policy makers. In fact, some years ago when Public Agenda surveyed professors in the nation's education schools, 6 in 10 said that "when a public school teacher faces a disruptive class it probably means that he or she has failed to make lessons engaging enough to the students."[1] The implication is that any teacher who is motivated and effective wouldn't face any problems on this score—it's an issue of classroom management and planning. But teachers, parents, and, notably, students themselves see it as a more pervasive and fundamental problem—one that merits more robust answers. Here's an overview of what they have to say:

Finding No. 1: Discipline is a far more important issue for teachers, parents, and students than many reform experts realize.
Majorities of parents and the general public say problems like bullying, illegal drugs, and physical fighting are either very or somewhat serious problems at local schools.[2] Nearly 7 in 10 middle and high school teachers say there are serious problems in their schools with students who disrupt classes. By large majorities, most parents and teachers say that in local high schools, poor student behavior and social issues are a bigger problem than low standards and out-of-date curricula.[3]

Students see the problem too, and surveys conducted by Public Agenda over the years provide the dispiriting details. Nearly 8 in 10 students (77%) say they often hear cursing in the hallways at their schools; 4 in 10 report that there is a serious fight at least once a month.[4] About the same number say there are serious problems with cheating in their schools, and nearly half say their teachers spend more time trying to keep order than actually teaching.[5]

Finding No. 2: Many teachers are frustrated and demoralized by lack of respect and effort from students.

Public Agenda surveys, and surveys by others, are rife with findings detailing teachers' concerns about uncooperative, disrespectful students and the time and energy these students consume—time and energy that teachers believe could be spent on teaching and learning. Most teachers believe that parents need to do much more to prepare their children to work hard and cooperate at school. More than 8 in 10 teachers say parents who fail to set limits and hold their kids accountable for their behavior or academic performance are a serious problem where they teach. Only about 4 in 10 teachers report that all or most of their students "have a sense of responsibility for their own education."[6] But sometimes teachers' words offer better testimony than a litany of numbers.

Here are some sample comments about student misbehavior and lack of effort from teachers in Public Agenda focus groups over the years: "It just amazes me," said one teacher from New Jersey. "The gum chewing . . . the yawning aloud or putting their feet up on the desk. [It's] like they didn't know that was inappropriate." Another teacher talked about "students [who] just terrorize other students, and we can't get rid of them, and they know this."

A Florida teacher, like many we have interviewed, said most of her students are well-behaved and cooperative, but that a handful of difficult students repeatedly cause trouble: "It's a low number . . . but the effect is disproportionate. You can have one kid blow up a whole class." Another teacher was frank about how student misbehavior sometimes derails and undercuts her work: "Instruction becomes—I don't want to say the minimal piece, but often it does become that."[7]

Many teachers are also shaken and demoralized by what they see as disrespect from students and some parents as well. Many teachers complain about litigation-tinged attitudes of contempt and second-guessing. Nearly 8 in 10 teachers (78%) say students are quick to remind them that students have rights and that their parents can sue. Nearly half of teachers (49%) say that a parent has accused them of unfairly disciplining a child.[8]

Finding No. 3: There is evidence that concerns about student behavior drive would-be teachers from the field.

According to the Public Agenda/AIR survey of teachers nationwide in 2009, 50 percent say that "too many kids with discipline and behavior issues" is a major drawback of the job, and strikingly, this is a concern that outranks teachers' concerns about low salaries and lack of prestige.[9] Given the level and depth of teachers' frustration with student behavior and parental support issues, it shouldn't be surprising that teachers routinely say they prefer working in schools with good administrative and parental support than in schools where they could earn higher salaries.

There's also evidence that the perceptions about unruly classes and disrespectful students deter people who might like to teach from entering the field. When Public Agenda explored ideas for attracting more students from top colleges into K—12 teaching, worries about school climate and discipline emerged as a key hurdle. Many of the college students we interviewed—all of whom had considered a teaching career but chosen another field—described the problems they believed today's teachers face. A college student from Philadelphia said, "I wouldn't mind teaching. It's just the fact that a teacher is more than just a teacher. You also have to be a disciplinarian. That's the part that I really wouldn't want be concerned with." Another worried about having to be a "babysitter" rather than actually teaching. Some saw public schools as "combat zones" where teachers were continually distracted trying to keep order, with little time left for teaching. Many of the students had friends who had gone into teaching; they often described them as exhausted and demoralized by their job, sometimes even feeling physically threatened by students.[10]

Finding No. 4: Many parents admit that they struggle to raise well-behaved children who work hard in school.

It's routine to see public opinion polls criticizing "parents these days." In one Public Agenda study, more than 8 in 10 teachers (82 percent) and 7 in 10 parents (74 percent) said that "parents' failure to teach their children discipline" was one of the biggest causes of discipline problems in the schools. Rightly or wrongly, many Americans have come to believe that too many parents just aren't providing the stability, structure, and consistency that help children grow into responsible, compassionate, considerate adults.[11]

What may be slightly more surprising is the degree to which parents themselves sense that they are not accomplishing these goals with their own children. For example, even though 8 in 10 parents say it's "absolutely essential" to teach their children to always do their very best in school, only 50 percent say they have succeeded in this area.[12] The vast majority of parents consider it absolutely essential to teach their children to "have self-control and self-discipline, but only 34 percent say they have succeeded there.[13] Consequently, many parents are looking for advice on how they can transmit to and reinforce with their children the values of hard work, persistence, respectfulness, and self-discipline—values that most Americans view as essential to living a productive, responsible life. This is why Jo Frost the Supernanny and Dr. Phil have done so well on TV.

It is easy to criticize today's parents—and many Americans do just that—but for many, raising responsible, honorable children in today's celebrity-drenched, "scandal of the moment" culture can seem like an uphill battle. As

GOOD INTENTIONS, MIXED RESULTS

In 2002, Public Agenda asked parents in the survey how essential each of the following character values were to teach their children, and whether they have succeeded. This chart shows the resulting gap between goal and performance.[1]

Table 9.1.   A Report Card for Parents

Item	% of Parents Saying Item is "Absolutely Essential"	% of Parents Saying They have Succeeded in Helping Children Master Item	Gap
Have self-control and self-discipline	83%	34%	49
Save money and spend it carefully	70%	28%	42
Be honest and truthful	91%	55%	36
Be independent and do for themselves	74%	38%	36
Always do their very best in school	82%	50%	32
Have good nutrition and eating habits	68%	40%	28
Be courteous and polite	84%	62%	22
Have strong religious faith	61%	53%	8
Help those who are less fortunate	62%	55%	7
Exercise and to be physically fit	51%	53%	−2
Enjoy art and literature	33%	51%	−18

Source: Public Agenda

From Steve Farkas, Jean Johnson, and Ann Duffett, with Leslie Wilson and Jackie Vine, *A Lot Easier Said than Done,* Public Agenda, 2002, Page 18, http://www.publicagenda.org/files/pdf/easier_said_than_done.pdf.

Public Agenda researchers wrote in a national study of parents called *A Lot Easier Said than Done,* "Whether they are affluent or struggling, whether they raise their child alone or with a spouse, whether they live in the cities or the suburbs, whether they are raising a young child or a teen, today's parents voice a gnawing unease about society's impact on their children. According to parents, there are just too many dangers, too many temptations, and too many harmful influences for them to be able to relax."[14] In truth, most parents are eager for allies in the cause of bringing up their children well.

AS CONDITIONS WARRANT

Obviously, problems with school climate and unruly student behavior manifest themselves in different ways in different schools. Some schools do offer a climate that nurtures the process of teaching and learning. Some have problems, but problems that are confined to a handful of students. Other schools have problems that are more widespread. And the problems themselves can run the gamut: some problems pose physical dangers for teachers and students, while others are mainly a threat to civility and learning.

Schools have made progress on addressing the most terrifying risks for teachers and students since Columbine and several other nearly unfathomable tragedies. Even so, according to government statistics, nearly 2700 students were expelled in the 2006–2007 school year for bringing a firearm to school.[15] In 2006, about 1 in 10 teachers reported "threats to teachers or staff by students," according to a survey by Met Life. The modestly good news is that less dangerous problems like "disorderly student behavior" and absenteeism are the ones that are more prevalent. About 4 in 10 teachers report problems here.[16]

THE TAKEAWAYS

Nationwide, more than half of teachers say that conditions in their schools are "very good" when it comes to "having an orderly, safe and respectful school atmosphere," while 39 percent say conditions are "manageable."[17] As far as I am concerned, that's little better than a split decision. The fact that some 4 in 10 teachers nationwide can't give their schools a thumbs-up in this basic area suggests that school leaders have work to do here. Turning a blind eye to these problems undercuts the nation's goal of raising academic achievement. And given that some schools are doing better than others in providing a good atmosphere for teaching and learning, just "living with" these circumstances undercuts our claim that we want a just society where all children have an equal chance. So what are the takeaways?

Takeaway No. 1: School climate and lack of student cooperation simply have to be on the table as priority issues.
Based on surveys of teachers and students who are in our schools every day, incivility, distraction, and disorder are commonplace. Yet we expect teachers to teach to high standards, and youngsters to obtain world-class academic skills in this kind of unsettled atmosphere.[18]

Some of the problems are deadly serious, while others are merely youthful high jinks, but the bottom line is this: 77 percent of secondary teachers say that they could be teaching a lot more effectively if it "weren't for discipline problems."[19] More than 4 in 10 parents say that their own child could accomplish more in school if teachers weren't so distracted by discipline issues.

Meanwhile, there is nearly universal support among teachers and parents for some measure to address the situation: 91 percent of teachers and 88 percent of parents support the idea that "enforcing the little rules sets a tone so that bigger problems can be avoided." Nearly as many—87 percent of teachers and 74 percent of parents—support the idea of "establishing alternative schools for chronic offenders." Teachers often comment in focus groups about how ineffective suspension is as a punishment, especially for alienated teens who often seem to regard it as a holiday from school or even a badge of honor.

According to 2006 government statistics, "about 1 out of every 14 students (or 7%) was suspended from school at least once during the year," with higher figures for boys and African American students.[20] Suspension is an unsatisfactory solution, one, frankly, that hasn't shown much success in changing the behavior of seriously troubled, alienated youngsters. The degree to which schools continue to rely on suspension as an enforcement tool also raises the question of whether, as a society, we're all merely choosing the path of least resistance. Are we really comfortable abandoning repeat troublemakers as lost causes and consigning them to education oblivion?

There is very little in the public opinion data to suggest that this is the course of action most Americans want. According to surveys, most Americans believe that nearly all youngsters can be helped, even if they have veered seriously off course as teenagers. Three-quarters of the public says that given enough adult attention, just about all kids can learn and succeed in school. Only a handful of Americans say that the most troubled teens "are beyond the point where they can be helped."[21]

I am not sure why education's top echelons don't invest more time and energy in understanding why discipline problems arise; which policies work best; and what schools, teachers, parents, and others need to do to change the status quo. Leaders in academia, business, government, and foundations have certainly come together to invest money in research and tackle other important educational topics. Sometimes, it's easy to lose track of the scores of reports and symposia devoted to improving teacher quality, teacher evaluation and performance pay, school leadership, and deciding on a core curriculum. Yet there's much less real work being done on this issue that causes so much anguish within schools and steals so much time and energy from teachers and students. Why isn't there more deep thinking about how to solve this problem?[22]

I am certainly not suggesting that school leaders can solve this problem by themselves, but I am suggesting that it may be time for them to use their collective voice to get this issue higher on the research and reform agenda. And school leaders can reach out to their communities and schools to consider what useful steps can be taken at a district and school level.

Takeaway No. 2: Disrespect and incivility are taking a toll.
For school leaders, it's natural to focus on first things first. When you're juggling more challenges than you can possibly handle, you obviously need to address the most serious threats to school safety and order first. But the rough-edged adolescent culture that prevails in many schools is also taking a toll—as most school leaders clearly recognize.

According to students, profanity and cheating are commonplace, as is disrespect for teachers and disrespect among students for each other as well. Seventy-five percent of the general public and 7 in 10 parents say that "students treating teachers with a lack of respect" is a very or somewhat serious problem.[23] Most Americans think we can and should do better here.

Public Agenda's research among parents suggests that many are looking to schools—and the culture of the school—to reinforce their efforts to raise more considerate, honest, diligent children. Many view contemporary culture as an outright enemy in this regard. In Public Agenda focus groups on the media, both parents and teachers are as bothered by the mouthy, smart-aleck role models in TV sitcoms as they are about more blatant sex and violence.[24] In many respects, parents believe they are fighting an uphill battle against a prevailing popular culture, and for some it seems that the climate in local middle schools and high schools isn't an ally.

This doesn't mean most people want schools to become rigid, soul-crushing institutions where children cower before adults, and silence is the rule. This is not at all what most parents or teachers have in mind. Both say sparking a child's curiosity and love of learning are absolutely essential elements of good schooling. For teachers and parents, better discipline simply means a little more order, fewer disruptions, more student cooperation and effort, and perhaps a little more courtesy all round. It doesn't seem too much to ask.

From a communications and engagement perspective, it may be in these "softer" areas of school culture where reaching out to parents, teachers, and students could have the greatest impact. Organizing meetings where a school community talks about expectations and discusses the standards of behavior acceptable at school may reveal more consensus in this area than anyone realizes. Giving parents, students, and teachers an opportunity to help define and clarify what's expected at school can help prevent the misunderstandings that lead to administrative red tape, hearings, and can even end up in court. Educational research has demonstrated persuasively that teacher and parent expectations have an outsized impact on children's academic learning.[25] Maybe it's time to tap the power of adult expectations to improve student behavior and respectfulness as well.

Takeaway No. 3: Lack of student effort and concentration is the next frontier.
Most teachers accept responsibility for engaging and motivating students: 9 in 10 say that whether students are engaged in their school work is a good or excellent measure of their success as a teacher. Teachers are somewhat more divided on whether they can reliably unleash effort from all of their students or whether some portion of student effort stems from attitudes students themselves bring into the classroom—39 percent of teachers say that "the effort students make is mainly determined by the level of motivation they bring to the classroom," while 59 percent say it's "mainly determined by what teachers do to motivate them once they get there."[26]

A small-scale study conducted by Public Agenda and the FDR Group suggests that motivating teens and getting them to put in their best effort in school could be a tall order among today's wired, multitasking students. The study looked at a small number of secondary school students, most considered high- or mid-to-high achievers.[27] Here are some highlights:

- Although there were a few exceptions, "about an hour is the maximum amount of time most of these students spend on a given subject in one sitting."
- Most tended to multitask, even though most also acknowledged that they didn't do their best work in these circumstances. According to the study, "listening to music or TV while studying is typical for many. When it comes to the computer, some students told us that they make a conscious effort (an effort at which they often fail) to stay away from it while doing homework or studying. The biggest distraction appears to be instant messaging."
- Most also described their classrooms as "noisy and full of wasted time," and many didn't regard reading, group work, or homework as particularly useful aspects of their school and learning experiences. Most didn't really make a connection, for example, between reading for pleasure and doing well in school.
- Virtually all indicated exposure to group work in class, but none described it as particularly helpful—at worst it made learning more difficult and at best it was benign.
- Homework was perceived mainly as "busy work."

This is a huge conundrum for educators, one that shouldn't just be dumped on teachers. To me, it's odd that student motivation and concentration aren't widely seen as vital, intellectually challenging, and supremely important subjects for researchers. Teachers, parents, and others are looking for more effective ways to help young people develop focus and the ability to concentrate in school. Educators across the country are looking for better ways to help youngsters who don't thrive in traditional settings and doing traditional school work.

Most school leaders can't commission studies and set up task forces to hone in on this challenge, but as the key decision makers in schools and districts nationwide, it might be in the interest of all of us for school leaders to call for a lot more research in this area.

TEN O'CLOCK SCHOLARS: STUDENTS TALK ABOUT HOW THEY STUDY AND WHAT THEY'RE LEARNING IN SCHOOL

Several years ago, Public Agenda conducted a small, but fascinating, set of interviews with high-achieving and mid-to-high-achieving students asking them to tell us about their classes and their views on what it takes to do well in school.[1] Here's a sampling of what we heard:

> "The big things like essays, I'd procrastinate to the last minute. I would basically put as much pressure on myself as possible, like 'I have to do this now. I cannot do this any other time.' I'd have to be in a situation like that to buckle down."

> "I don't study at all. If I didn't learn it already, for me to cram the night before, it's not worth it. If I don't know it then, I can't do anything about that."

> "I want good grades. The way I see it, you work as hard as you can up until college and during college too, and then that determines what you're going to be when you grow up. I could choose to slack and not be as successful, and then later on, that won't sit well with me."

> "Some teachers just read it. They'll give you the lesson with no spunk or anything. They just read [to] you. It's so boring sometimes, and that's not what keeps you. I remember I had one teacher—I had her for global—and she made sure that everybody worked. She got into it. She put her emotion into it. She gave you a little bit about how she felt about the lesson or whatever."

> "I think it depends on how it's being taught. For example, in U.S. [history] my first term, I had a teacher who taught college style. He would lecture us—no writing on the board, just lecture, but he would say it in a way that was very understandable. The next following term, I had a teacher who wrote everything on the board and said things right out of the text book. I felt like I didn't know anything but what she had just said."

"In math I was learning how to do long division, and I was not good at it at all, so I just kept trying to get it, and everybody was screaming in the classroom. . . . They were yelling, so then I just concentrated and tuned everything out, so that was really hard for me."

"I pick up things that I know I'm probably going to use ahead. So that's why I was doing so bad in math, cause for me, the math we were learning was stuff like I knew in ten years I'm not going to use it. . . . I was trying to keep my grade level, so I would pass, but it wasn't like I need it, so it was so hard to pay attention in class . . . like, why would I need to know how to find the angle of some triangle?"

1. Ruth Wooden, Jean Johnson, Paul Gasbarra, and Ann Duffett, "Key Observations from an Exploratory Look at Student Views on Studying and Concentration," Public Agenda and the FDR Group, August 18, 2008. Contact info@publicagenda.org for additional information.

Takeaway No. 4: Insuring that all schools are safe, orderly, and focused on learning is a matter of justice.

Here's how we think about what's acceptable and fair for adults. If an employee works in an environment where disrespect, profanity, fighting, substance abuse, and other troubling behavior is tolerated or winked at by management, we call this a hostile workplace and consider it a violation of the law. But roughly a third of African American youngsters face a school environment with exactly those problems.[28] In fact, when Public Agenda asked students to rate their schools on key academic and social dimensions— resources, promotion policies, dropout rates, truancy, fighting, drug and alcohol abuse, and others—African American and Hispanic students were more likely than their white counterparts to report very serious problems in nearly every category.

As Public Agenda's research has shown, most students regardless of race or ethnic background voice concern about lack of respect, profanity, and drug and alcohol abuse in their schools, but the levels of concern are routinely higher for minority students—disturbingly higher.

According to research, about 3 in 10 African American students attend schools with considerable turmoil.[29]

- Thirty percent of black students report that teachers spend more time trying to keep order than teaching.
- Thirty percent say their schools have very serious problems with drug and alcohol abuse.

- Thirty-two percent report very serious problems with fighting and weapons.
- Thirty-three percent say their schools are not consistent in enforcing discipline and behavior rules.
- Thirty-seven percent say their schools have very serious problems with kids cutting classes.
- Fifty-two percent say their schools have very serious problems with kids who lack respect for teachers and use bad language.
- At the same time, nearly half of Hispanic students (44%) report that their schools have very or somewhat serious problems with kids dropping out. [30]

As we pointed out when we issued our report, this is not "grumbling from a group of easily shocked adults who haven't been inside a school in years and still haven't come to grips with today's teen fashions." This is what young people report themselves. They say problems like truancy and disrespect for teachers are very serious in their schools—not just "somewhat serious," but "very serious."

Surveys of minority parents and teachers who work in mainly minority schools confirm much of what the teens report. Thirty-one percent of African American parents and 20 percent of Hispanic parents give local school superintendents fair or poor ratings for ensuring that schools are safe and orderly; just 13 percent of white parents make this complaint. Twenty-seven percent of African American parents and 30 percent of Hispanic parents say that too much fighting and too many weapons are serious problems in their local schools; again only 13 percent of white parents say the same.[31]

The findings from this work are not uniformly bleak: Healthy majorities of all students—black, white, and Hispanic—told us that they had had a teacher who was able to get them interested in a subject that they hadn't really liked before.[32] And across all racial and ethnic groups most parents believed that their children's schools are better than the ones they attended when they were young.[33]

But the differences among the student experiences are too jarring to ignore. For far too many minority youngsters, rowdy, unsettled schools are the norm. That has to be discouraging and distracting for them, and it should be a warning bell for anyone who believes in an equal educational chance for all.

NOTES

1. Steve Farkas and Jean Johnson with Ann Duffett, *Different Drummers: How Teachers of Teachers View Public Education,* Public Agenda, 1997, Page 31, http://www.publicagenda.org/files/pdf/different_drummers_0.pdf.

2. Public Agenda, "Nearly Three In Four Americans Say Bullying Is A Serious Problem In Their Local Schools," April 2010, http://www.publicagenda.org/pages/bullying-2010.

3. Jean Johnson, Ana Maria Arumi, Amber Ott, and Michael Hamill Remaley, *Reality Check 2006, Issue No. 1: Are Parents and Students Ready for More Math and Science?* Public Agenda, 2006, Page 4, http://www.publicagenda.org/files/pdf/rc0601.pdf, and Public Agenda, *Reality Check 2006,* Contact info@publicagenda.org for full question results.

4. Jean Johnson, "Isn't It Time for Schools of Education to Take Concerns about Student Discipline More Seriously?" *Teachers College Record,* February 14, 2005.

5. Ibid.

6. MetLife, Inc. *Collaborating for Student Success, Part 1: Effective Teaching and Leadership,* Page 17, http://www.metlife.com/assets/cao/contributions/foundation/american-teacher/MetLife_Teacher_Survey_2009_Part_1.pdf.

7. Reported in Jean Johnson, "Why Is School Discipline Considered a Trivial Issue?" *Education Week,* June 23, 2004.

8. Public Agenda, *Teaching Interrupted: Do Discipline Policies in Today's Public Schools Foster the Common Good?* Public Agenda and Common Good, 2004, Pages 2–3, http://www.publicagenda.org/files/pdf/teaching_interrupted.pdf.

9. Jean Johnson, Andrew Yarrow, Jonathan Rochkind, and Amber Ott, *Teaching for a Living: How Teachers See the Profession Today,* Survey by Public Agenda and Learning Point Associates/AIR, Originally published in *Education Week,* October 21, 2009, http://www.publicagenda.org/pages/teaching-for-a-living-full-survey-results.

10. Public Agenda, "What Would It Take To Attract More Talented, Accomplished Americans To Teaching?" A Pilot Study Conducted by Public Agenda for the Woodrow Wilson Foundation, 2007.

11. For example, when the Pew Research Center queried members of the public about families today, most voiced concerns about single women raising children and nearly 4 in 10 worried about the impact of women with young children working outside the home. More than 4 in 10 said they were pessimistic about the education system, and even more (51%) said they were pessimistic about the country's moral and ethical standards. Pew Research Center, "The Decline of Marriage and Rise of New Families," November 18, 2010, http://pewresearch.org/pubs/1802/decline-marriage-rise-new-families.

12. Steve Farkas, Jean Johnson, and Ann Duffett, with Leslie Wilson and Jackie Vine, *A Lot Easier Said than Done,* Public Agenda, 2002, Page 18. http://www.publicagenda.org/files/pdf/easier_said_than_done.pdf.

13. Ibid.

14. Ibid., Page 9.

15. U.S. Department of Education, Report on the Implementation of the Gun-Free Schools Act in the States and Outlying Areas: School Years 2005–06 and 2006–07, 2010, http://nces.ed.gov/fastfacts/display.asp?id=54.

16. Met Life, *The MetLife Survey of the American Teacher: Expectations and Experiences,* September 2006, Page 56, http://www.eric.ed.gov/PDFS/ED496558.pdf.

17. Jean Johnson, Andrew Yarrow, Jonathan Rochkind, and Amber Ott, *Teaching for a Living: How Teachers See the Profession Today,* http://www.publicagenda.org/pages/teaching-for-a-living-full-survey-results.

18. Jean Johnson, "Why Is School Discipline Considered A Trivial Issue?" *Education Week,* June 23, 2004.

19. Public Agenda, *Teaching Interrupted,* Page 2, http://www.publicagenda.org/files/pdf/teaching_interrupted.pdf.

20. U.S. Department of Education, School Characteristics and Climate, Student Suspensions and Expulsions, http://nces.ed.gov/programs/coe-indicator_sdi.asp.

21. Ann Duffett, Jean Johnson, and Steve Farkas, *Kids These Days '99,* Public Agenda, 1999, Page 7. http://www.publicagenda.org/files/pdf/kids_these_days_99.pdf.

22. Jean Johnson, "Why Is School Discipline Considered A Trivial Issue?" *Education Week,* June 23, 2004.

23. Public Agenda, "Nearly Three In Four Americans Say Bullying Is A Serious Problem in Their Local Schools," April 2010, http://www.publicagenda.org/pages/bullying-2010.

24. Jean Johnson, "What Parents Are Saying About TV These Days," Public Agenda, 2002, http://www.publicagenda.org/files/pdf/parents_tv.pdf.

25. See for example, National Education Association, *Research Spotlight on Parental Involvement in Education: NEA Reviews of the Research on Best Practices in Education* at http://www.nea.org/tools/17360.htm, and Michigan Department of Education, *What Research Says about Parental Involvement in Children's Education,* 2002, http://www.michigan.gov/ . . . /Final_Parent_Involvement_Fact_Sheet_14732_7.pdf.

26. Jean Johnson, Andrew Yarrow, Jonathan Rochkind, and Amber Ott, *Teaching for a Living: How Teachers See the Profession Today*, http://www.publicagenda.org/pages/teaching-for-a-living-full-survey-results.

27. Ruth Wooden, Jean Johnson, Paul Gasbarra, and Ann Duffett, "Key Observations from an Exploratory Look at Student Views on Studying and Concentration," Public Agenda and the FDR Group, August 18, 2008. Contact info@publicagenda.org for additional information.

28. Jean Johnson, Ana Maria Arumi, and Amber Ott, *Reality Check 2006, Issue No. 2: How Black and Hispanic Families Rate Their Schools*, Public Agenda, 2006, http://www.publicagenda.org/files/pdf/rc0602.pdf.

29. Jean Johnson, Ana Maria Arumi, and Amber Ott, *Reality Check 2006, Issue No. 2: How Black and Hispanic Families Rate Their Schools*, Page 8, http://www.publicagenda.org/files/pdf/rc0602.pdf.

30. Ibid., Page 7.

31. Ibid., Page 14.

32. Ibid., Page 5.

33. Ibid., Page 2.

Chapter 10

The Big Turnaround

Whether or not to close a persistently failing school or take other clear-cut steps, such as replacing the principal and staff, has to be one of the toughest choices superintendents face. These decisions are always controversial. They can be thorny even when school leaders make every effort to be transparent and fully explain the issues involved. Making the right decision can mean genuine progress in giving children the high-quality, high-standards education they deserve.

As for making the wrong decision—well, there are multiple ways to derail. Backing away from tough decisions because of pushback from the community can mean leaving students, teachers, and principals working in environments that crush teaching and learning. Pushing changes through in the face of strong opposition from the community can mean that reforms will be short-lived—they simply can't be sustained given the level of resistance and antagonism.

Sometimes school leaders decide to put new schools, principals, teaching teams, and practices into place "from the top," often with strong support from mayors and other elected officials. But the "my way or the highway" approach can damage trust and cohesion in the community. It can leave principals working with alienated, suspicious parents, teachers, and students. It can provoke political opposition, as happened in Washington, DC, with the reforms of Michele Rhee. It can leave school leaders fighting a lonely battle, and in most cases, that's not the best formula for long-term, turnaround success.

IS THERE A WAY TO TURN DOWN THE VOLUME?

For school leaders, there are questions galore:

- Is there anything school leaders can do to tone down the unhealthy dynamic that has emerged in cities and towns across the country when schools are closed or when popular, but ineffective, principals and teachers are replaced as part of school turnaround reforms?
- What about negative reactions that accompany proposals to break up large, underperforming schools into smaller, more manageable units?
- What about the uproar that often ensues when charter schools are added to the choices available in a community?
- What about when schools have to be closed for financial reasons or when declining school populations make keeping them open untenable and unacceptably costly?
- How can superintendents and principals play a positive role in these discussions when the proposed changes are so confusing and threatening for so many parents, students, teachers, and members of the broader community?

Step number one is developing a better understanding of why people react so strongly to these proposals and being clearer about what kinds of concerns, fears, and gaps in knowledge are driving these controversies. I would argue that leaders with integrity need to do what's best for the students, and sometimes that may be a very unpopular choice. But recognizing and understanding the perspective of those who oppose change doesn't have to mean backing away from reform.

In some cases, leaders may be able to make better choices by listening to and incorporating community concerns. In others, at least they will be better able to help communities cope with unwanted change if they understand and show respect for parent and neighborhood concerns.

Public Agenda has looked carefully at the views of parents and local advocates in communities that are facing or have already faced the prospect of school closings or other major changes related to transforming persistently failing schools.[1] Here are some key points school leaders need to consider.

Finding No. 1: Most parents with children in low-performing schools do want change.
New York City Mayor Michael Bloomberg is often considered a master politician, but he dramatically misread community feelings when he said this

about parents opposed to his plans to close 22 low-performing city schools: "Unfortunately, there are some who just come from—they never had a formal education, and they don't understand the value of education."[2] Public Agenda research reveals a very different mindset.

It is certainly true that most parents can't recite the facts and figures about school performance that school leaders (and mayors) pore over. It is also true that parents of children in persistently low-performing schools are likely to be poorer and less-well-educated. But in years of conducting research for Public Agenda, I have rarely seen parents who didn't grasp "the value of education." In fact, parents who have not had the benefits of a good education themselves often have a special goal of making sure that their own children get better chances than they had. Minority parents, for example, are more concerned about low standards and the state of math and science education in local schools than white parents—and justifiably so in far too many cases.[3]

In Public Agenda's focus groups in communities with low-performing schools, parents routinely voiced gnawing doubts about the quality of local schools even before the moderator broached the subject. In Washington, DC, for example, one mother of a seventh grader worried about her child's teachers: "My [son's] teachers are just not engaging with the students," she complained. "They're just there. You wonder why you go into a profession to teach. . . ."

A mother of a 10-year-old in Denver complained about ineffective school leadership: "I'm pretty much [at my child's school] all the time. . . . [As for] how the school has been run for the last year, it's unorganized." A Detroit father was not at all reassured just because his child was getting good grades: "I can't be happy that my daughter is on the honor roll knowing that those teachers in her school might be [failing her]." Another Detroit parent decided it was time to pull the plug on the local public schools: "When it was time to put my kids in school, the public school down the street [had] a police car there for the second graders . . . that was a great deterrent for me, so I found the nearest charter school."

Many of the parents also voiced anger and outrage at anonymous, bureaucratic school administrations that they saw as deeply dysfunctional and even corrupt. Here's what a Detroit mother said to Public Agenda's New York-based focus group moderator (He had mentioned where he lived when he introduced himself to the group): "Can I ask—in [New York City], do people come into your office and then just pillage and rape and . . . take everything that is not nailed down? Because in Detroit . . . as far as the mayor, the police department . . . whatever they can take, whatever false charity they can set up, whatever they can do to . . . suck all the money out of it is what happens."

A mother in Washington said that the school system there "is not backing our students up. You know what I mean? They're really not interested in our students." In Denver, a mother pointed to the lack of responsiveness of the school system and local government: "[They] pretend to listen. They say what you want to hear." Not only are most parents in communities with low-performing schools anxious about the quality of local schools, they are also often deeply distrustful of local government and school officials who, in their view, have ignored and underserved their children for far too long.

Finding No. 2: Local public schools are profoundly important to communities even though they are often dissatisfied with them.
Given parents' longing for better schools for their children, you might assume that most would be eager to have new charter schools in their neighborhoods or to be able to send their children to higher-performing schools in other parts of the city.

Many parents are looking for better options, and Public Agenda's qualitative research suggests that many are familiar with charter schools and often admire their practices. In 2009, the researchers at *Education Next*/HPEG found that about 4 in 10 Americans supported the formation of charters (described as "publicly funded, but not managed by the local school board"). The researchers also found that support increased to roughly half when survey respondents were told that President Obama supported charters or that a research study had shown positive academic results for charter schools.[4]

But receptivity to charters doesn't mean people are ready to close down public schools or change the current public school system into one based on competition and choice. Parents and community members often see "their" local public schools as a symbols of their communities. They often voice deep affection for these schools even as they recognize their flaws.

At the most basic level, what most of the parents in the Public Agenda study wanted was for their local public schools to be good public schools. Replacing a failing school with a new entity or giving people the option to send their children to better schools elsewhere did not ease their sense of loss and disappointment that the school they were familiar with—right there in their own neighborhood—was closing. In Detroit, where the city has closed dozens of public schools due to declining enrollment and financial problems, one mother said this: "Detroit Public Schools represent our history . . . our legacy. Detroit public schools are a part of Detroit. If Detroit public schools fail, Detroit fails. They look bad—we look bad. It's a big picture. We want to succeed." This is a very common view—and often an intense and emotional one.

Table 10.1. Public Views on What to Do about Persistently Troubled Schools

% of the General Public Responding:	
54%	Keep the school open with existing teachers and principal and provide comprehensive outside support.
17%	Close the school and reopen with a new principal.
13%	Close the school and reopen as a public charter school.
11%	Close the school and send the students to other, higher performing schools.
5%	Don't know.

Source: Phi Delta Kappa/Gallup Poll, September, 2010

Finding No. 3: For people in a community, having their school closed is a defeat and a loss.

Even in the abstract, the idea of closing a school bothers most Americans. Table 10.1 shows results from a Phi Delta Kappa/Gallup survey that asked what should be done about a "consistently poor-performing school in your community."[5]

More than half of Americans immediately push back on the idea of closing a school, even one that is severely underperforming. Most people see the better approach as trying to help and reform the existing school.

Based on Public Agenda's research, the opposition is even more intense when parents and community members consider the prospect that a local public school, one they are actually familiar with, will be closed. Parents bring a number of concerns to the table. Here are just a few of them—and in Public Agenda's work, most people actually had more than one of these concerns:

- Many parents fear sending their children to a new and unfamiliar school, and often the children object as well.
- Many feel a rapport with their children's teachers, seeing them as hard-working, nurturing people who have the children's best interests at heart.
- Many are suspicious of people "downtown" making the decisions.
- Many are skeptical and resentful that "outsiders" who don't understand "our neighborhood" are deciding what to do about "our school."
- Many do not know about or understand the information showing how poorly a school is performing. Many do not understand how brutally inadequate some of these schools are.
- Some question whether the information that's being reported in local papers or provided by the school department is accurate. Some suspect that this information is being manipulated so that their school is closed while schools in other neighborhoods remain open.

- Most lack the framework that drives reformers—the need for a fresh start, the need for improved management and leadership in the school, the benefits of bringing in more innovative and creative educators.
- Many parents cannot envision what the alternative schools are really like.

Instead, people see the school closing as a defeat and a loss. They often feel that their community is being written off or abandoned. A parent advocate in Seattle pointed out that "people, no matter what their school is doing, love their school, because schools are such a neighborhood thing. People sort of use them as a touchstone."

A New York City community advocate highlighted the fallout from closing a school regardless of whether some students benefit from the decision. "Unless someone can prove to me that [closing schools] has worked somewhere in the country to improve outcomes overall, not just for the kids who were once educated in that building, I'd say it's extremely disruptive and extremely damaging."

Finding No. 4: Closing a school seems like such an extreme solution.
For many people, closing a school seems like an extreme, drastic decision, and they have a hard time seeing how it could possibly help teachers and students. In the Public Agenda focus groups, we talked at length about why school leaders sometimes propose closing schools and explained some of the thinking behind it—the benefits of bringing in new schools and school programs and principals and teachers with good track records of helping troubled students. The focus groups also emphasized that, in many cases, there have been repeated attempts to help troubled schools by providing more resources and support and that little seemed to change. The parents in the group thought about the issues carefully, and some did change their minds about some ideas—such as bringing in a new principal and staff with good experience turning struggling schools around. But in focus groups around the country, hardly anyone thought that closing a school is the best choice, even after getting more information and having a chance to think about the arguments in favor of it. In the end, the arguments against it, in most people's minds, are simply too powerful.

Finding No. 5: For most parents and community residents, lack of support for schools is seen as the more pressing problem.
Another reason parents and community members resist the idea of closing a school so strongly is that they believe that these persistently failing schools operate under very trying circumstances—a whole variety of them. For many people, that means that a) it is understandable why the principal and the teachers are having problems helping children learn, and/or b) any school or

group of educators is going to have problems given the circumstances. They often charge that society and the larger community have failed to support schools and learning on a number of fronts.

Many believe that schools in general don't get enough financial support. Others focus on their belief that the money the city or state has for schools is not getting to their neighborhoods or to the classroom where it can help the teachers and the students.

There are also concerns that some parents don't support the teachers or don't do a good job teaching their children to cooperate with teachers and respect them. Community residents are often very concerned about negative social forces—that some "kids these days" aren't respectful and hardworking in school. Many point out that some students are difficult for any teacher to handle because of the prevalence of drugs, gangs, pop culture, and/or apathetic or indulgent parents. One Detroit father told us: " I think there is an education problem in America, because a lot of young people—they don't have enough role models . . . [and] education is on the back burner." Another parent said: "I'm thinking these kids [at my children's school] are so disrespectful. I mean—it's ridiculous. I'd be there with my kids, and I find myself snatching kids up [to discipline them]. I'm forgetting they aren't mine." Public Agenda's survey research with students, teachers, and parents in low-income and mainly minority schools show that many of them share these very same concerns.

THE TAKEAWAYS

Some decisions to close schools stem from financial issues facing the cities and states, but many stem from educators' commitment to remedy one stunning and heartbreaking statistic. Half of the country's high school dropouts come from just 12 percent of the nation's schools.[6]

In 2009, Secretary of Education Arne Duncan called on the nation to solve this problem: "I want to challenge the country to think about the schools that are at the bottom nationally. . . . Schools that have become dropout factories . . . where 50, 60, 70 percent of students drop out."[7] These schools are by nearly every measure schools that are fundamentally broken.

Deciding how to address this problem—and deciding whether closing the school is the right thing to do or whether other steps will be effective—is a genuinely daunting and heart-wrenching decision for many school leaders. The resentment and distrust that follows these decisions can haunt school leaders for years. These controversies have derailed the careers of more than one superintendent.

So this has to be an instance when a school leader looks into his or her own heart and renders the decision carefully and compassionately. What would help in terms of working with communities and handling the almost unavoidable doubts and fears that arise from bold and assertive change? Here are some takeaways.

Takeaway No. 1: Talk with parents, students, teachers, and community leaders and residents early and often.
In May 2011, Public Agenda convened a small conference entitled "What's Trust Got to Do with It?" The subject was how to help school leaders do a better job engaging the public in transforming broken, failing schools. The conference, funded by the Broad, Joyce, and Skillman Foundations, included national education experts, parent and community representatives, and communications and engagement experts.

One piece of advice from the communications pros—talking to people after the decision has been made is too late. School leaders need to reach out to parents, teachers, students, and others in the community early and often to hear their concerns and ideas about how best to improve the schools locally. There are three important reasons to do this.

* In too many cases, communications between communities and "the central office" have been virtually nonexistent for decades.
* School leaders need to establish their credentials as leaders who do care about the community and who are committed to hearing and weighing different points of view.
* School leaders who take on bold change need allies in the community. Talking to people, hearing their ideas and concerns, is a good way to establish these crucial connections.
* When parents and others in the community believe that they have been routinely "left out" or "pushed away," the negative residue from controversial decisions is even tougher to overcome.

In Public Agenda's research, some of the most potent and angry comments we encountered circled around people's perceptions that their views were ignored or that they were deliberately being pushed out. A New York City community advocate described what she saw: "Most people objected to the decision [to close their schools]. They were less interested in the actual process, except for the fact that the process did not include the stakeholders." In Seattle, a parent advocate told us: "As a parent I feel like my voice is not being heard very much; all the decisions being made are being made . . . by the central office, by the superintendent . . . and they haven't been listening to parents enough. . . ."

An expert observer of the controversies in Detroit emphasized the need for trust in the communications and how difficult it is to establish trust when decisions seem to be coming from a leader whom many people considered an "outsider." "We'd love to have a neighborhood school in as many neighborhoods as possible, but it's just not feasible. . . . I think there's a real good-faith effort to communicate that. The difficulty is, people are suspicious of the messenger."

Another expert described how important giving people some way to participate in these decisions can be. "When you take a 2,000-student, dysfunctional school and redesign it completely, it is something that the whole community has to be aware of, understand and feel that they were consulted at least in the approach to changing this old, traditional school—that many of the parents went to themselves and in many ways is a source of pride to the community. So, just to walk in and say, 'we're going to turn this thing upside down'—we saw some of the early work in this area, and it was very confusing to parents."

Takeaway No. 2: Keep the human touch. Beware of too much PR on the one hand, or an anonymous, legalistic, bureaucratic approach on the other.
School leaders need to find new ways of talking with parents, teachers, students, and others, ways that are more authentic and maintain the human touch. A flashy Power Point complete with facts and figures has its place, but by itself, it may be seen as just "PR." Most school systems cannot afford public service announcements or attractive brochures, but even if they could, the level of distrust in many communities might render them useless or even counterproductive. At the other end of the spectrum, communicating through cold announcements from officialdom just feeds resentment and confusion.

In the Public Agenda "What's Trust Got to Do With It?" session, more than one communications expert bemoaned the standard "public hearing" format as especially alienating and counterproductive. School leaders and city officials sit at tables in the front of the room; community residents are allotted a minute or two to make their comments while partisans on both sides of the issue hold up placards and roll their eyes—this is not a setting that encourages thoughtfulness or any viable exchange of viewpoints. Basically, everyone makes the point they came in with. They often go home even angrier than before.

Smaller, more informal discussions with key groups on a regular basis may help build a better basis for communication and mutual respect. Later on, I discuss some more planned and targeted engagement approaches that may help.

Takeaway No. 3: And don't forget Communications 101.
In the Public Agenda work, we were often astounded at the number of times districts seem to make a difficult situation like a school closing even worse by ignoring the most basic rules of good communications. Here's how a Boston parent, an activist in her community, described how she learned that her child's school was being closed:

> "So the [district] sent a letter home on Wednesday . . . in the kids' backpacks that said, 'Your school is slated to be merged with [another school] . . . This will be presented at the meeting of the school committee tonight at 6 o'clock.' That's how we found out. . . . The teachers found out at a staff meeting at 8:00 that morning. . . . This is [not] how you . . . talk to families if you want them to stay."

> —Boston Parent Committee Co-Chair

There are some basic rules to follow, even when there's no money for sophisticated press help—basics that are essential when the news is likely to be upsetting to many.

- **Don't surprise people.** People need time to adjust and absorb troubling information, and just suddenly announcing changes that will affect thousands of families and community residents "out of the blue" inflames the shock and anger. One of the communications pros in the "What's Trust Got to Do with It?" session described her experience in the corporate world announcing plant closings. When the decision was made, the company lined up senior staff to personally call key people in the community to let them know. The calls went out simultaneously so that none of the key leaders were caught off guard. In the calls, senior staff explained why the company made the decision and outlined the plans to help workers who would be laid off.
- **Be ready with a plan.** In the plant closing example, the company had thought through how to mitigate the pain their decision would cause, and they were ready from day one to explain where and how workers could get help and exactly what was going to happen, when, and why. When people don't know the facts, rumor and hearsay get the upper hand. And when people can't envision the future, they focus intently on the immediate loss. Proposals to close schools unleash deep fears about change, and communities, students, teachers, and parents typically focus almost exclusively on what could be lost, as opposed to the goal of creating better schools. School leaders need to be ready with a plan that helps people envision what the future will hold for them.

• **Line up allies and communicate through trusted sources.** When schools are targeted for closing, the news often reaches the community in the form of a press conference or a press release from the district office. Given the legacy of distrust that prevails in many poor communities with low-performing schools, "the district" acting alone is probably not going to be an effective messenger, especially when the message is so feared and unwanted. Reaching out to local employers and higher education leaders, teachers and other community leaders whose views might be more trusted by the community can help people cope with the news. With time, it may help them see the planned changes as a time to move forward, and less as the district "giving up" on them.

Takeaway No. 4: Ask for help.

Most parents and members of the broader public welcome the increased focus on turning around failing schools, improving teacher effectiveness, and insuring that all students graduate from high school with the knowledge and skills that will enable them to go to college. But most Americans also acknowledge that lack of parent participation and poor student behavior and lack of effort are major hurdles to accomplishing these goals. Most people don't put all the blame on the schools.

This is a widely held perception that school leaders can build on. Schools need parents and other adults pitching in to address problems like truancy and high dropout rates. Teachers need parents who reinforce the importance of learning and are willing to work with teachers to help students who struggle to stay focused. Educators can't just "deliver" good schools unless parents and students are more accountable too. In Public Agenda's research in districts with persistently failing schools, parents and community members frequently pointed out that the community itself had work to do.

Public Agenda is not the only organization urging school leaders working on turnarounds to reach out to other groups, especially those most closely connected to the schools. In their helpful summary of research on school turnarounds, AIR/Learning Point advises school leaders to seek "greater engagement among building stakeholders, including teachers, parents, and students in the development of school goals and objectives." This is a way, their analysis suggests, to "replace an army of one with a platoon of many."[8]

That's an invitation to school leaders to reach out to parents and community institutions, to local law enforcement and local higher education to join in efforts to increase school attendance and completion, to provide mentors, to work with students who need extra help. There are many ways communities and schools can work together to bolster what teachers and students do in the classroom. Asking for help demonstrates that school leaders value and respect what the community can bring to the table. Asking for help can also dissolve some of the distrust and miscommunication that bedevils so many school turnaround projects.

FIRST THINGS FIRST

School leaders are under pressure from state and federal government to address the problem of persistently low-performing schools squarely and forcefully, and there are no guarantees about which options work best in every circumstance. In fact, one chief issue facing the field today is that the success rate on school turnarounds is mixed no matter what strategy is chosen.[9]

But here is one guarantee based on everything Public Agenda has discovered in its research. School leaders who take the time to listen to parents, teachers, students, and members of the community with empathy and open-mindedness will make better decisions. And even if the decision runs counter to popular opinion, school leaders who promote and welcome dialogue with the community are far more likely to earn its respect and cooperation in the future.

NOTES

1. With support from The Broad Foundation, The Joyce Foundation ,and The Skillman Foundation, Public Agenda conducted one-on-one interviews with national experts, district leaders, parent advocates who have publicly spoken out on the issue, and leaders working locally with school turnarounds or on community engagements. The project also included focus groups with parents/guardians of children in Washington, DC; Denver; and Detroit. The results will be published in Fall 2011.

2. Fernanda Santos, "Spontaneity Again Causes Mayor Trouble," *The New York Times,* May 20, 2011, http://www.nytimes.com/2011/05/21/nyregion/bloomberg-causes-new-stir-with-remark-on-school-parents.html.

3. Jean Johnson, Ana Maria Arumi, and Amber Ott, *Reality Check 2006, Issue No. 2: How Black and Hispanic Families Rate Their Schools,* Public Agenda, 2006, http://www.publicagenda.org/files/pdf/rc0602.pdf.

4. William G. Howell, Paul E. Peterson, and Martin West, "The Persuadable Public," *Education Next,* Fall 2009, Pages 20–29, http://educationnext.org/persuadable-public/.

5. Phi Delta Kappa/Gallup Poll, *Highlights of the 2010 Phi Delta Kappa/Gallup Poll,* September 2010, Page 11, http://www.pdkintl.org/kappan/docs/2010_Poll_Report.pdf.

6. Alliance for Excellent Education, *Issue Brief: Prioritizing the Nation's Low-Performing High Scho*ols, April 2010, Page 1, http://www.all4ed.org/files/PrioritizingLowestPerformingSchools.pdf.

7. Alliance for Excellent Education, Issue *Brief: Prioritizing the Nation's Low-Performing High Schools,* Page 6, http://www.all4ed.org/files/Prioritizing LowestPerformingSchools.pdf.

8. American Institutes for Research, *A Learning Point: What Experience from the Field Tells Us about School Leadership and Turnarounds,* 2010, http://www. learningpt.org/pdfs/leadership_turnaround_schools.pdf.

9. See, for example, David A. Stuit, "Are Bad Schools Immortal? The Scarcity of Turnarounds and Shutdowns in Both Charter and District Sectors," December 14, 2010, http://www.edexcellence.net/publications-issues/publications/are-bad-schools-immortal .html.

Chapter 11

An Alternative Model of the Informed Public

Nearly everyone has been to a meeting gone wrong. Maybe it was a school board or city council meeting. Maybe it was at work or at a committee meeting at an association or club where a group gets together to address a problem. There are generally two ways things go south. On the one hand, you have the classic expert panel format, and on the other, you have the classic public hearing.

Think about the expert panel for a moment. There is a group of people sitting up front who have come to share their knowledge with the people in the audience. Sometimes it works, but when there's a complex, controversial issue on the docket, it often veers off course. The panelists spell out their ideas and work their way through their Power Points. They show their charts and graphs and let statistics and the jargon flow. Maybe the people on the panel discuss some points of contention among themselves, but, frequently, the audience is simply bored (or checking their e-mail) while the experts "drone on and on." Information goes out; very little of it actually gets through to the audience. It's one-way communication, if it can be described as communication at all.

This format is omnipresent as a form of citizen education, and it's widely used by the media as the preferred method for helping people understand complex policy problems. Here's how Dan Yankelovich describes its impact: "Serious news shows, for example, are filled with discussions and debates among experts in the economics and foreign policy fields. Often these programs have the opposite effect of what is intended. Instead of making people feel they understand the issues better, detailed expert talk confirms viewers' assumptions that the discussion could not conceivably be aimed at them."[1] Rather than bringing experts and leaders closer to the public, this approach often has the opposite result.

At the other end of the spectrum, there is the classic public hearing. Something's gone wrong, and the people who have come to the meeting are not happy. They demand solutions. The leaders up front are in the hot seat trying to explain, but few in the audience buy their justifications. Not only do people question the leaders' decisions, they often question their sincerity and integrity as well. Maybe the venting helps people get some of their anger off their chests, but the communication is still only going one way. The leaders in the dock and the people in the audience don't actually listen to each other, and, typically, there's not much progress in solving the problem. If anything, meetings like this often set things back, instead of moving them forward.

This type of public gathering where people "talk past each other" is not at all unusual of late. The "public hearings" on the Obama healthcare plan were infamous for their incivility and antagonism, with audience members screaming at elected officials and at one another. In some meetings, members of Congress were shouted down by chanting members of the audience. There were even a handful of arrests.[2]

In one New York City hearing on proposed school closings, audience members jeered at then-Chancellor Cathy Black, and she jeered right back. The video clip of the audience heckling the Chancellor and her mocking retort was played over and over again on the news and online. Depending on your point of view, it was either a symbol of how unreasonable the community was or proof positive the Chancellor was out of touch and that city's education leaders just didn't care what parents and community members thought.

THE SEARCH FOR AN ALTERNATIVE

The two "wrong ways to hold a meeting" phenomena exemplify the communications gap between leaders and the public today, and it's at the heart of much of the crosstalk among different stakeholders in education. Public Agenda's key mission is changing this dynamic and looking for more effective ways for leaders to talk with people and for people to participate more meaningfully in policy development. Pursuing this mission has led the organization to develop a different model of "the informed public," one that builds on our research into how people learn and how all of us wrestle with and cope with change.

In the next few pages, I will lay out the two main concepts at the heart of this new model of the informed public and at the heart of Public Agenda's work. They are:

- The three stages of public opinion—how people learn about new issues and cope with the need for change.

- The public learning curve—what stops people from moving from stage to stage and what can help them push through.

But first, let me say a little about how it all began.

In the 1970s, Dan Yankelovich joined with Cyrus Vance, the widely admired diplomat who served as the secretary of state in the Carter Administration, to envision and found Public Agenda. During that period, the two men often met for lunch to talk about issues and politics and exchange ideas and perspectives. During one meeting, they began to talk about what seemed to be a potentially treacherous gap between the country's leaders and the broader public.

Having served at the top levels of government, Vance spoke about concerns among elected officials and senior policy makers that the American public didn't seem to understand many of the most pressing challenges facing the country or that people expected quick, easy solutions to problems that were enormously difficult and complex. In many cases, Vance suggested, leaders felt hamstrung by public opinion—unable to move ahead with promising solutions because of the public's unreasonable expectations or lack of interest.

Having spent decades delving into public thinking on nearly every issue and topic imaginable, Yankelovich talked about the public's state of mind. Americans often felt confused and disoriented by what they saw on the news. Despite being flooded with information, many lacked even the most basic facts needed to understand the major issues facing the country. Most lacked the context needed to absorb and assess them. And many resented leadership's seeming incapacity to solve the country's problems—why didn't elected officials do more to fix things?

But Dan added another key observation. Even though people are often shockingly short on the details, they can bring a much-needed perspective to the table: Most Americans approach issues with a pragmatism and sense of fair play that are essential to problem solving. While leaders often argue among themselves in a swirl of ideology and professional rivalry, the public is often more open-minded and more disposed to address problems in a practical way.

What both men knew, based on long experience, is that it is nearly impossible to solve big problems in a democracy like ours without public buy-in. Leaders can tinker around the edges, but whether the issue is healthcare or education or energy or foreign policy, authentic, long-lasting solutions require broad public acceptance and sustainable support.

It was this insight—and this conversation between Dan Yankelovich and Cyrus Vance—that led to the creation of Public Agenda. It is an organization devoted expressly to understanding how to enhance the American public's role in public policy. It works to narrow the gap between leaders and the public and to reduce among different sectors in the society the rifts that have led to stalemate and political gridlock time and time again.

In its work over the years, Public Agenda has developed two innovative concepts that help explain how people learn about and adapt to changing situations and challenges. Fleshed out in years of opinion research and through dozens of pilot studies and field tests, these concepts can help leaders understand why people often resist change and what might help them adapt. School leaders who absorb these concepts and begin to incorporate them in their work with teachers, parents, students, and the broader community will be far better positioned to make progress on the problems facing schools today.

Concept # 1: The three stages of public opinion—how people learn about issues and cope with the need for change
Most of us do reasonably well coping with change when the benefits are apparent and when we don't need to reshape our lives or viewpoints in fundamental ways. We've all adapted to e-mail and smart phones and online check-in readily enough. Sometimes, there are glitches and periods of adjustments, but these changes aren't radical enough to genuinely upset most of us. But some of the changes facing our society today aren't so easily accommodated—that's true for education and for other social and economic issues as well.

When faced with new issues and circumstances, people typically move through a series of stages as they come to terms with them. People's views aren't static, and understanding that can be helpful in and of itself. Appreciating how the three phases differ and becoming aware of the glitches that arise in each stage can help leaders improve their communications and engagement strategies for working with the public and other stakeholders. Here is what to watch for:

Stage 1: Consciousness-raising. Stage one is exactly what it says it is— people become aware of a problem. This is the stage where the news media generally excel and where standard public relations and communications strategies are most helpful. Sometimes events themselves hurl problems to center stage. September 11 catapulted the problem of international terrorism into the public's mind. The BP oil spill alerted people to the trade-offs of offshore oil drilling.

But there are distinctions leaders should be alert to. If you ask people to name problems in their community (or in the country or in education), most can come up with a pretty long list given enough time. But not all of these problems are equally important to people. There is usually only a small circle of issues that truly command public attention. One Public Agenda rule of thumb is: there are typically only three or four issues that people truly see as urgent at any one time. Another rule of thumb is to be skeptical about polls showing that Americans say that "X" is an important issue. Most people are hesitant to brush off any problem as "unimportant," even if it's way down on their own list of urgent issues. So when polls show that people say that an issue is "important," the question has to be: "Yes, but how important, and compared to what?"

Stage 2: Working through resistance and wishful thinking. This middle stage is the most crucial and least well understood. It's the phase when some very common human failings come to the fore, and where people begin to work through them. Here's how Dan Yankelovich summarizes what happens: "As observers of human psychology know well, all change is difficult. People caught in cross pressures must overcome the temptation to fall back on denial and wishful thinking. . . . They must face and resolve the conflicts, ambivalences, and defenses the issues arouse. Rarely does the course of change proceed smoothly."[3] Not surprisingly, this is where public learning often stalls and where problem solving often stalls with it.

When people are in denial or engaged in wishful thinking, they don't move forward. When they are ambivalent and conflicted, needed decisions get postponed. Getting through this stage to the next depends on their coming to terms with these emotions.

Stage 3: Resolution. At some point (and often years later), we decide that we have to decide and begin to take action. Elected officials and others offer ideas and proposals. Citizens debate them, and the pros and cons of different approaches come more clearly into view. Getting to this phase is often messy, but once we're here, the United States does have democratic institutions that function reasonably well. People begin to accept change and adapt to it.

But "it's not over until it's over," to quote the quotable Yogi Berra. There are still a few wrinkles late in the game. People often accept change intellectually before they can act on it fully. People buy gym memberships because on an intellectual level, they know they need to get in shape. On an emotional level, though, many still aren't ready to make going to the gym part of their daily lives. To take a more consequential example, this is why some people give lip service to equality for all regardless of race or background, yet they still harbor resentment and prejudice toward people who are different from themselves. Intellectually, they accept the idea of equality, but emotionally and psychologically, they aren't there yet.

In this final stage, people sort through their feelings, make decisions, and begin acting on them. This happens on an individual level, and it happens in communities, and on a national level as well.

HOW PEOPLE LEARN

In many respects, the stages of public opinion reflect inherent qualities in the way people think and learn. Over time, people absorb new ways and ideas from others around them. They learn from experience. Information wends its way through the body politic. Having been around when computers and the Internet first started arriving in offices and homes, I can easily remember when very savvy people would confuse an e-mail address with a website address. Now that distinction is second nature to anyone who uses a computer.

For leaders, the challenge is not that people don't learn. The challenge is to find ways to expedite people's progress through that troublesome middle stage of public opinion, when we're most likely to get bogged down by denial and wishful thinking.

Concept # 2: The public's learning curve
Take a look at Figure 11.1 which captures Public Agenda's concept of the public's learning curve.

The Public's Learning Curve:
Why Information Isn't Enough

Resolution

Resistance to change
Lack of Urgency
Grasping at straws
Lack of context
Lack of practical choices
Leadership miscommunication
Wishful thinking / denial
Mistrust

Consciousness Raising

Figure 11.1

What's most interesting about the long climb in the middle stage is how little it depends on absorbing lots of detailed, expert information. That's what makes this new model of the informed public so different and potentially useful for leadership.

In the traditional model, leaders assume that giving people more facts, a better grasp of history, detailed white papers on how to solve problems, debates and more debates between experts with opposing views, and more facts and more data is the way to bolster citizen participation and engagement. Well, yes, but . . .

We now live in a society that's awash with information from around the world, from every perspective, 24 hours a day from a myriad of sources. Information is more easily available than at any time in our history. Yet, the gaps between leaders and the public, and the divisions between different groups of Americans, are as wide as ever. In fact, for many Americans, it's too much information, rather than too little, that confounds them, especially the information that inundates them without context or a framework for thinking about it.

Here are some of the chief obstacles that emerge and need to be resolved in the middle stage of public learning:

- People are unrealistic and deny that the problem exists.
- People indulge in compartmentalized thinking.
- People resist change.
- People fear loss.
- People have ambivalent or conflicted views that they need to work through.
- People can't decide whom to believe, and they have no context to help them judge.

These aspects of public opinion have bedeviled the country's progress on solving the problem of routine federal deficits and the country's ballooning federal debt. And only the first obstacle—the lack of realism—is mainly an information issue. People unrealistically believe that cutting spending that they personally dislike will balance the budget—it could be foreign aid or the National Endowment for the Humanities or the honey subsidy. A few minutes with a pie chart of current government spending ususaly remedies that misconception.

The other obstacles, though, have a more psychological and emotional component. The whole country has indulged in compartmentalized thinking,believing that we can continually reduce taxes and increase spending without it coming back to bite us. This is avoidance and lazy thinking—not a lack of information. Anger at leadership for putting us in this situation, fears of losing services we've come to rely on, wanting government to do more than we're willing to pay for, not being able to decide what to give up, not knowing whom to trust—these aren't issues that can be addressed by giving people more information. Yet, overcoming these obstacles is the very essence of advancing the public's learning curve. Wrestling with some key facts is one factor, to be sure, but coming to grips with the issue emotionally is the much more important and difficult hurdle.

Think for just a moment about some of the major changes taking place in education today:

- Teachers are facing new expectations, and the rules governing their employment and pay are changing throughout the country.
- Students are being pushed to achieve higher standards. Entering the workforce with only a high school diploma and no specific skills just doesn't work anymore.
- The entire education system is being asked to ramp up learning to meet the competition from well-educated workers in other countries.
- School leaders are trying to rally parents, students, and teachers to turn around broken and persistently failing schools—we've tolerated the dropout factories for long enough.
- School leaders are being asked to do more with tighter and less-predictable budgets.

These are not minor technical issues. Changes of this magnitude present enormous emotional and psychological challenges for the people going through them. Giving people better information will help, but as Dan Yankelovich has put it: "People's minds are much more stormy and emotional. Part of [Public Agenda's] contribution is to describe the [learning curve] process as it really exists . . . the way people act in real life."[4]

Faced with threatening and unwelcome changes in our circumstances and life prospects, very few of us can sit back and calmly sort through the facts and cooly come to a quick resolution. Whether it's losing a job or facing a serious illness or divorce, most of us need considerable time to absorb the reality of what's facing us. It's not just a question of weighing the facts before us. Yet, in a world flooded with information, that's often what leaders expect typical Americans to do. It hasn't been working very well lately. No, it's time to try a different approach.

NOTES

1. Daniel Yankelovich, "How to Achieve Sounder Public Judgment," *Toward Wiser Public Judgment,* Daniel Yankelovich and Will Friedman, Editors, Vanderbilt University Press, 2011, Page 15.

2. David Gardner, "Violence Breaks Out in America's Town Halls over Obama's Healthcare Reforms," *Daily Mail Online,* August 8, 2009, http://www.dailymail .co.uk/news/article-1205063/Violence-breaks-Americas-town-halls-Obama-battles -healthcare-reforms.html#ixzz1QylaVj79.

3. Daniel Yankelovich, "How to Achieve Sounder Public Judgment," *Toward Wiser Public Judgment,* Page 15.

4. Ibid., Page 45.

Chapter 12

Dialogue and Choicework—Two Ways to Help People Cope with Change

Understanding the trajectory of how most of us come to terms with new problems is useful for anyone who leads an organization. It helps leaders anticipate how people may react and makes it clear that giving people information only goes so far. Given the emotional work most human beings have to do to accept change and flourish in new circumstances, you might think it's time to add a psychologist to the management team. After all, Captain Picard had the empathic Counselor Troi to help him lead the Starship Enterprise.

As fascinating as it might be to work with an "empath," Public Agenda's experience in education and many other issues shows that it's not necessary. There are two complementary techniques that can help people better comprehend and come to grips with new challenges. In some cases, these two techniques can even help groups begin to collaborate on addressing these challenges. One of the techniques is dialogue; the other is choicework.

THE "MAGIC" OF DIALOGUE

We're all used to debates. In political campaigns, these choreographed discussions between and among candidates are often the high points. They give voters the chance to see the candidates side by side and to compare and contrast their approaches to the issues. We evaluate the way the candidates conduct themselves under pressure. We ask ourselves whether we're confident that this person could lead and represent us.

Debates are extraordinarily useful in helping people decide among competing political candidates, but the act of voting, as important as it is, doesn't represent a fundamental change in people's lives. Voters aren't being asked to change their accustomed ways of doing their jobs or planning their lives. They aren't being asked to do more, or to do things differently. If anything, candidates running for office typically reinforce the voters' existing beliefs and priorities. The voters are always right, and candidates generally tell them what they want to hear.

But that's not the situation in education today. Leaders who believe that our education system must improve in fundamental ways are pushing people to struggle with new ideas. They are asking them to change long-ingrained assumptions about their jobs (in the case of teachers) and their patterns of behavior and plans for the futures (for students and parents). School leaders need people with competing priorities and different points of view to work together. Plus leaders themselves need to understand the insights and contributions these groups can bring to solving education's problems. School leaders need to plant the seeds for some forms of cooperation and collaboration down the line for anything real to change.

This set of circumstances calls for a very different kind of conversation, one that informs, but in a very different way. It calls for dialogue, rather than debate.

For anyone who has been reading this book from start to finish, it's clear that I am a great admirer of Dan Yankelovich's book, *The Magic of Dialogue.* I consider it an indispensible guide for anyone trying to organize and corral people to tackle tough challenges, whether in business, politics, or education. Here's what Yankelovich has to say about the essence of dialogue: "Webster defines the purpose of dialogue as 'seeking mutual understanding and harmony. . . . I hew closely to the dictionary definition, straying from it in only one respect."[1] The caveat Yankelovich highlights is crucial, because, as helpful as dialogue can be, it is not a silver bullet for producing consensus.

It is, however, an underutilized pathway for opening up more genuine communications among people with different points of view, and it has been shown time and time again as an effective way to diminish antagonism and misunderstanding. As Yankelovich explains: "I put less emphasis on harmony than the dictionary does because the outcome of dialogue is not always harmony. In fact, as a consequence of dialogue, you may come to understand why you disagree so vehemently with someone else; there will be better understanding, but not necessarily more harmony."[2]

In writing about dialogue and the distinctive role it can play in helping leaders lead and people begin to communicate more openly and candidly, Steve Rosell and Heidi Gantwerk of Viewpoint Learning (another group that specializes in public engagement) describe it as "the step we can take, before decisions are made, to uncover assumptions, broaden perspectives, build trust, and find common ground."[3] Here are some of the advantages dialogue offers:

- It provides a deeper and richer understanding of public and stakeholder sentiment than polls. Polls can be a useful roadmap. Dialogue is more akin to getting out of the car and taking a walk around town.
- It reduces crosstalk and wariness between groups (between teachers and parents on discipline issues, for example). It opens different channels of communication between leaders and the led. Remember that statistic up front about the percentage of teachers (It was 70%) who say district leaders usually come to tell them about the decisions they've made and get their support—not to get their insights based on their experience working directly with students. I'd be willing to bet that number would drop dramatically with a little more dialogue.
- It helps people see what other people can bring to the table—a process that can jump start collaboration and problem solving. Public Agenda has used dialogue to help communities come together to improve early childhood education and reduce the rate of high school dropouts. The details are coming up.

Courtesy of Steve Rosell and Heidi Gantwerk at Viewpoint Learning, Table 12.1 shows how dialogue differs from its well-known cousin, debate.[4]

Table 12.1. Debate and Dialogue: Differences to Look For

Debate	Dialogue
Assuming there is one right answer (and you have it)	Assuming that others have pieces of the answer
Combative: attempting to prove the other side wrong	Collaborative: attempting to find common understanding
About winning	About finding common ground
Listening to find flaws and make counter-arguments	Listening to understand
Defending your assumptions	Bringing up your assumptions for inspection and discussion
Searching for weaknesses and flaws in the other position	Searching for strength and values in the other position
Seeking an outcome that agrees with your position	Discovering new possibilities and opportunites

Source: Steven A. Rosell and Heidi Gantwerk

In the next chapters and the appendix, I list a number of organizations and sources that can help school leaders incorporate dialogue into their own leadership work. But I would like to conclude this short "Dialogue 101" with another reflection from Yankelovich based on his work with the process over decades: "One of the empirical things that impressed me, and I would not have predicted, is that dialogue almost always leads to more respect for differing points of view. The process of coming to judgment through dialogue rather than advocacy creates a climate of civility. It creates civic virtue."[5]

It's a fundamental insight. Dialogue is not just a useful technique for solving specific problems; it's what should be happening every day in a democracy—especially one as complex and diverse as ours.

CHOICEWORK

The term "choicework" was coined by David Mathews, the president of the Kettering Foundation, a research foundation that focuses directly on citizens and politics and how citizens learn about issues and participate in resolving them (See Appendix for more). The word means just what it says—it's the work of making choices.

When the goal is to help people get through that troublesome middle stage of public learning—when denial and wishful thinking must be resolved—choicework can work wonders. I have seen focus group participants enrich their grasp of issues and make surprising leaps in their understanding within 45 minutes of starting on choicework. That's true even on the issue of the federal debt and deficits where public opinion has been mired in wishful thinking for decades.[6] To Yankelovich, "nothing advances the public's learning curve more effectively than the opportunity to discuss and deliberate a concrete set of choices, with their value implications cogently set forth."[7]

CHOICES—NOT TOO MANY, NOT TOO WONKY

So what is choicework and what kinds of choices does it include? First of all, it helps to be clear on what it's not. Choicework is not presenting people with every choice under the sun—most of us can only grapple with three or four choices at a time in any real sense.

What's more, choices for laypeople—teachers, students, parents, community members—are quite different from the choices a legislator or education expert might consider. We're talking about broad, strategic directions for change that are described without jargon and without a data dump. The choices aren't simple or simpleminded, though. They clarify risks and trade-offs. They bring the essential values imbedded in the choices to the fore. They make dilemmas about right and wrong, fair and unfair, risk and reward explicit and vivid.

To me, the military options that top generals prepare for the president are a good analogy. These options lay out an array of choices for the president to consider in response to threats to the nation. They are not detailed plans listing what every unit commander will do or exactly which combat units will go where. Instead, the military's obligation is to insure that the president has the information he or she needs to make the best decision for the country. The options lay out the military's best analyses on possible loss of life, risks of retaliation, dangers to the homeland and to Americans abroad, budgetary implications, diplomatic concerns, competing priorities, whether there is a clear exit plan, and the chances of success and failure. The choices couldn't be tougher, but they are choices developed precisely to be understandable and straightforward for someone who is a civilian, not active-duty military. The options are designed to explain and clarify—not to persuade or prettify the situation.

DEVELOPING CHOICES THAT PROMPT CHOICEWORK

So what are the guidelines for developing the kinds of options that generate choicework? Public Agenda's work, along with the experience of organizations like Viewpoint Learning and the Kettering Foundation suggest that these criteria are crucial:

- Choices for choicework start where the audience starts, whether the audience is teachers, parents, students, a school community, or the broader public. Each of the three or four choices is couched in language and concepts that are easy for people to understand and grapple with. At Public Agenda, focus groups are used to develop and pretest choices. People have to understand them and be able to work with them, or the exercise will be useless.
- The choices are described fairly from a neutral point of view. Each should be presented with its best foot forward and with its risks and trade-offs clearly spelled out. If there's a choice around that doesn't have any risks or trade-offs, then, in all likelihood, leaders would have already acted on it. You wouldn't be in a situation that requires choicework if there were effective but easy answers available.
- The choices emphasize the ethics and values embedded in each option. Who might get hurt if we go this direction? What does this choice mean for

the way we like to see ourselves? Does it match our vision for the future and our aspirations for our children? Why is it that some people oppose this choice?

- They are designed to get people thinking about the overall direction to take. In nearly every choicework discussion I have seen, people begin to adapt or expand the choices as soon as they start to wrestle with them. It's not "Choose A, B, or C, and the deal is sealed." The purpose is to help people advance along the learning curve, to help them work out their own ambivalences and conflicts and to compare their views with the views of others.
- The choices provide a framework that helps people cope with the "too much information" phenomenon. In some respects, the most magical aspect of choicework is its ability to clarify problems that previously seemed overwhelming, slippery, and totally unmanageable to most people. Choices define the lay of the land, and once we get outside our own field of endeavor, nearly all of us need to understand the lay of the land in order to make sense of an issue or problem.

Obviously, preparing choices and pretesting them to make sure they are helpful and easily understood takes time and a good grounding in both the issue and the attitudes and perceptions people bring to it. (There's an example of choicework following this chapter, and Public Agenda's website at www .publicagenda.org includes a number of choicework guides on educational issues and many others.)

But just having choices is only the beginning. Giving people the opportunity to wrestle with them means setting up meetings, including them in publications, putting them online, getting media to cover them—all the tried-and-true techniques for getting people's attention. So it's hardly an everyday activity.

Frankly, the benefits of choicework might dwindle if the process was used day in and day out for every decision that comes up. Choicework is best saved for times when it can truly be a game changer. Here's my list of situations where choicework might be genuinely helpful:

- Big changes are underway that will directly affect people's lives and futures.
- People are divided among themselves, and there's a stalemate.
- People are unrealistic or internally conflicted.
- Ideas are on the table, but few people understand their implications.
- Ideas are on the table, but people fear or resent change.
- A working consensus, decisions, and follow-through are needed.

WHAT MAKES CHOICEWORK SO EFFECTIVE

Typically, choicework is a door opener. It encourages people to think about the need to respond to a situation. It allows them to look at a range of alternatives for addressing it. Since people often approach these situations with a blend of confusion, skepticism, and defensiveness, choicework has shown a remarkable ability to open up their thinking. It addresses a number of specific hurdles in the traditional way people learn and think about issues:

- People are less likely to feel manipulated or like they are targets of spin when they are presented with an array of choices. In effect, offering people choices establishes that leaders respect and value the public's views and are themselves open to different ways of addressing a problem.
- People are less likely to feel daunted or bored by a top-down, leadership or expert presentation. Since the kind of choices used for choicework are specifically developed to be understandable to lay people, there's less likelihood that people will tune out or see them as too wonky. Choices that are developed for the public help experts and nonexperts start on the same page.
- People generally become more realistic when presented with choices. In fact, the act of struggling with choices advances realism and diminishes wishful thinking more effectively than any method I know of. Since people look at the choices side by side, the trade-offs and downsides of all the choices become readily apparent.
- People are less likely to indulge in continual venting and more likely to be curious about the nature of the problem and how different solutions might work. Public Agenda's Will Friedman and Alison Kadlec have used choice-work in public engagement projects nationwide on a wide range of issues. They describe why less venting and more curiousity is so pivotal based on research they conducted: "When the conversation got bogged down in vent-ing about corrupt and greedy leaders . . . it seemed to circumvent people's curiosity about the nature of the problem. . . . Venting about malfeasance furnished a kind of explanatory framework that made [them less] curious or interested in exploring the causes and nature of [the problem]. Or perhaps it simply gave people an excuse not to work very hard by letting them fall back on pat explanations."[8]
- People are less likely to indulge in scapegoating and blaming. Since all of the choices have downsides that are made explicit, it's harder for people to try to pin the blame solely on one person or one group.

- People are less likely to want to wait for a perfect solution. A related, but equally important advantage is that choicework can short-circuit the phenomenon I call "waiting for the perfect solution." Until people juxtapose choices side by side, they can always assume that there is a better idea out there somewhere—one that is easier, cheaper, less bothersome, and more popular. But on most tough issues, all of the choices present costs and trade-offs. When people look at the choices together, they are generally more inclined to choose one of the less-than-perfect options rather than waiting for the perfect solution.
- Choicwork expedites public learning. By giving people a framework and a context, choicework can empower people to be more skeptical of politicians and others who overpromise and gloss over the costs and trade-offs to their own preferred solutions.

IF CHOICEWORK IS SO GREAT . . .

Given how effective choicework can be in advancing public engagement, it's fair to ask why there isn't more of it. One reason is that it's not really in the interest of most of the groups that typically deliver information to the public.

The news tends to focus on daily events—the president announced this, congress did that, the governor is proposing a plan, etc. The news media basically assume that people will work out the choices for themselves if they receive all the bits and pieces of information as they emerge on a daily basis. Unfortunately, that's simply not true for most of us. I am often struck by the fact that people in focus groups can often readily tell you about recent news events, yet they don't understand the issue, and they certainly don't understand the choices.

Experts, political leaders, and advocacy groups generally have preferred solutions that they have developed from their work, often over many years. Most are intent on persuading people to back what they back. Most are far less interested in seeing their favored solution juxtaposed against other solutions with its own trade-offs clearly spelled out.

However, for leaders who are interested in problem solving and moving the needle on issues where progress has stalled, well-planned choicework can change the conversation dramatically. By itself, neither choicework nor dialogue will solve a problem, but using these techniques can give leaders the opening they need to move forward. What's more, they will be armed with a better understanding of what really matters to people, and sometimes they may find themselves with allies and collaborators they never knew they had.

LOOKING AT SOME PUBLIC CHOICES ON IMMIGRATION

Want to see what "public choices" look like on a hot topic issue facing the country? Here's an example—a choicework that Public Agenda put together for its *2008 Voter's Survival Kit*. It presents a few key facts to

VOTER'S SURVIVAL KIT: IMMIGRATION

CITIZEN'S SURVIVAL KIT

🚹🚺IMMIGRATION: WHO GETS TO COME, WHO GETS TO STAY

☆THE FIX WE'RE IN NOW

- **The U.S. admitted more than 400,000 new immigrants in 2007**, and more than 600,000 people were given permanent legal status, adding up to more than a million legal immigrants a year. More than 12 percent of the U.S. population is foreign-born.

- **There are an estimated 11.7 million illegal or undocumented immigrants** in the country. U.S. border agents say they apprehended more than one million people in 2006.

- **Although legal immigration rates are historically high**, they have fallen since the early 1990s.

- **Current laws emphasize family ties for admission**, and most legal immigrants are, in fact, relatives of people already here.

Read More...

HOW WE GOT HERE

If you want to get people arguing these days, there's no better topic than immigration. For talk show hosts who specialize in showcasing irate callers and displaying how angry they are themselves, devoting a show to immigration, especially illegal immigration, is a no-brainer. The topic is so bitter, and Americans are so divided about it, that we seem to have decided to live with a broken system rather than compromise on crafting a new one. Read More...

SO WHAT'S THE PLAN?

There are many ideas about how to reform the American immigration system – and frankly it's going to take a while to really make sense of the situation and fix all the problems Americans complain about. Here are three different directions a lot of politicians talk about - directions in which the country might move.

Dramatically strengthen the enforcement of current laws and reduce the level of legal immigration	Reform immigration law to match the needs of the economy – bring in more highly-skilled immigrants and create a guest worker program for low-skilled immigrants	Reform the system to take advantage of the enormous contributions immigrants make to the U.S. and give decent, honest undocumented workers a clear path to citizenship
Our immigration system is out of control. With about 11.7 million illegal immigrants living in the United States and nearly half a million new ones arriving each year, the current system undercuts American workers and risks allowing dangerous criminals and terrorists into the U.S. It's just wrong to tolerate the widespread breaking of the law. Read More...	About 15 percent of U.S. workers are immigrants, and over the last decade they have accounted for about half of the growth in the work force. Our economy just won't function well without them, but we need to adjust the system so that we really do bring in the people who can help us most. Read More...	The United States is a nation of immigrants, and our whole society benefits from having a humane policy that recognizes the vast majority of undocumented workers have become valued members of our society. Plus, the country basically allowed illegal entry for decades. To suddenly pull the rug out from under people who have built good lives here is just wrong. Read More...

Figure 12.1

start—chosen by Public Agenda to address very common gaps in knowledge and misconceptions on the immigration issue. It poses three broad approaches to the issue, each emphasizing the values and concerns associated with it.

Maybe you're wondering why I didn't spotlight a choicework on a controversial education issue. It's essentially because it's easier to grasp the usefulness of choicework on issues where you yourself are not an expert. It's very common for experts (and school leaders are clearly experts on school issues) to initially consider a public choicework too simple and sketchy. But simplicity and brevity are the "magic potion" in public choices. Good public choices start where most lay people start, and that's often right at the beginning. That way, typical citizens have a chance to get their grounding so the conversation can begin.

See the Appendix for information on where to find choiceworks available from Public Agenda, the Kettering Foundation, and other organizations. There is also a list of groups to contact for help in developing choiceworks on specific questions and issues in education.

NOTES

1. Daniel Yankelovich, *The Magic of Dialogue: Transforming Conflict into Cooperation,* Touchstone, 2001, Page 14.

2. Ibid.

3. Steven A. Rosell and Heidi Gantwerk, in "Moving Beyond Polls and Focus Groups," *Toward Wiser Public Judgment,* Daniel Yankelovich and Will Friedman, Editors, Vanderbilt University Press, 2011, Page 112.

4. Ibid., Page 113.

5. Daniel Yankelovich, "Further Reflections: A Dialogue Between Dan Yankelovich and Will Friedman," *Toward Wiser Public Judgment,* Page 47.

6. Public Agenda, *It's Time to Pay Our Bills,* May 2007, http://www.publicagenda .org/files/pdf/facingup_leaders_report_0.pdf.

7. Daniel Yankelovich, "How to Achieve Sounder Public Judgment," *Toward Wiser Public Judgment,* Page 47.

8. Alison Kadlec and Will Friedman, "Thirty-Five Years of Working on Public Judgment at Public Agenda," *Toward Wiser Public Judgment,* Page 102.

Chapter 13

From Ideas to Action—School Leaders Use Dialogue and Choicework to Spur Change

For Public Agenda, dialogue and choicework are the heart and soul of public engagement. Over the last 30 years, the organization has refined its understanding of how these concepts operate, probed them, and written extensively about them. It has also encouraged leaders and the news media to embed them in their own work.

But a major strand of Public Agenda's work is developing and testing different ways to integrate dialogue and choicework into community or school-based projects that make sense for school leaders. That means designing projects that are practical and doable, that encourage and implant engagement skills within the community and that help local leaders move the needle on the challenges they face.

JUMP-STARTING ACTION

Public Agenda has conducted public engagement projects in scores of communities and school districts "of every kind, large to small, rural to inner city, fairly homogenous to incredibly diverse."[1] Typically, these projects are collaborations between Public Agenda and local community groups and/or state education or district leaders.

Some public engagement projects are "campaigns" lasting six months to a year. These are specifically designed to ignite and support local leadership action. (See the box following this chapter for some key principles behind these campaigns.) In other cases, the formal aspects of the projects are much simpler—the development of a choicework brochure or helping with planning for a single community town hall. These smaller projects can help school leaders identify potential communications pitfalls and avoid them. They can also break the ice for conversations about a key problem or challenge, and then local school and community leaders can take it from there. In some communities where Public Agenda has worked, the habits of dialogue and choicework become embedded. They have been used repeatedly over a period of years to nurture engagement on education and other issues as well.

Although Public Agenda has been a pioneer in researching and developing engagement projects featuring dialogue and choicework, other organizations and individuals have been honing similar approaches and doing remarkable work advancing the field. The Kettering Foundation and Viewpoint Learning are two of the most perceptive national organizations working in this area, and Public Agenda has collaborated with both. There are also several state and local initiatives incorporating engagement approaches. For example, Advance Illinois is a "group of high profile political, civic, business, and educational leaders" serving as "an independent, objective voice to promote a public education system . . . that prepares all students to be ready for work, college, [and] democratic citizenship."[2] The organization collaborated with the state board of education, teachers' unions, elected officials, and others on legislation reforming teacher evaluation policies in the state.[3]

In this chapter, I will describe several Public Agenda projects using dialogue and choicework, showing how school leaders have put these two key concepts into practice. There's more information in the Appendix about obtaining engagement materials and exploring engagement partnerships with Public Agenda and other groups.

LOCATION: SAN JOSÉ, CA

The Challenge: Like school districts nationwide, San José has worked hard to raise academic standards and increase parental involvement. Its work began in the 1990s led by Schools Superintendent Linda Murray, along with members of the school board. The goal, as Dr. Murray describes it, was to "put together a comprehensive public engagement strategy to test the waters and ask the question of all district stakeholders: 'How good is good enough in San José Unified School District?'"[4]

Reaching Out: The district initially approached Public Agenda to "test the waters" by conducting local opinion research. Public Agenda organized "focus groups with Anglo parents, bilingual Hispanic parents, Spanish-only Hispanic parents, students of various backgrounds and teachers on the topics of student achievement, diversity and equity."[5] The results showed a solid, broadly shared hunger for higher student expectations, and, in response, the district raised high school graduation requirements. This was a step that some in the community had been hesitant to take, but listening to parents, students, and teachers provided the impetus for the district to move forward. After this initial step, the district moved to a broader, community-wide dialogue called "Standards and Expectations for Our Students." School leaders worked with Public Agenda and the Institute for Educational leadership to organize a broader community conversation.[6] Public Agenda helped prepare choicework discussion materials (available in English and Spanish) and train local moderators to lead breakout discussions. A committee of local "parents, members of the clergy, employers and others" took responsibility for much of the planning and operations.[7] The community event included some 150 parents and other community stakeholders, along with front page coverage in the *San Jose Mercury News*. As Dr. Murray puts it: "We knew we had a mandate to proceed, and in January 1998, the Board of Education adopted the University of California system's entrance requirements as our graduation requirement, to begin with the entering freshman class of 1991.[8]

Moving Forward: With community and stakeholder support, the San José schools aimed high and realized remarkable progress. As Dr. Murray notes, "higher standards and expectations did not lead to more dropouts, but to greater achievement. Graduation rates have remained steady," while the district has seen higher SAT scores and twice as many Hispanic students taking AP courses. [9] The district's decision to use a public-engagement strategy was of course only one element in a multifaceted drive to improve public education in San José. But the district has remained committed to the process. The district created a "plan to increase parental involvement, began regularly surveying students and parents, and started holding neighborhood conversations on standards policies and other school issues."[10] It also established a public engagement unit that conducts focus groups and surveys and convenes community conversations on a regular basis. For San Jose, public engagement centered on dialogue became "an established mode for communications and collaboration in the district and an integral part of its planning process."[11]

LOCATION: THE STATE OF NEBRASKA

The Challenge: How can a leader responsible for schools in close to 500 districts launch a conversation about setting statewide learning standards?[12] That's the challenge that faced Nebraska State School Superintendent Doug Christensen in the 1990s when he joined with Pubic Agenda to engage his state's citizens in discussion about the issue. At the time, many Nebraska residents were nervous about proposals to set statewide standards, and the issue was contentious.

Reaching Out: Public Agenda worked with state officials to conduct a series of community forums built on the principles of dialogue and choicework. In these sessions, parents, students, teachers, and a cross section of community members "wrestled with alternative approaches to the standards issue."[13] Nebraskans talked with one another, and, although most endorsed the general thrust of the proposed state standards, they also suggested refinements and additions. State officials listened, and building on the results of those forums, the State Board of Education adopted new statewide guidelines, confident that their decision reflected the perspectives of a broad spectrum of Nebraskans.[14]

Moving Forward: Nebraska relied on engagement again a few years later, when the state worked with Public Agenda to help develop a process that would allow the state's citizens to weigh in on how to define an "essential education" for Nebraska students. The state prepared a planning document, "Equitable Opportunities for an Essential Education for All Students— Recommendations for Nebraska Public School Districts" that served as the impetus for the discussions. In the first round, Public Agenda conducted focus groups with educators from some 25 districts across Nebraska to gather feedback. Then, Public Agenda worked with state officials to develop discussion materials and train local organizers, moderators, and recorders for dialogues that brought together nearly 400 Nebraska citizens in different sites across the state. The dialogues included parents, students, teachers, principals, superintendents, and members of the broader public. Again, a broad swath of Nebraskans voiced support for the key ideas in the planning paper, but there were a few areas "where Nebraskans saw gaps in the existing opportunities, as well as cautions they wanted state education leaders to take to heart."[15] Even so, most Nebraskans believed that the State Board could and should play a leadership role in defining what kinds of courses should be offered in Nebraska's schools, a role it has taken and has continued to pursue in the years since.[16]

CARLSBAD, NEW MEXICO

The Challenge: Superintendent of Carlsbad Public Schools, Dr. Sheri Williams was inspired by the dropout prevention campaign launched by America's Promise, the child and youth advocacy organization founded and led by General Colin Powell and his wife Alma Powell.[17] Dr. Williams attended an America's Promise "Graduation Summit" event where New Mexico Governor Bill Richardson encouraged districts throughout the state to hold similar summits in their own communities. The question was whether it was possible to hold an event that would move people from concern and inspiration to collaboration and action.

Reaching Out: Dr. Williams called Public Agenda in July 2009 for advice about putting together a community-action plan to reduce the number of high school dropouts in Carlsbad (about 36% in the public high school) The project started simply, with several telephone calls to exchange information and explore what a plan might look like. The result was an innovation—a distinctively designed Graduation Summit that combined the America's Promise model with Public Agenda's experience in developing community conversations. Together, the partners planned a daylong session that would bring together parents, students, community residents, local employers, heads of local religious organizations, and others. Participants could attend a morning session devoted to learning about the dropout problem and weighing potential solutions. For those who wanted to go further, the afternoon centered on a "more action-oriented deliberation aimed at identifying and prioritizing specific next steps."[18] Public Agenda developed a Choicework Discussion Guide called "A Quality High School Education For All" that focused on three different approaches to increasing the high school graduation rate.

Moving Forward: On May 8, 2010, Carlsbad's Graduation Summit drew over one hundred community residents of all ages, professions, ethnicities, and backgrounds. The participants talked as a group and then convened in 10 small-group sessions to talk through different ideas for reducing the community's dropout rate. Some of the suggestions that emerged in the conversations included improving data systems to identify students at risk of dropping out early on, training teachers to better engage parents in their children's education, increasing the use of technology in the classroom, and helping students understand (beginning in junior high) how the material they learn in school connects to the jobs and careers they will seek later.

In the afternoon, 35 participants stayed on to pursue the conversation. They broke up into "action teams" and produced a list of priorities and actionable next steps. Some specifics: setting up phone trees to inform parents about upcoming parent-teacher meetings and developing lists of people willing to serve as mentors. After nearly 8 hours of discussion, dozens of people stayed to exchange contact information and talk about potential partnerships and collaboration. For the Carlsbad community and local school leaders, the event moved the needle from concern and inspiration to the seeds of action.

A PRACTICAL TOOL

Three different situations and three different approaches, but, in each, school leaders were able to use the principles of dialogue and choicework to engage broader portions of the public. In none of these instances was engagement the sole tool used by leaders, but, for each, the process provided an opening that hadn't been apparent before.

Based on Public Agenda's experience, and the experiences of other groups working on public engagement, dialogue and choicework are practical methods with a proven track record. They are flexible enough to be useful in different communities and different circumstances to spur change. They can be used to focus attention on a specific challenge or to reveal problems and concerns that leadership has not anticipated. They can be used to ascertain a direction for improvement; often they can reveal a budding consensus for action. At the very least, engagement that incorporates dialogue and choicework can reduce the miscommunication that often stalls progress. In the best cases, it can propel it.

THE ESSENTIALS—10 CORE PRINCIPLES OF PUBLIC ENGAGEMENT

Most school leaders are already excellent communicators. Nearly every day, they use their communications skills to rally people, explain goals, clarify strategies, establish rapport, deliver bad news tactfully, and to listen and read between the lines. Whether they're superintendents, principals, or senior administrators, school leaders rely on their ability to communicate well on a virtually daily basis.

But using dialogue and choicework to help communities and colleagues engage in more constructive conversations about education and how to improve it sometimes forces school leaders to flex their communications muscles in some slightly different ways.

"The Essentials"

If you're a movie buff, you've probably encountered Robert Osborne, the host of Turner Classic Movies, introducing his classic film series, "The Essentials." Osborne and a guest select a marvelous film and talk a little about how it got made, the director, the stars and so on before showing it. More often than not, you learn something new about the film—even one you've seen many times before.

Borrowing on Osborne's idea, Public Agenda has developed 10 basic principles for public engagement—a step-by-step roadmap to bringing people together and using dialogue and choicework to advance understanding and problem solving. And even though the list contains some classic and widely known principles of good communication, it's still revealing and informative.

These 10 core principles grow out of the work of my Public Agenda colleagues Will Friedman and Alison Kadlec, and they are described more fully in *The Essentials—Public Engagement: A Primer from Public Agenda.* It's available for free download from Public Agenda at http://www.publicagenda .org/files/pdf/public_engagement_primer_0.pdf. Here's the preview:

1. **Begin by listening.** To engage people effectively, you need to know what's on their minds. That means getting a better feel for the concerns and fears they bring to an issue, along with the hopes and aspirations they attach to it. It means letting go of the jargon and shop talk and speaking with people using terms and concepts that nonexperts can easily grasp.

2. **Take people's concerns seriously.** A genuine dialogue has three requirements—equality, empathy, and surfacing assumptions nonjudgmentally. That means listening to people's concerns, priorities, and proposals carefully and respectfully. It means trying to understand their point of view and appreciate the experiences and beliefs they bring to the issue.

3. **Reach beyond the usual suspects.** All of us learn and grow when we meet and talk with people from different walks of life, and one way to advance dialogue is to include those who might not normally be included. In education, most school leaders routinely think about dialogue with teachers, parents, and students. Those groups are essential. But bringing in local employers who hire local graduates, local professors, recent graduates, and representatives from community groups and local government agencies can open up the conversation in unexpected, very useful ways. In *The Magic of Dialogue,* Yankelovich recommends that leaders interested in promoting dialogue "err on the side of including people who disagree."[1]

4. **Use dialogue and choicework.** These techniques can change the conversation, but it's important to remember that they don't by themselves solve the problem. However, they often set the stage for problem solving by helping leaders identify submerged issues and promising new ideas, and find new allies and collaborators. And Public Agenda's work has shown time and time again that dialogue and choicework can help leaders establish mutual respect and rapport.

5. **Give people the information they need and want, but avoid the data dump.** Here's what Public Agenda suggests in *The Essentials:* "It is helpful to provide people with carefully selected, essential, nonpartisan information upfront . . . but too much all at once can result in people feeling overwhelmed. . . . It plays to the experts in the room while disempowering regular citizens." Having people feel overwhelmed and disempowered is not a promising start to dialogue. Concise, well-chosen "intro" information that helps everyone start on the same page can be far more effective than a 50-slide Power Point— and it leaves people more time to talk, which is the real objective. Choicework, with its blend of key facts and its explicit discussion of people's concerns, values, aspirations, and priorities, is a superior way to package information for lay people.

6. **Help people move beyond wishful thinking and blaming.** Choicework offers another advantage—it helps people quickly grasp the trade-offs entailed in different solutions, and it helps them move beyond easy answers, wishful thinking, blaming, and venting. Training moderators specifically to lead choicework and promote dialogue is also helpful,[2] as is bringing diverse groups together. People with different points of view can help each other become more realistic and subtle in their thinking.

7. **Expect obstacles and resistances.** As Public Agenda puts it: "People are used to doing things in a particular way, and it is hard work to grapple with new possibilities." In many cases, people will need time to absorb, think, ruminate, and decompress. Dialogue and choicework are powerful tools to increase understanding, but change is still difficult and can be threatening to many people, depending on the circumstances. Leaders need to expect that some people will be frustrated, and they need to find ways to help them process their fear and disappointment.

8. **Once is not enough.** When an issue involves significant alterations in the way people conduct their daily activities and major changes in what's expected of them, engagement initiatives need to provide repeated opportunities for people to think and talk. Here's Public Agenda's advice: "A strong engagement initiative will be inclusive as well as iterative, giving people multiple and varied opportunities to learn about, talk about, think about, and act on a problem at hand. Community conversations, "study circles," online engagement strategies, and media partnerships are a few of the possibilities."

9. **Respond thoughtfully and conscientiously to the public involvement.** Sometimes leaders assume that reaching out to the general public and other stakeholders in education means putting every decision up for a "yea" or "nay" vote. But leaders still need to lead, and part of that is making the most thoughtful decision you can based on authentic dialogue, good research, and considering the realities at hand. Even when—and perhaps especially when—leaders can't do the popular thing, explaining why some suggestions and viewpoints could not be incorporated in the ultimate decision is respectful and builds trust.

10. **Build long-term capacity as you go.** Dialogue and choicework are useful techniques to address specific problems, but they should be part of the fabric of life in a democracy. That means that engagement actually operates on two levels. Again from Public Agenda: "On one level it is about addressing a concrete problem, such as improving education, public safety, or jobs. On another, it is about building what philosopher John Dewey called, 'social intelligence,' the capacity for a democratic community to communicate and collaborate effectively in order to solve its common problems and enrich its public life."

1. Daniel Yankelovich, *The Magic of Dialogue,* Touchstone, 2001, Page 127.
2. Public Agenda, the Kettering Foundation, the National Coalition for Dialogue and Deliberation all have programs to help moderators master these skills. See the Appendix for more.

NOTES

1. Jean Johnson and Will Friedman, "Dear Public: Can We Talk? Public Engagement Encourages a Broad, Lasting Base of Support," *The School Administrator,* February 2006.

2. Advance Illinois, "Our Mission and Priorities," Accessed June 27, 2011, http://www.advanceillinois.org/.

3. Statement of Robin Steans, Executive Director of Advance Illinois, "About Illinois Senate Bill 7: The Negotiated Education Reform Package Passed by the Illinois State Senate," Accessed June 27, 2011, http://www.advanceillinois.org/education-news-pages-6.php?listing_id=707, and Ellen Alberding, "The New Leader in Education Reform," *The Chicago Tribune,* June 13, 2011, http://www.chicagotribune.com/news/opinion/ct-oped-0613-reform-20110613,0,7530822.story.

4. Dr. Linda Murray, "The San Jose Unified School District Story," *Profiles in Leadership,* All4Ed.org, Accessed June 27, 2011, Page 90, http://www.all4ed.org/files/Murray_PIL.pdf.

5. Jean Johnson and Will Friedman, "Dear Public: Can We Talk?" *The School Administrator.*

6. Dr. Linda Murray, "The San Jose Unified School District Story," *Profiles in Leadership,* Page 90, http://www.all4ed.org/files/Murray_PIL.pdf.

7. Jean Johnson and Will Friedman, "Dear Public: Can We Talk?" *The School Administrator.*

8. Dr. Linda Murray, "The San Jose Unified School District Story," *Profiles in Leadership,* Page 90, http://www.all4ed.org/files/Murray_PIL.pdf.

9. Ibid., Page 91.

10. Jean Johnson and Will Friedman, "Dear Public: Can We Talk?" *The School Administrator.*

11. Ibid.

12. Nebraska has 492 school districts, http://www.setda.org/c/document_library/get_file?folderId=322&name=DLFE-852.pdf.

13. Jean Johnson and Will Friedman, "Dear Public: Can We Talk?" *The School Administrator.*

14. Ibid.

15. Ibid.

16. Ibid.

17. http://www.americaspromise.org/.

18. Public Agenda, Dropout Prevention in Carlsbad, New Mexico, 2010. Contact info@publicagenda.org for additional information.

Chapter 14

Is It Time for School Leaders to Speak Up for Themselves—and Speak Out for the Rest of Us?

Most of this book has been about listening—how school leaders can benefit from listening to parents, teachers, students, colleagues, community residents, and others. One of my chief themes is how understanding the perspectives of these different groups can empower school leaders to engage them more successfully, and how that improves the chances for sustainable reform.

DIFFERENT STROKES . . .

As important as that is, though, it's now time to focus on what school leaders themselves have to say. Many of course have different points of view about how best to help and motivate their teachers and how best to turn around persistently failing schools. That's as it should be—school leaders work in different kinds of schools in markedly different kinds of communities. School leaders themselves bring different talents and skills to the job. Leadership shouldn't be cookie-cutter. Education overall could gain from leaders taking different approaches to problem solving and being innovative and breaking new ground.

This chapter focuses on some broadly shared concerns among school leaders today that should get more attention. In fact, it may be time for school leaders themselves to be more vocal and assertive, highlighting these problems. I propose a four-item agenda that needs to be addressed so school leaders can do a better job improving the country's schools:

1. Leaders need to have time to lead.
2. Leaders need the flexibility to make good decisions on behalf of kids and schools.

3. Leaders need to speak up about practices that aren't working.
4. Leaders need better preparation and support.

Here's what I've seen in Public Agenda's research and my own conversations with educators around the country. See if you agree.

LEADERS NEED TO HAVE TIME TO LEAD

Michael Keany, an experienced administrator who blogs on school leadership issues, recently wrote a piece entitled: "CEOs and School Leaders: The Good Ones Are More Alike than Different."[1] Keany makes some excellent points. For example, he comments: "Gone are the days when a school leader could simply cause change by the sheer act of will. The educational system is too complex. All aspects of the system must see the change. This implies a sense of team unity and that is very much the responsibility of the leader." Well said. I couldn't agree more.

But there are also major differences between CEOs and school leaders, and one crucial one is that CEOs are typically surrounded by teams of senior vice presidents who manage everything from finances to personnel to government relations and future planning. Big city school leaders have small (and usually overworked) teams around them, but, across the country, most school leaders have nothing like the coterie of support enveloping the typical corporate CEO.

To me, the better comparison is someone starting a small business—someone who is thinking, planning, strategizing, and investing his or her entire being into the effort. Small business people—like school leaders—typically work long hours with few breaks in order to develop the enterprise and keep it humming. They are masters of invention and making do.

In Chapter 1, I mentioned a small-scale study Public Agenda conducted for the Wallace Foundation called *A Mission of the Heart: What Does It Take to Transform a School?* In it, Public Agenda looked at the views of principals in high-needs schools and districts in different parts of the country. As the report spells out, the principals had many common concerns and experiences, but they typically fell into one of two distinct categories. They were either *transformers* and had "an explicit vision of what their school might be like and brought a 'can do' attitude to their job," or they were *copers* who were often "struggling to avoid being overwhelmed."[2] One chief difference between the two groups was whether the principals were able to overcome the intimidating problem of having too many things to do with too little time to do them.

The problem of finding time to accomplish the most important tasks—and not be distracted by less important ones—emerges pointedly in the area of instructional leadership. Many reformers see instructional leaders as the key to creating the schools the country needs. They want school leaders to play a much stronger role in identifying, developing, coaching, supporting, and motivating effective teaching, and there's plenty of research to suggest they're right.[3] The question is whether we have a system that enables school leaders to tackle that urgent role head-on.

Public Agenda's surveys of principals show that about three-quarters (74%) say that they spend more time "than they used to when it comes to working on the substance of teaching—for example, curriculum, teaching techniques, mentoring, and professional development."[4] But only 1 principal out of every 10 believes that he or she has enough time to work on this: 70 percent of principals say they would like to do a lot more; 19 percent would like to do a little more.[5] Many principals appear to be frustrated because they can't find enough time for instructional leadership. Nearly three-quarters (74%) say that "daily emergencies rob them of time that could be better spent on academic or teaching issues."[6]

As Public Agenda reported, principals who are transformers make the instructional leadership mission a top priority. One transformer talked about why working directly with teachers on instruction simply has to take precedence: "At the end of the day, with high-needs schools, it's really about student achievement and the instruction. If we're not able to be in the classrooms to observe instruction and make sure . . . students are receiving high-quality instruction, the . . . moving the budget is not going to do anything."[7]

The copers, in contrast, often allow instructional leadership to get derailed by the school's daily flare-ups and eruptions. One told Public Agenda: "I find myself wearing so many hats . . . it's unbelievable. I just cannot free myself up."[8] Another told us what a typical day looks like: There are "seven teachers grabbing me going down the hallway while I'm trying to get to an observation [that I've] got two minutes to get [to]."[9]

Based on Public Agenda's research, school leaders at every level and in schools and districts of all kinds are also frustrated because they see their time eaten away by distractions that administrative or clerical personnel could easily handle. This is where the world of school leaders departs so sharply from the world of most corporate CEOs. Most principals spend considerable time defusing problems that emerge with teachers, students, or parents. Most CEOs never even talk to a customer or line employer—their vice presidents and other managers do that for them.

There are two takeaways here. One is that the best and strongest school leaders find ways to put first things first. But the second takeaway is equally important. If school leaders see instructional leadership as a key reform that will help them give students the education they deserve, then it's time to speak up. School leaders need to explain that, and explain it forcefully. The central question for the field overall is whether the broad interest in instructional leadership is accompanied by an equally broad commitment to reorganizing schools in ways that make it possible.

LEADERS NEED THE FLEXIBILITY TO MAKE GOOD DECISIONS ON BEHALF OF SCHOOLS AND KIDS

Schools are places with a lot of rules. When Public Agenda convenes superintendents and principals to talk about schools, the issue of red tape and bureaucracy generally leaps out as an exhausting and frustrating obstacle. "Keeping up with state and federal mandates . . . is extremely time-consuming," one superintendent told us. "We have an education code that is over 3,500 pages, and that doesn't even include all the laws . . . within the health and safety code and government codes to which we must adhere. Add regulations from the federal government—which can often conflict with state codes or our local labor contracts—and we spend a lot of time trying to straighten out the confusion."[10] More than 8 in 10 school leaders—86 percent of superintendents and 84 percent of principals—agree that "keeping up with all the local, state, and federal mandates handed down to the schools takes up way too much time," with roughly 4 in 10 in each group saying that this is "very close" to their view.[11]

When Public Agenda asked superintendents why talented people in their field sometimes leave the job, 82 percent picked "politics and bureaucracy," as the major reason, compared to just 13 percent who said the major reason was "unreasonable demands brought about by higher standards and accountability," and just 3 percent said the major reason was "low pay and prestige."[12] These results are a forceful testament to how frustrated school leaders are at the mountains of paperwork that come with their jobs.

Again, there are two takeaways. In a thought-provoking article called "Cages of Their Own Design,"[13] Fred Hess, the prolific education expert at the American Enterprise Institute, urges school leaders to fight back. Hess believes that too many school leaders are entrapped in a "debilitating timidity." He urges "reform-minded leaders [to] make much better use of their existing autonomy."[14] Among other measures, he encourages school leaders to request waivers from laws that hamstring them and to confer often with managers from other fields so they don't become bogged down in a narrow, education-only mindset.

And once again, maybe it's time for school leaders to speak up and cry foul. Corporate leaders have certainly pushed back against what they see as overregulation and mind-numbing bureaucratic micromanagement. School leaders might be surprised by how powerful their voices could be if they spoke out strongly and as one.

DO THEY EVEN READ THE BILLS THEY PASS?

As a group, school leaders tend to be a diplomatic bunch. Since they are often speaking publicly on behalf of their schools and districts, they often have to think carefully about the impact their words will have on the various constituencies they work with.

But when school leaders go off the record, some of their frustrations and annoyances spill out, and more than a few of them concern bureaucracy and red tape. Here's just a small sampling of what some school leaders across the country told us about the flood of administrative minutia they have to deal with—minutia that many feel steal time and energy from improving schools and helping kids.

"Some items are well-intended, [but] most of the lawmakers don't have a clue what the unintended consequences of their laws will be. . . . I really don't think they read most of them."[1]

"Our district [of 4,000 students] decided we had to . . . hire our own special ed director. There was simply too much paperwork to attend to. Plus our teaching staff was not filling out the forms the way the state felt they should. We also budget a healthy amount for legal fees in this area since parents and lawyers find it worthwhile to litigate for just about any reason."[2]

"Take [away] some of my responsibility. . . . Transportation—I mean give me a break. How am I responsible for a bus driver being rude at a bus stop?"[3]

"I'm sure you've noticed by now that very little of what I mentioned above [about bureaucracy and red tape has] anything to do with leading instructional change, supervising 25 school sites, or becoming a known and respected member of my school community."[4]

Re: using data: "We're sitting here trying to—where are the AIM scores? Where [are] the language scores? That's ridiculous, and that will take you two weeks to compile all that together. What has happened to the child?"[5]

Re: special education legislation: "You can certainly quote me, and I'll be happy to testify before Congress if necessary. . . . We've gone so far overboard that we can no longer even hope to meet our [special-needs students'] real education needs. We're far too busy satisfying bureaucratic demands to be bothered with actual teaching and learning. Can you tell that I'm frustrated and disgusted?"[6]

One superintendent provided this list to show how it all adds up. By law, his schools must provide:

- provide oral health instruction
- provide information about organ donation
- institute anti-bullying policies
- insure that children say the Pledge of Allegiance,
- make sure that social studies classes celebrate Freedom Week
- organize parent involvement committees at every school
- set up committees on certain employee policies
- set up school and district committees on "closing the gap"
- arrange for employees such as bus drivers to have two paid breaks
- see that each teacher has a specific amount to spend on classroom supplies
- include the body mass index of each child on his or her report card

His parting shot: "Oh, [and] by the way, remember No Child Left Behind."

1. Steve Farkas, Jean Johnson, and Ann Duffett with Beth Syat and Jackie Vine, *Rolling Up Their Sleeves: Superintendents and Principals Talk About What Is Needed to Fix Public Schools,* Public Agenda, 2003, Page 12, http://www.publicagenda.org/reports/rolling-their-sleeves.
2. Ibid.
3. Public Agenda, *A Mission of the Heart: What Does It Take to Transform a School?* Conducted for The Wallace Foundation, 2008, Page 13, http://www.publicagenda.org/files/pdf/missionheart.pdf.
4. Steve Farkas, Jean Johnson, and Ann Duffett with Beth Syat and Jackie Vine, *Rolling Up Their Sleeves,* Page 13, http://www.publicagenda.org/reports/rolling-their-sleeves.
5. Public Agenda, *A Mission of the Heart: What Does It Take to Transform a School?* Page 5, http://www.publicagenda.org/files/pdf/missionheart.pdf.
6. Steve Farkas, Jean Johnson, and Ann Duffett with Beth Syat and Jackie Vine, *Rolling Up Their Sleeves,* Page 14, http://www.publicagenda.org/reports/rolling-their-sleeves.

LEADERS NEED TO SPEAK UP ABOUT PRACTICES THAT AREN'T WORKING

Most people don't spend all that much time in schools, and ideas that look good on paper or worked well in other settings sometimes just don't transfer very well. This is where school leaders need to speak out—for themselves and their colleagues, certainly, but also for the teachers and students they are responsible for.

As a group, superintendents and principals have experiences and insights into what works and what doesn't that few others have. They have the perspective of being managers, but also the on-the-ground touch and feel for what happens in schools daily.

Public Agenda's research suggests some contenders—issues that the majority of school leaders seem to believe need reconsideration and that rarely make it onto the national reform agenda. The red tape issue is certainly one of them. The vast majority of superintendents and principals also have serious reservations about the way special education operates.

Personally, I have never met a school leader who wasn't fully committed to giving children with special needs the help and support they deserve, but that doesn't mean that they believe that the current system works well. Some 83 percent of superintendents and 65 percent of principals say that administrators are obligated to spend a disproportionate "amount of money and other resources on special education issues."[15] Among both superintendents and principals, 8 in 10 say the "special education laws have encouraged a sense of entitlement among parents, making them too quick to threaten legal action to get their way."[16] This is a difficult and sometimes deeply emotional issue for parents, but if that many school leaders have qualms about special education, they need to voice those concerns. They need to play a constructive role in considering ways special education could be improved.

Teacher training and certification is another area. Just 5 percent of superintendents and 11 percent of principals say that in their states "being fully certified guarantees that the typical teacher has what it takes to be a good teacher."[17] Only 28 percent of superintendents and 25 percent of principals say that in their districts, having tenure means that "a teacher has worked hard and proved themselves to be very good at what they do."

Huh! If this is what judges thought about lawyers passing the bar exam or what hospital administrators said about board-certified physicians, the nation would be scandalized. School leaders have an ethical responsibility here. For the good of us all, school leaders should be speaking out and demanding and leading the way to get improvements here.

LEADERS NEED BETTER PREPARATION AND SUPPORT

I opened *You Can't Do It Alone* with a story about how school leaders in Public Agenda focus groups often exchange business cards so they can talk later to exchange ideas and compare notes. Superintendents and principals are routinely looking for practical advice on how to do their jobs better. That's a tribute to their motivation and commitment. I have seen it in the cities, suburbs, and rural areas, and in affluent and low-income school districts alike.

But this observation also suggests that there's something important missing in how the field prepares and supports superintendents and principals. When Public Agenda asked school leaders to choose what was "the most valuable in preparing you for your current job," just 2 percent of superintendents and 4 percent of principals pointed to their academic preparation. About a third of superintendents and about half of principals said it was the mentoring and guidance they've gotten from people they work with. The rest say it's just plain old experience.[18]

One school leader we interviewed said bluntly that "training in universities is irrelevant."[19] Another commented that "universities are too far removed from the realities of working in education. They are gifted at research, but off-base [about] what is actually going on in schools."[20]

In the end, just 14 percent of superintendents and 10 percent of principals say that the graduate program they completed to be certified "has proved indispensable in my job." Most say the program contained "some useful things." Given the amount of time and money invested in training school leaders—and given how much this country needs more good ones—we simply have to do better than that. Who is more qualified to speak out about how to improve leadership training that school leaders themselves?

And training is just the beginning. How do we support school leaders once they are on the job so their energy and know-how are directed right where we need it—in helping teachers be more effective and motivating students to do their best? Do we really want principals spending their time working out lunch schedules and deciding how much paper to order? School leaders shouldn't have to devote even one second to tasks like this if it's taking time away from the teachers, the kids, and what's happening in the classroom.

My last comment, again, grows out of our report on principals in high-needs schools and districts called *A Mission of the Heart*. We chose the title because it is exactly what we saw while doing the research—"inspiring people who were putting heart and soul into their mission." That is genuinely inspiring and admirable, but we also said this: "Most seemed to be working many, many hours a day at very stressful, albeit rewarding jobs. Our questions is how long human beings can be expected to keep this up—even individuals as gifted and committed as our transformers. What are they giving up to be able to do the jobs they are doing? . . . Is it reasonable to believe that they can maintain this level of energy and sparkle and passion years in the future?"

School leaders hold the key to reinventing the nation's public education system and giving America's children the uniformly excellent, caring, and effective schools and teachers they deserve. Understanding the perspectives different groups bring to the education enterprise is fundamentally important. Incorporating dialogue, choicework, and better-planned strategies for engaging the public and communities in education reform can help our schools turn the corner. But sometimes school leaders don't seem to be aware of their own importance and their own power. You need to hear from us, but we need to hear from you as well.

It's time for the country's school leaders to speak up and speak out—for themselves and for the rest of us.

IF SCHOOL LEADERS RAN THE WORLD . . .

We all have to live in the real world, and we don't necessarily get to impose our views on how to solve problems and make progress on everyone else. But we all deserve the chance to say our piece, and in a book that's focused mainly on encouraging public-school leaders to listen to parents, teachers, students, and others, there certainly should be room for superintendents and principals to have their say.[1] What do Public Agenda surveys show about their priorities for improving teaching and enhancing school leadership? Take a look:

Table 14.1. Public School Superintendents' Priorities for Improving the Quality of Teaching:

Would [this idea] be a very effective, somewhat effective, not too effective, or not effective at all in improving teacher quality?

Proposal	Very Effective %	Somewhat Effective %	Not too Effective %
Increasing professional development opportunities for teachers	57	36	5
Requiring new teachers to spend much more time teaching in classrooms under the supervision of experienced teachers	45	47	6
Eliminating teacher tenure	43	32	15
Increasing teacher salaries	36	49	14
Reducing class size	34	49	15
Tying teacher rewards and sanctions to their students' performance	20	37	31
Requiring teachers to earn graduate degrees in education	11	46	33
Relying more heavily on alternative certification programs	4	24	50

Source: Public Agenda

Table 14.2.   Public School Superintendents' Priorities for Improving Their Ability to Lead:

Would [this idea] be a very effective, somewhat effective, not too effective, or not effective at all in improving leadership?

Proposal	Very Effective %	Somewhat Effective %	Not too Effective %
Making it much easier for superintendents to remove bad teachers—even those who have tenure	77	19	2
Making data from student testing available in a more timely and useful way so that administrators can use it to make better decisions	73	22	2
Markedly reducing the number of mandates on schools and the bureaucracy and paperwork associated with them	64	30	4
Giving school leaders more autonomy to deal with school discipline	43	42	13
Giving school leaders more autonomy to choose teaching methods, texts, and curricular programs	33	45	18
Putting more business practices into how school systems are run	11	30	36

Source: Public Agenda

Table 14.3.   Public School Principals' Priorities for Improving the Quality of Teaching:

Would [this idea] be a very effective, somewhat effective, not too effective, or not effective at all in improving teacher quality?

Proposal	Very Effective %	Somewhat Effective %	Not too Effective %
Increasing professional development opportunities for teachers	62	34	3
Requiring new teachers to spend much more time teaching in classrooms under the supervision of experienced teachers	54	36	10
Reducing class size	54	37	8
Increasing teacher salaries	45	46	8
Eliminating teacher tenure	29	30	26
Requiring teachers to earn graduate degrees in education	20	45	26

Table 14.3.   Public School Principals' Priorities for Improving the Quality of Teaching: *(Continued)*

Would [this idea] be a very effective, somewhat effective, not too effective, or not effective at all in improving teacher quality?

Proposal	Very Effective %	Somewhat Effective %	Not too Effective %
Tying teacher rewards and sanctions to their students' performance	17	35	29
Relying more heavily on alternative certification programs	4	21	50

Source: Public Agenda

Table 14.4.   Public School Principals' Priorities for Improving Their Ability to Lead:

Would [this idea] be a very effective, somewhat effective, not too effective, or not effective at all in improving leadership?

Proposal	Very Effective %	Somewhat Effective %	Not too Effective %
Making it much easier for superintendents to remove bad teachers—even those who have tenure	72	23	3
Making data from student testing available in a more timely and useful way so that administrators can use it to make better decisions	71	26	1
Markedly reducing the number of mandates on schools and the bureaucracy and paperwork associated with them	67	30	1
Giving school leaders more autonomy to deal with school discipline	38	48	11
Giving school leaders more autonomy to choose teaching methods, texts, and curricular programs	35	48	14
Putting more business practices into how school systems are run	16	31	35

Source: Public Agenda

1. Findings reported here are from Jean Johnson, Ana Maria Arumi, and Amber Ott, *Reality Check 2006, Issue No. 4:The Insiders: How Principals and Superintendents See Public Education Today,* Public Agenda, 2006, http://www.publicagenda.org/reports/reality-check-2006-issue-no-4. Contact info@publicagenda.org for details.

NOTES

1. Michael Keany, "CEOs and School Leaders: The Good Ones are More Alike than Different," SchoolLeadership20.Com, May 23, 2011, http://www.schoolleadership20.com/profiles/blogs/ceos-and-school-leaders-the.

2. Public Agenda, *A Mission of the Heart: What Does It Take to Transform a School?* Conducted for The Wallace Foundation, 2008, http://www.publicagenda.org/files/pdf/missionheart.pdf.

3. See for example, Jane Cogshall, Amber Ott, Ellen Behrstock, and Molly Lasagna, *Retaining Teaching Talent: The View From Gen Y*, Public Agenda and Learning Point Associates/AIR, November, 2009, http://www.learningpt.org/expertise/educatorquality/genY/SupportingTeacherEffectiveness/index.php.

4. Steve Farkas, Jean Johnson, and Ann Duffett with Beth Syat and Jackie Vine, *Rolling Up Their Sleeves: Superintendents and Principals Talk About What Is Needed to Fix Public Schools*, Public Agenda, 2003, Page 66, http://www.publicagenda.org/reports/rolling-their-sleeves.

5. Ibid.

6. Ibid., Page 51.

7. Public Agenda, *A Mission of the Heart: What Does It Take to Transform a School?* Page 4, http://www.publicagenda.org/files/pdf/missionheart.pdf.

8. Ibid., Page 3.

9. Ibid., Page 4.

10. Steve Farkas, Jean Johnson, and Ann Duffett with Beth Syat and Jackie Vine, *Rolling Up Their Sleeves,* Page 13, http://www.publicagenda.org/reports/rolling-their-sleeves.

11. Ibid., Page 53.

12. Ibid., Page 49.

13. Frederick M. Hess, "Cages of Their Own Design," *Educational Leadership*, October, 2009, Pages 28–33, http://www.ascd.org/publications/educational-leadership/oct09/vol67/num02/Cages-of-Their-Own-Design.aspx.

14. Ibid.

15. Ibid., Page 29.

16. Steve Farkas, Jean Johnson, and Ann Duffett with Beth Syat and Jackie Vine, *Rolling Up Their Sleeves,* Page 52, http://www.publicagenda.org/reports/rolling-their-sleeves.

17. Ibid., Page 51.

18. Ibid., Page 65.

19. Ibid., Page 70.

20. Public Agenda, *A Mission of the Heart: What Does It Take to Transform a School?* Page 10, http://www.publicagenda.org/files/pdf/missionheart.pdf.

21. Ibid.

Epilogue

Reconnecting the American People with Their Schools

Most of this book has been about problem solving within the schools—how reaching out to teachers, parents, students, and others can help school leaders accomplish needed change. My argument is that even the most thoughtful, best-laid plans leaders can devise will falter unless these groups come into the fold and become genuine partners in reform. Fundamental change depends on having them think and act differently than they do now. And leaders need to think and act differently as well: Developing better solutions and more effective ways to implement them depends on understanding and incorporating the ideas and experiences teachers, parents, students, and other key stakeholders bring to the table. That's pretty much my bottom line.

But there's another reason leaders need to engage (or reengage might be a better word) a much broader group of Americans in the national effort to improve the nation's schools. Public schools are part of the fabric of our communities. These are educational institutions to be sure, but they are far more than that in the eyes of most Americans. They are the places where people's children enter the broader society. They are the contact point where neighbors meet. In rural areas and smaller cities, they are frequently the heart of community social life. Even in large cities, communities often feel a strong connection and tremendous loyalty to neighborhood schools—especially when they believe they are at risk of closure or other fundamental change.

As I mentioned earlier on, the Kettering Foundation's David Mathews has written about the relationship between schools and communities and explored what it means when people talk about "our" schools as opposed to "the" schools.[1] It's an expression of pride, but also one of responsibility, connection, and ownership. The use of "our" instead of "my" is significant. It suggests a strong and lasting relationship between the schools and the entire

159

community—not just between the school and the individual whose children attend it.

Mathews is not alone in his judgment that this distinct relationship has become less intense in recent decades. Experts have suggested a number of plausible and probably valid explanations. The percentage of Americans with school-aged children has declined—we're an older population than we used to be. We're also a more mobile society, and fewer of us maintain life-long relationships with the same communities and schools. We're all busier. Most mothers now work, and with both parents in the workforce (and with more single parents as well), there's just less time for parents to be closely involved with their children's schools. Then there's the failure of schools themselves—in far too many cases, they simply haven't served children and families well.

But the strategy the country has pursued to improve public education over the last 10 to 15 years could be another contributing factor. We've basically skipped over teachers, parents, and communities in the movement to build the better, stronger education system America needs. There's a broad sense among many Americans today that "our schools" are being redesigned and controlled by a disconnected and largely distrusted power elite.

Here are some thought-provoking results from a Public Agenda survey conducted in 1994, right at a moment when the reform movement that has swept through schools nationwide was just beginning to take shape. The survey asked typical members of the public which groups they most trusted to make decisions on how schools in their communities should be run. A healthy 6 in 10 Americans gave strong endorsements to "parents in [their] community" and "teachers in [their] local public schools." In stunningly sharp contrast, just 14 percent gave similarly strong ratings to "elected officials in Washington, DC." Fewer than 3 in 10 people put a lot of trust in local elected officials, governors, or teachers' union representatives.[2] Yet it is precisely these groups—elected officials, national and state policymakers, and union officials—that have been most visible in shaping the reform accountability measures that are transforming in public education.

GOOD INTENTIONS, MINIMAL DIALOGUE

Based on my experience, the vast majority of national and state policymakers propelling reform are genuinely concerned about the serious inadequacies in public education. They believe the nation's children deserve better, and they deserve ample credit for putting the ball into play. But they have mainly been in dialogue with each other—not with teachers, parents, students, and communities. From the public's point of view, the reforms that are reshaping their schools are coming from the sources they trust the least. The groups they trust the most have had relatively little say in the matter.

Not only does this mean that reforms have to be carried out in an atmosphere of skepticism and doubt, it also loosens the public's sense of connection to—and responsibility for—what happens in local schools. If someone else is making the decisions, people seem to be saying, and they're not even bothering to consult the people we think matter most, then these aren't really our schools anymore.

Strong public schools depend on strong public support, but there is reciprocity as well. Schools that have broad public support and participation tend to "return the favor." They nurture and sustain the sense of community and shared responsibility that makes problem solving possible.

As I complete work on this book, Public Agenda is just concluding a piece of research with the Kettering Foundation that explores how parents talk about their own accountability for their children's education and their community's schools. The study confirms some of the key themes laid out here—a strong sense that schools are more than educational institutions and that in too many instances, schools and school leaders do not communicate effectively with parents and the broader community. Many of the parents interviewed for the study voiced frustration with what they see as one-way communication.

But the strongest message from the research is the resounding belief voiced time and time again that schools cannot be successful unless parents themselves shoulder their own responsibilities and unless other key players— students, teachers, principals, and others—all fulfill their distinctive obligations with resolve and a spirit of cooperation.

"IT SHOULD BE IN PARTNERSHIP"

Here's my favorite quote from the study. It's from a father in Westchester, NY, who said: "[The work of helping children succeed in school] should be in partnership. I think that's the bottom line problem. We've ended up in a place where [educators and parents are] adversaries now, instead of . . . in partnership with each other."

Exactly. I couldn't have put it better myself. The mission now is to rebuild that partnership and move ahead together reimagining and rebuilding "our" public schools.

NOTES

1. See David Mathews, *Is There a Public for the Public Schools?* The Charles F. Kettering Foundation, 1996.

2. Jean Johnson and John Immerwahr with Adam Kernan-Schloss, *First Things First: What Americans Expect from the Public Schools,* Public Agenda, 1994, Page 52, http://www.publicagenda.org/reports/first-things-first.

Appendix

So You Want to Do Some Engagement?
Here's Where to Start

My keen hope is that this book will inspire school leaders to reach out to parents, students, teachers, community residents, and others and bring them into authentic, two-way conversations on how to improve schools and enhance student learning. The book is called *You Can't Do It Alone* to convey the message that involving these stakeholders is essential to authentic, long-lasting reform. Luckily, if you decide to take the plunge and engage more people in addressing the challenges facing your districts and schools, you won't have to do it alone either. There are some very good sources of help and advice on how to engage groups in dialogue. Here are some to get you started.

PUBLIC AGENDA

Nearly all of the research summarized in this book is available either online or for free download at Public Agenda's website at www.publicagenda.org. But that's just the beginning. Public Agenda's website has a section specifically designed for "public engagers." It houses guides to planning and moderating community conversations, video discussion starters, and reports on what other communities have done. One good place to start is Public Agenda's "primer" on public engagement. It's at http://www.publicagenda. org/files/pdf/public_engagement_primer_0.pdf.

THE KETTERING FOUNDATION

Public Agenda and the Kettering Foundation have been partners exploring ways to promote dialogue and engagement since the early 1980s. The Kettering Foundation has scores of publications detailing how communities and institutions are using engagement practices to address their own challenges. The Foundation's research on public education is particularly perceptive. It examines the relationship between schools and communities and the communications gaps between national education experts and typical citizens and parents. Visit the website at www.kettering.org and, while you're there, take a moment to see the video, *No Textbook Answer,* at http://www.kettering.org/achievementgap.

THE NATIONAL ISSUES FORUMS

NIF, which was founded by Kettering, is a "network of civic, educational, and other organizations and individuals, whose common interest is to promote public deliberation in America. It has grown to include thousands of civic clubs, religious organizations, libraries, schools, and many other groups that meet to discuss critical public issues." Since NIF promotes dialogue and deliberation, their website at www.nifi.org is chock-full of practical advice on how to organize and moderate forums based on the principles outlined in this book.

NATIONAL COALITION FOR DIALOGUE & DELIBERATION

NCDD is an "active network and community of practice centered around conflict resolution and public engagement." Not only does NCDD publish a number of useful tools and guides itself, it provides lists of materials available from other engagement-focused groups. Its *Resource Guide on Public Engagement* is an excellent introduction to the field. You can find it, along with much more on engaging the public, at www.ncdd.org.

PETER LEVINE'S CIVIC RENEWAL BLOG

Peter Levine, one of the nation's leading experts on engagement, is a widely admired academic who publishes regularly on youth engagement and civic renewal. But don't let the term "academic" scare you away. His writing is crystal clear and incisive, and he is at the center of a growing group of organizations and practitioners immersed in engagement topics. You might want to start with his civic renewal blog at http://peterlevine.ws/?page_id=11 and take it from there.

SOME ESPECIALLY GOOD READS

There are several books that offer helpful insights and very practical advice on dialogue and engagement. I consider *The Magic of Dialogue: Transforming Conflict into Cooperation* by Daniel Yankelovich a must-read. There's really no better way to get a handle on what dialogue is and how different it is from business as usual. *Toward Wiser Public Judgment,* edited by Daniel Yankelovich and William Friedman, is a collection of articles by authors with experience and expertise in engagement and dialogue. Some of the pieces discuss "the public's learning curve" and lay out the theory of change that is at the core of *You Can't Do It Alone.* Other articles describe real-life projects that encapsulate these principles. David Mathew's book, *Is There a Public for the Public Schools?* was first published over a decade ago, but his analysis of the urgent need to reconnect the public with the public schools is as timely as ever.

Acknowledgments

This book is the result of the work of an entire organization over the course of a decade or more. That means I have many people to thank.

The lion's share of the opinion research I have summarized was conducted by Public Agenda, and I want to thank my wonderful colleagues there. The lion's share of the opinion research I have summarized was conducted by Public Agenda, and I want to thank my wonderful colleagues there. First and foremost is the incredible and indefatigable Jon Rochkind who was Public Agenda's research director when most of the surveys and focus groups cited here were conducted. Jon was aided by a superb team including Amber Ott, who worked on key data analyses, along with Samantha DuPont, Paul Gasbarra, Jeremy Hess, and others. John Immerwahr and John Doble, two of Public Agenda's remarkable senior fellows, led our work on several important projects. Much of the earlier work was led by Steve Farkas and Ann Duffett when they worked at Public Agenda. Steve and Ann now have their own firm, FDR Research, and they continue to produce superb opinion research, some of the best in the country.

Through the years, Public Agenda has worked many partner organizations, and I am especially grateful to Sabrina Laine and her colleagues at AIR/ Learning Points Associates, including Jane Coggshall, Ellen Sherratt, Molly Lasagna, and Gretchen Weber among others.

I would also like to thank Dr. David Mathews and John Dedrick of the Kettering Foundation. Kettering's work in education has been a source of new ideas and insights for me for the past 20 years.

The later chapters of the book describe Public Agenda's public engagement operations. This is an extraordinary body of work led by Dr. Will Friedman and Alison Kadlec. Will, who is also Public Agenda's president, gave me helpful feedback on initial drafts of the book, and I thank him for his encouragement and support.

I want to say a word of thanks to my other Public Agenda colleagues who have been so supportive over the years, including Scott Bittle, David White, and Alex Trilling, along with my good friends Josu Gallastegui, Mary Georgiade, and Kate Sheaffer.

I am also very grateful for the good counsel and support I have received from Rowman & Littlefield, especially from my editor, Kristina Mann.

I have dedicated this book to three individuals whose intelligence, creativity, and passion have guided me through much of my career. Dan Yankelovich has been an inspiration and guiding star in everything I have written here and elsewhere. Deborah Wadsworth and Ruth Wooden, who served as Public Agenda presidents and now sit on our board, have been wonderful role models and great friends. If I hadn't had the good fortune of encountering Dan, Deborah, and Ruth along the way, this book would never have been written.

Index

About the Author

Jean Johnson is head of Public Agenda's Education Insights division and a writer and speaker who specializes in helping non-experts understand complex policy issues. She has more than 20 years experience in public opinion and public policy, and her work has focused on issues ranging from education and energy to the federal budget and foreign policy.

At Public Agenda, she has authored or co-authored opinion studies on K-12 education, higher education, families, religion, race relations, civility, and foreign policy. Among her most recent Public Agenda publications are *Don't Count Us Out: How an Overreliance on Accountability Could Undermine the Public's Confidence in Schools, Business, Government, and More* (2011), *One Degree of Separation: How Young Americans Who Don't Finish College See Their Chances for Success* (2011), and *With Their Whole Lives Ahead of Them: Myths and Realities about Why So Many Students Fail to Finish College* (2009). She has also published articles and opinion pieces on education issues in *USA Today, Education Week, School Board News*, and Columbia University's *Teachers College Record*.

Working with Public Agenda colleague Scott Bittle, Ms. Johnson is also the co-author of three books designed to help typical citizens grapple with some of the most confusing, controversial issues facing the nation. They are: *Where Does the Money Go? Your Guided Tour to the Federal Budget Crisis* (Revised edition, 2011); *Who Turned Out the Lights? Your Guided Tour to the Energy Crisis* (2009), and *Where Did the Jobs Go—and How Do We Get Them Back?* (2012).The writing team has been featured on Bill Moyers Journal, and the authors are regular contributors to *The Huffington Post* and *National Geographic*'s "Great Energy Blog."

Ms. Johnson has appeared on CNN, NPR's *Fresh Air*, the *Today Show*, *Lou Dobbs Tonight*, and *The O'Reilly Factor*. She graduated from Mount Holyoke College and holds master's degrees from Brown University and Simmons College. She is also managing director of Sugal Records, a small classical music recording company based in New York.

CPSIA information can be obtained at www.ICGtesting.com
Printed in the USA
BVOW011851041211

277501BV00002B/3/P

ED McCAFFREY

Catching a Star

by

Tony DeMarco

R.I.F.

SPORTS PUBLISHING INC.
www.SportsPublishingInc.com

Production manager: Susan M. McKinney
Cover design: Scot Muncaster, Todd Lauer
Photos: AP/Wide World Photos, Stanford University, Joe Robbins, Allentown Central Catholic High School, Brian Spurlock

ISBN: 1-58261-170-x
Library of Congress Catalog Card Number: 99-68303

SPORTS PUBLISHING INC.
SportsPublishingInc.com

Printed in the United States.

CONTENTS

Ed awaits a pass. (Joe Robbins)

CHAPTER ONE

A Super Feeling

For any professional athlete, winning a championship is the ultimate goal. Individual awards and achievements are nice, but to be part of a winning team is the prize that drives them through long hours of training, practices and games.

Ed McCaffrey had that dream as well as a boy growing up, when he couldn't decide if he wanted to be on a World Series winner, an NBA champion or a team that won the Super Bowl. He played all three sports as a youth, before finally deciding his future would be as a football player.

He was able to realize the goal of being on a winner early in his career, as a member of the San Francisco 49ers. He didn't feel like he had contributed as much as he would have liked to that victory, however, and wondered if he would have a chance to win again sometime in the future.

Not many players get the opportunity to win more than one Super Bowl, but Ed was one of the lucky ones. Not only did he win one more, he won twice, both coming as a member of a Denver Broncos team that won the Super Bowl in 1997 and repeated that victory in 1998. In a span of just five seasons, Ed had earned three Super Bowl champion rings.

"I don't think there's a best one when it comes to winning the Super Bowl," Ed said. "They're all special. When you win, you're the best. You don't take it for granted when you win one."

Ed felt better about his contribution to the 1998 victory, but he wasn't certain that was going to be the case. At halftime of the game against the Atlanta Falcons, Ed still had yet to catch a pass. The second half was better. He caught five passes, and narrowly missed a touchdown catch when the ball squirted out of his hands. That was a minor disappointment on an otherwise great day.

It was the kind of day Ed had dreamed about as a young boy.

Ed is tagged out during the Ed McCaffrey Field of Dreams Softball Classic, an event to raise money for Denver's public schools and underprivileged children. (AP/Wide World Photos)

CHAPTER TWO

Family Ties

From the time he was eight years old, Ed, the oldest of five children of Ed and Betty McCaffrey, recalls playing sports nearly every day.

"I can remember playing for four or five teams in a year," Ed said. "I'd change from my basketball uniform to my baseball uniform on the way to the field. It seemed like I always was involved in some sport. I loved playing sports and had a great time playing."

Following Ed, who was born in Waynesboro, Virginia, on August 17, 1968, was sister Monica.

She went on to play basketball at Georgetown University. Then came brother Bill, two years younger than Monica and three years younger than Ed. He played for the 1991 national championship basketball team at Duke University, and became an All-American after transferring to Vanderbilt University.

Youngest brother Mike, five years younger than Bill, currently plays basketball at Husson College in Maine. The youngest McCaffrey child, Meghan, 13 years younger than her famous brother, plays high school basketball.

Along with encouraging the children to play sports came a family emphasis on schoolwork. Ed, a computer systems analyst, and Betty, a nurse, insisted it be that way.

"Academics and athletics were two important parts of my childhood," Ed said. "But even though we were heavily involved in sports, we always knew that if our grades started slipping, we wouldn't be able to play."

Ed's first favorite sport as a child was baseball. It wasn't until after a move from Wilmington, North Carolina, to Allentown, Pennsylvania, when Ed was 11, that basketball became number one. In fact, in high school at Allentown Central Catholic, Ed was known more for his ability on the basketball court than on the football field.

At the time, Central Catholic was a basketball powerhouse in Pennsylvania, and Ed played a big part in the success. The team won state championships during Ed's sophomore and senior years, 1984 and 1986.

As a sophomore, Ed was the second-leading scorer on the team even though he wasn't a starter. A sprained ankle in a playoff game kept Ed out of the state championship game, but Central Catholic won anyway for the first of what would be a long line of championships for Ed.

Ed's high school basketball team won state championships in his sophomore and senior years.
(Allentown Central Catholic High School)

Ed was 6'4" as a high school senior.
(Allentown Central Catholic High School)

By his senior year, Ed was 6'4" and 230 pounds, and played center on a team that played a fast-break style. He led the team with a 21.4 scoring average. In the playoffs leading to the state final, brother Bill, only a freshman, played a key role in a win over Warwick, coming off the bench to score 11 points.

"That was the first time I got to play with him on a major level because there is a three-year difference between us," Ed said. "I remember how fun it was to play with him, and set picks for him."

In the state championship game, Ed's team played Aliquippa, a team that included Sean Gilbert, whom Ed later would play against in the National Football League. In the win over Aliquippa, Ed scored 29 points. Three years later, Bill, who has played professional basketball overseas and still hopes to catch on with a National Basketball Association team, scored 39 points in the state championship game in a losing cause.

"I can't believe there isn't a spot for him in the NBA," Ed said about Bill. "It's just a mystery to me. All through my college years, I was known as Billy's brother. He was All-American every year."

Ed also dabbled in baseball through high school. Playing mostly first base, Ed hit .540 during one summer league.

The football team at Central Catholic wasn't nearly as successful as the basketball program. In Ed's junior year, the team lost all 11 games. The following year, it improved only to 2-9.

Ed played several positions—running back, quarterback, tight end, wide receiver, linebacker and safety. But it was at the football camps he attended each summer where Ed began drawing attention from college scouts.

"Even though I didn't have any great statistics, or my team didn't have a winning season, I got a lot of recognition for football by my senior year," Ed said. "I got noticed in the camps, and by scouts who came to watch other players, and saw me."

By then, Ed knew his future was in football. He wouldn't be following in the footsteps of his father, who played collegiate basketball at St. Joseph's University.

"I think I was naturally gifted to play football," Ed said. "It seemed to me like that was my best chance to play professionally. Plus, I didn't want to sacrifice my education by signing to play pro baseball out of high school. I wanted to go to college. In basketball, I was 6' 4" and had played center most of the time. You have to be a guard to play in the pros at that height. I think I could have been successful in any of those three sports, but I think football was my sport to do really well."

Time would prove him right.

Ed chose to play football at Stanford, partly because he wanted to play wide receiver. (Stanford University)

CHAPTER THREE

Stanford Man

When it came time for college, Ed had his choice from among a handful of the nation's top football programs. Penn State coach Joe Paterno made trips to Allentown for a couple of Ed's basketball games. Twice, Ed visited Notre Dame, where new coach Lou Holtz was taking over the program. The University of Michigan and Purdue University also were on Ed's short list.

Because of his size, those programs wanted Ed to play tight end. Only Stanford coach Jack Elway offered him the chance to play as a wide receiver.

That, plus the combination of getting to play in Stanford's pro-style passing attack, the school's great academic reputation, and the persuasion of recruiter Tom Beckett and Elway convinced Ed to go west.

"I believed him," Ed said about Elway. "I felt he was honest. He allowed me to play wide receiver. He said I would be able to contribute early on, and I did. I played a lot my freshman year. I thought he was a great coach. I loved playing for him."

Ironically, the connection with the Elway family would remain long into Ed's pro football career, as he later played with Jack's son, John, on the Denver Broncos.

"I first got to meet John when Stanford went out to play a game at the University of Colorado," Ed said. "John already was a star quarterback for the Broncos. It was a thrill to meet him. Never in a million years did I think I'd be catching passes from him."

Ed finished his freshman year with only two catches for 12 yards, both at Oregon State. But he was part of a team that included a handful of future NFL players and finished the season 8-4 by losing to Clemson University in the Gator Bowl. That was the only bowl game Ed played in during his collegiate career.

Ed rose to a starting position by his sophomore season, and caught 30 passes for 533 yards and two touchdowns. His best game came against the University of Washington, when he caught four passes for 108 yards. But the team was in transition, as five quarterbacks saw action, and it struggled to a 5-6 record. As it turned out, Ed wouldn't play for Jack Elway again.

The 1988 season brought Ed's first injury, and his most frustrating moment in sports to that point.

Ed earned bachelor's and master's degrees at Stanford. (Stanford University)

During pre-season practice, Ed ran into a defensive back teammate and suffered a deeply bruised quadriceps muscle. Then, after returning to practice in the week before the first game of the season, he got hit in exactly the same spot, causing more damage.

By the time Ed could run full speed again, it was the seventh week of the season. With most of the season already gone, Ed took a medical redshirt, meaning he still would have two seasons of eligibility remaining.

The extra year Ed would spend on campus allowed him to obtain a bachelor's degree in economics, as well as a master's degree in organizational behavior before his NFL career began.

"It was no coincidence that when I got hurt, my grades skyrocketed," Ed said. "I knew there was no guarantee with football. At that point, I doubted what my future would be as a football player. I was a B, B+ student to that point, but I was close to a 4.0 student after that."

Ed played under future NFL head coaches Dennis Green and Brian Billick while at Stanford. (Brian Spurlock)

Ed was healthy again for the 1989 season, but found himself listed as a second-stringer on the first day of practice under new coach Dennis Green.

"That was a shock, and a wakeup call," Ed said. "I always thought things would progress, and I'd get better in my junior and senior years, and then get a chance to play in the NFL. But here I was, listed on the second team. I worked hard, and was a starter by the time the season began."

Ed flourished in the new offense installed by Green, who later would move on to coach the Minnesota Vikings. Ed's wide receiver coach, Brian Billick, followed Green to Minnesota, and eventually landed the head coaching job of the Baltimore Ravens.

Ed was named Stanford's Most Valuable Player as a junior, and also earned All-Pacific 10 Conference honors after catching 53 passes for 871 yards and four touchdowns. He set season highs with 10 catches for 165 yards and two touchdowns against San Jose State, and caught eight for 150 yards against Washington State.

During his junior year, Ed also met a female soccer player named Lisa Sime. The two were introduced by a mutual friend, and eventually were married after Ed's first season in the NFL.

As a senior, Ed was even better on the field. He caught 61 passes for 917 yards and eight touchdowns, bringing his career totals to 146 catches, 2,333 yards and 14 touchdowns. He set a career high with 11 catches in a 29-23 loss to San Jose State, caught nine for 123 yards and two touchdowns in a 31-21 loss to UCLA, grabbed seven for 176 yards and a career-best three touchdowns in a 31-13 victory over Washington State, and finished with seven catches, 127 yards and two touchdowns in a 37-22 loss to the University of Southern California.

That was enough for Ed to earn All-Pacific 10 Conference honors again, as well as be named to the Kodak All-American team, and be selected to play in the East-West Shrine game. His chance in the NFL was coming, and it wouldn't be long before he would run into Green and Billick, this time on opposing teams.

"After I left Stanford, I thanked both of them for being true professionals," Ed said. "They treated players with respect. They ran it like a pro team. They were very organized and very prepared. I was lucky. I had great coaches who gave me a chance to play, and the offense we ran there helped me prepare for the NFL."

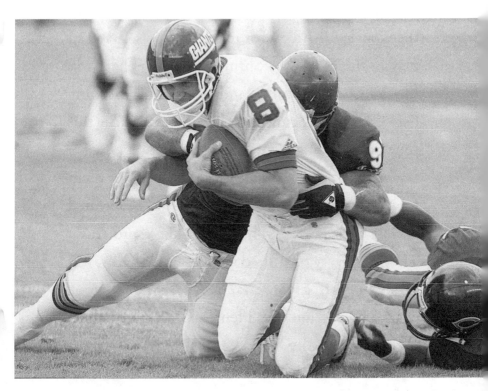

***Ed was picked by the New York Giants in the 1991 NFL draft.
(AP/Wide World Photos)***

CHAPTER FOUR

Giant Steps

With his All-America status, Ed looked to the NFL draft with anticipation. On draft day, he sat in front of the television set, and sat, and sat, and sat.

Finally, after the ESPN cameras had stopped rolling, Ed got a telephone call from New York Giants coach Bill Parcells.

The good news was that Ed had been picked by the defending world champions, who were coming off a Super Bowl victory. Also, their two leading wide receivers had only 26 catches apiece in the

Ed grabbed a pass that led to a touchdown against the Redskins. (AP/Wide World Photos)

previous season. The bad news was that after being told he would be picked as high as the first round, and almost certainly in the second round, Ed was the last pick of the third round.

"I was surprised and disappointed," Ed said. "I was one pick away from dropping to the fourth round. It seemed like an eternity when I was watching the draft on television and my name wasn't picked. Over time, I've learned where you're drafted isn't a predictor of what kind of career you're going to have."

As it turned out, teams shied away most likely because of Ed's average time in the 40-yard dash. But Ed proved wrong the college recruiters who wanted him to play tight end rather than wide receiver, and he would do so once again with pro coaches who doubted him.

"Most teams really make receivers' 40-yard dash times the end-all, be-all," Ed said. "With guys who run great 40-yard dash times, it's almost like being a 7-footer in basketball. They will take you just to see if they can develop you. Fortunately, there are coaches who know football players, and will take a player they think will do well on the field, regardless of his 40-yard dash time."

Ed got another surprise just a few weeks after the draft, as Parcells stepped down as head coach, citing health problems. That elevated Ray Handley to the top job. Ed got a lot of playing time in the preseason because both starting wide receivers—Stephen Baker and Mark Ingram—held out of training camp in contract disputes. That helped Ed earn a spot on the roster and fulfill his dream of playing in the NFL.

"It wasn't until they announced the final cuts that I knew for sure I had made the team," Ed said.

In his first season, Ed finished with 16 receptions for 146 yards as the team's fourth wide receiver. He caught three passes against the Los Angeles Rams on September 8, and three against the Philadelphia Eagles on November 4. His best game came November 24 against the Tampa Bay Buccaneers, when he caught four passes for 35 yards, including two on the Giants' game-winning drive in a 21-14 win.

The numbers weren't much, primarily because the Giants relied mostly on running the ball. On top of that, there remained a lingering quarterback controversy involving starter Phil Simms and backup Jeff Hostetler, who was so effective in the run to the Super Bowl victory in the previous season after Simms was injured. But Ed considered his rookie year a personal success despite the team going a disappointing 8-8.

"I felt good in that of all our rookies, I got the most playing time," Ed said. "I did whatever I could do to contribute, played on special teams. It was a

Ed's wife, Lisa, right, helps decorate "The World's Largest Super Sunday Cake." (AP/Wide World Photos)

learning experience. I considered it a requirement to break into the NFL."

After the season, Ed married Lisa on April 4, 1992, in Miami. Their first son, Maxwell, was born May 17, 1994. Christian followed on June 7, 1996, and the third, Dylan Thomas, came in 1999. By then, Ed's career had taken two major changes of direction, and he had three Super Bowl championship rings.

Ed blossomed into a quality NFL receiver in the 1992 season. He started three games, saw extensive playing time in all 16, and ended up leading the Giants in receiving with 49 catches for 610 yards. He also scored five touchdowns. Ed caught five passes in each of the Giants' first two games, and had then-career highs of six receptions and 105 yards including a 44-yard catch against the Dallas Cowboys on Thanksgiving Day. Unfortunately, Ed's improvement wasn't matched by the Giants, who dropped to 6-10.

"After my second season, I was hoping it would be a stepping stone to better things," Ed said. "I saw a lot of action, got a lot of balls thrown my way. I felt like I knew the offense better. We threw the ball more because we were losing most of the time, and we had to throw."

Two bad years in a row brought a change in coaches, as Handley was replaced by Dan Reeves, the former coach of Ed's future team, the Denver Broncos.

The transition was a difficult one. With Reeves came the signing of free-agent wide receivers Mark Jackson and Mike Sherrard to big contracts. That dropped Ed back to the team's fourth receiver, and his playing time and production during the 1993 season were reduced as a result. He finished with 27 catches for 335 yards and two touchdowns. At least Ed enjoyed the team's success, as the Giants advanced to the playoffs and won a first-round game over Chicago before losing to the San Francisco 49ers.

"It was extremely fun to be a part of that," Ed said. "But I was disappointed because I thought I had a lot more to offer. After that season, I felt I had to work hard, and somehow would have to impress the coaches more in the next training camp."

That opportunity never came—at least not in New York.

Ed played three seasons in New York. (AP/Wide World Photos)

CHAPTER FIVE

Going West Again

As Ed readied for training camp before the start of the 1994 season, he got a phone call that changed the path of his career. It was Reeves calling with some shockingly bad news. Ed was unsigned at the time, but fully expected to report to camp and reach a deal on a new contract. But Reeves told him not to bother, that the Giants no longer wanted his services. He would have to look elsewhere to continue his career.

The Giants had added Omar Douglas, Arthur Marshall and Thomas Lewis to Chris Calloway, Sherrard and Jackson, and Reeves felt Ed wasn't needed. Ed had been cut from the team despite 92 catches, 1,091 yards and seven touchdowns in three seasons.

"I was shocked," Ed said. "Not only did I think I was going to compete for a starting position, but by telling me they already had enough receivers in camp, it was like they didn't even want me to compete for a job. I couldn't understand that at all. I think I got caught in a situation where somebody in that organization didn't want me.

"It really took me by surprise. It was a reality check. If I learned anything from it, it's never to take anything for granted. Be prepared for anything. But it turned out to be the best thing that ever happened to me."

It wasn't until three and one-half years later that Reeves admitted his mistake.

Ironically, Reeves' Atlanta Falcons were the Super Bowl XXXII opponent for Ed's Denver Broncos, and during the week leading up to the game, Reeves took the opportunity to say he was wrong about letting Ed go.

"I don't think I've ever made a mistake that bad," Reeves said. "If a guy is that talented, you ought to be able to see it. I certainly didn't see him as the type of receiver he's turned into. He's worked really hard."

Ed was pleasantly surprised to hear what his former coach had to say.

"No one has to admit something like that," Ed said. "I took that as one of the biggest compliments I've been paid. He didn't have to say anything. It meant a whole lot to me."

***Ed battles a Redskins defender for the ball.
(AP/Wide World Photos)***

But at the time of his release, Ed was devastated. He, Lisa and then-two-month-old son Maxwell had just settled into a bigger apartment, and were thinking they would be with the Giants for a long time. Instead, it was July 18, and Ed was forced to find a new team in a hurry. At least he knew where to look.

The San Francisco 49ers had expressed some interest in Ed when he came out of Stanford, and were looking for another receiver to back up Jerry Rice and John Taylor. It didn't hurt that Ed had been the most productive receiver on the field for the Giants in their playoff-game loss to the 49ers the previous year. Ed signed on with the 49ers, and began what would be an important association with Mike Shanahan, then the 49ers offensive coordinator.

Ed caught only 11 passes during the season, and was just a small part of one of the game's most-

Ed played with the San Francisco 49ers for a short season before ending up with the Broncos. (Joe Robbins)

productive offenses ever assembled. But that was enough to earn a championship ring, as the 49ers went all the way through the playoffs and defeated San Diego in Super Bowl XXIX. Ed caught one pass in the game for five yards.

"I felt that I was lucky to be a part of one Super Bowl-winning team," Ed said. "You dream of getting back to another one, but there are so many things involved that you never know if you will."

Ed's stay in San Francisco didn't last long. Better things awaited at a new stop.

The record-setting success of the 49ers offense during Shanahan's stint as offensive coordinator helped him land the job as head coach of the Broncos just a few days after the 49ers' Super Bowl win. Six weeks later, Ed followed Shanahan to Denver, signing with the Broncos as an unrestricted free agent.

Ed works on drills during practice. (AP/Wide World Photos)

"If there is anything I learned from San Francisco, it was that hard work could pay off," Ed said. "I never was sure what Coach Shanahan thought of me while I was there. I didn't know that he was watching so closely, but I tried so hard. When he went to Denver, I didn't know if he would be calling me or not. I didn't expect him to. When he did, I was thrilled."

Ed finished his first season with the Broncos with 39 catches for 477 yards and two touchdowns. At that point, it was the second most productive season of his career, as he started four games and played in all 16 as the Broncos finished 8-8.

Ed saved his best for last, catching nine passes for 99 yards and a touchdown in a 31-28 victory over the Oakland Raiders in the season finale. His four-yard touchdown catch tied the game with 5:46 remaining in the fourth quarter.

"After spending the year in San Francisco with him, and seeing what kind of person he was, how good his work ethic was, I really thought Ed would have a chance to start in Denver," Shanahan said. "When you see him on an everyday basis, you see that he will do anything he possibly can to make himself better. He takes pride in everything he does, whether it be his pass catching, route technique or blocking. I thought he had a chance to be a great player."

By the 1996 season, Shanahan made Ed a starter once again, this time for good. Ed caught 48 passes for 563 yards and a career-high seven touchdowns during the Broncos' brilliant regular season, which saw them go 13-3 and win the AFC West title. They were beaten only once in their first 13 games, and at one point, won nine games in a row.

Ed's biggest game came against the Baltimore Ravens on October 20. In a 45-34 victory at Mile High Stadium, Ed caught a career-best three touchdown passes, tying a club record. He caught seven passes for 76 yards in all in the game.

There was no more important catch than the one Ed made in the final seconds of a 21-17 victory over the Minnesota Vikings. Elway's pass was tipped three times by Viking defenders, only to fall into Ed's arms as he dove backwards into the endzone for the game-winning touchdown with 19 seconds left. Ed also caught Elway's 250th career touchdown pass, which came against Seattle on December 1.

But the season ended on a bad note for Ed and the Broncos, as they were upset by the Jacksonville Jaguars, 30-27, in a first-round playoff game at Mile High Stadium even though they were heavy favor-

Ed had 477 yards and two touchdowns during his first season in Denver. (AP/Wide World Photos)

ites. Ed caught a touchdown pass with 1:50 remaining in the game, but it wasn't enough.

"That was incredibly disappointing," Ed said. "We felt like we were the best team in football that year. We played against a team that played extremely well, but our team definitely didn't play as well as it had during the regular season. That's the great thing about the playoffs. It doesn't matter how good you are, if you lose one game, you're out. That's what makes it so exciting, and what makes winning so wonderful."

At least the crushing loss would lead to bigger and better things.

Ed pulls in a pass at training camp. (AP/Wide World Photos)

Back in the Winner's Circle

The 1997 season began on a positive note for Ed even before training camp started, as he was rewarded with a four-year contract extension. The deal gave him the security he wanted for his family, which now included a second son, Christian.

By the season's end, Ed would have something else to treasure—a second Super Bowl championship, one that he would play a big part in winning.

***Ed caught 45 passes for 590 yards and eight
touchdowns during the 1997 season. (Joe Robbins)***

The playoff loss to Jacksonville served as a motivator for the Broncos, who picked up where they left off in the previous regular season, and rolled to a 9-1 start behind a high-powered offense that averaged 30 points per game.

"We definitely didn't lack focus going into that season," Ed said. "We didn't take anything for granted. I think losing to Jacksonville was one reason why we really, really appreciated winning the Super Bowl the last two years."

Ed's 1997 regular season was very similar to 1996, as he finished with 45 receptions, 590 yards and eight touchdowns. His first two-touchdown game of the year came in game two against the Seattle Seahawks. Later in the season, he had another two-TD performance against the San Diego Chargers. Some national attention finally came Ed's way when he made a diving catch for a 35-yard gain that started the Broncos on a 38-3 rout

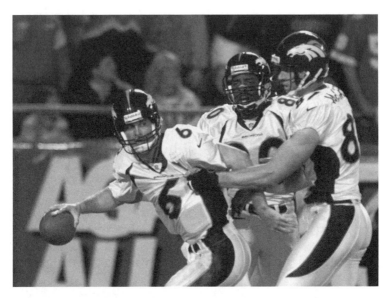

Ed tries to help out a friend in need.
(AP/World World Photos)

of the Oakland Raiders on a Monday Night Football telecast.

"Rod Smith, Shannon Sharpe and myself really started to develop something special that season," Ed said. "We started to gel as a trio. That made playing football a lot of fun. Every week, a different guy would have a great game. We'd go back and forth, and that made it very hard on defenses. We had so many weapons, with Terrell Davis developing into the best running back in football. Defenses would try to take away one receiver, and that would leave one-on-one matches for another receiver."

The Broncos hit a rut late in the regular season, losing three of their final six games to finish 12-4. That left them with only one home playoff game, and forced them to go on the road and win twice to advance to the Super Bowl. But on what

Ed and the Broncos were 14-point underdogs in Super Bowl XXXI. (Joe Robbins)

became known as the "Revenge Tour", the Broncos did just that.

Jacksonville was the first playoff opponent, and there would be no upset this time, as Denver pounded the Jaguars, 42-17, with Ed catching two passes for 35 yards, including a 25-yarder that set up the first touchdown.

"That was one of the most intense games I've played in during my career," Ed said.

Next came arch-rival Kansas City, and Ed caught three passes for 56 yards, including a 42-yard gain that set up Davis' game-winning touchdown in a 14-10 victory. The AFC championship game at Pittsburgh gave the Broncos the opportunity to avenge another regular-season loss, and they did, winning 24-21. Ed had five catches for 37 yards and a touchdown.

"It was tough going on the road, no doubt about it," Ed said. "You're going into stadiums that

Ed caught 11 passes for 190 yards in the 1998 postseason. (AP/Wide World Photos)

are packed with cheering fans going crazy, making it extremely tough on offense. You can barely hear yourself think.

"But we had a lot of confidence. We knew we could beat those teams if we played well. It felt good to be an underdog against Kansas City and Pittsburgh, to tell you the truth. There's no added pressure, like when you're expected to win. Once we got past Kansas City and Pittsburgh, the pressure was off. We knew it would be easier to play in the Super Bowl, where it's a neutral field."

The Broncos headed into Super Bowl XXXI as a decided 14-point underdog to the Green Bay Packers, who were back to defend their title after beating up the New England Patriots the previous year. It would be another opportunity for Elway to win his first Super Bowl after losing three early in his career, and that, along with the Packers' supposed dominance, was the focus of pre-game hype.

Ed makes one of his 10 touchdown catches in 1998. (AP/Wide World Photos)

"Nobody was giving us a chance," Ed said. "That was one of the few times where I was tired of being an underdog because people were blowing the talent difference between the two teams so far out of proportion. We went in knowing we could win. We didn't see why there was a 14-point spread."

When the Packers quickly went ahead 7-0, it appeared as if the "experts" were correct. But the Broncos went right back down the field and scored to tie the game, setting the stage for one of the best and closest Super Bowls in history.

Ed's 36-yard catch was a key play in a 92-yard third-quarter drive that put Denver ahead 24-17, and the Broncos held on to win 31-24, making Ed only one of 30 players at the time who had won Super Bowls with two different teams.

"After winning the Super Bowl with San Francisco, I dreamed about getting back to another one," Ed said. "I didn't know it would happen so quickly."

The game's final play saw Elway take the snap and put his knee on the ground to ice his first Super Bowl win. After Elway's retirement following the 1998 season, Ed still called that moment of glory his favorite Elway memory.

"Playing in that game meant a lot," Ed said. "Everybody wanted to win as badly as John did, but he added another element to so many guys on our team. Rod Smith and I were in the backfield, and John knelt on the ball, and the clock hit zero. To see the emotion on his face was overwhelming. That's a vision that's imbedded in my mind."

There would be more Super Bowl success to come.

CHAPTER SEVEN

Superstar

Super Bowl XXXII was half over, Ed had no catches, and the game was very much in doubt with the Broncos leading 17-6 over the Atlanta Falcons. A sideline reporter asked Shanahan about Ed's lack of production in the first half, and the Broncos' coach responded, "there's a lot of time left."

Sure enough, the Broncos built on their lead in the second half and rolled to an easy 34-19 vic-

Ed, left, heads upfield with the ball after catching a pass in front of Arizona Cardinals quarterback Corey Chavous. (AP/Wide World Photos)

tory for their second consecutive Super Bowl championship, and Ed played a big part in the second half. He caught an 18-yard pass on the very first play after the intermission, another for 14 yards on the Broncos' first drive, and two more before the third quarter ended.

The latter catch gained 15 yards down to the Falcons' five-yard line, and two plays later, Howard Griffith scored a touchdown that gave the Broncos a commanding 24-6 lead. Ed finished with five catches for 72 yards, and barely missed one for a touchdown when he made a diving attempt, only to have the ball squirt out of his hands. It was a minor disappointment in an otherwise dream-come-true day.

The game turned out to be the last one in the career of Elway, who threw for 335 yards, third-most in Super Bowl history, then announced his retirement four months later.

*Ed battles with cornerback Chris Watson during practice.
(AP/Wide World Photos)*

Said Shannon Sharpe: "If Ed McCaffrey was black, I don't think you would hear it mentioned that he is slow. It's a misconception. How many receivers have Anthony Miller-type speed? There aren't many—black, white, red, yellow, green or Chinese."

"I feel very fortunate to have played with arguably the greatest quarterback whoever played the game," Ed said. "He was a true leader on and off the field. He was given a lot of talent, but it was his personality, charisma and dedication to the game that earned him the respect of teammates.

"He was an example to me. Coach Shanahan needed a great quarterback and a leader to convince players from other teams to come and play for the Broncos. Guys came because they thought Coach Shanahan could build a championship team around John Elway."

***Ed went to his first Pro Bowl after the 1998 season.
(AP/Wide World Photos)***

With 64 receptions, 1,053 yards and 10 touch-downs, despite missing one game with a strained hamstring muscle, Ed became a star in his own right during the 1998 season. And the longer the Broncos went unbeaten through the regular season—they went 13 games without a loss—the more the rest of the NFL grew to respect Ed's abilities. No longer was he standing out for his size, but for his productivity.

"I feel like I've worked as hard as I possibly could for as long as I can remember to be the best possible football player I could be," Ed said. "I've also learned over the years what it means to eat right, how to work out right, how to get faster, how to get stronger, how to study film, how to run better routes, how to catch the ball better.

"As you get older, you learn and you grow, and you become a better player. It's a slow, steady pro-

Ed holds up the ball after making a touchdown catch.
(AP/Wide World Photos)

cess. But I always felt that I needed somebody to believe in me and put me on the field and give me an opportunity to play. Coach Shanahan gave me that opportunity.

"I've never been slow, and I'm not slow now. My speed is comparable to most of the starting receivers in the league. But when you're big, you don't look that fast. It took this year to really erase that impression in people's minds."

Said Sharpe: "If Ed McCaffrey was black, I don't think you would hear it mentioned that he is slow. It's a misconception. How many receivers have Anthony Miller-type speed? There aren't many—black, white, red, yellow, green or Chinese."

Spread throughout the season were big catches from Ed at key moments. In a victory over division rival Kansas City, his 47-yard reception led to a touchdown that gave the Broncos a fourth-quarter comeback win. It was the longest play of a very defensive-oriented game, a mix-up in the Chiefs secondary let Ed get all the way to the one-yard line. In a crushing 31-3 victory over the Oakland Raiders on November 20, Ed made a spectacular catch for a 35-yard gain that led to the Broncos' first touchdown.

Ed also played a big part in the AFC Championship Game victory over the New York Jets. The Broncos found themselves trailing 10-0 in the third quarter in Mile High Stadium, and in need of a big play to get back in the game. And it was Ed who provided it, but not without a bit of confusion.

On the first play of the Broncos' drive following a Jets' touchdown, Ed and the other wide receiver, Rod Smith, both lined up on the wrong side of the formation.

But before the play started, Elway told Ed to run a post pattern, and it worked for a 47-yard gain that put the Broncos on the Jets 17-yard line. Two plays later, Howard Griffith caught an 11-yard touchdown pass, starting the Broncos on a 20-point run that led to a 23-10 victory.

Following the Super Bowl victory, another honor arose for Ed, as he played in his first Pro Bowl. Ed was elected as a starter, along with Jimmy Smith of Jacksonville, beating out New York's Keyshawn Johnson and Buffalo's Eric Moulds.

"I dreamed of playing in the NFL, I dreamed of playing on a championship team, but I had given up on dreaming about going to the Pro Bowl," Ed said. "That was another thrill, especially because the players and opposing coaches—the guys you go against every week—get to vote on that. That meant a whole lot to me. Finally, I had earned some respect around the league. It's a great feeling when you've worked as hard as you could for so many years."

Said Shanahan: "I'm not surprised Ed has become a Pro Bowl player. In fact, knowing what I do about him, and what kind of work ethic he has, I would be surprised if he didn't become a Pro Bowl player.

"Everybody stereotypes people with talent. But 12 of the 22 starters on our team were either cut or released by other teams, or not drafted. People think if you don't get drafted in the first four rounds, your chances of sticking in the NFL are slim and none. That shows you people don't know heart and drive, and what makes a person go. One of the reasons Ed is the type of player that he is the type of heart that he has."

Pitch Man

The lanky wide receiver found himself in a predicament. Or to be more specific, a locker. Locked inside a locker by his offensive line teammates, who were angry that he didn't bring them McDonald's hamburgers, just as he had done for his quarterback. He pleaded for his release, promising to deliver food to the linemen as well.

All part of a clever and popular television advertising campaign Ed starred in during the Bron-

Appearing on the Jay Leno Show with teammate Bill Romanowski was one of Ed's extracurricular activities. (AP/Wide World Photos)

cos' first run to a Super Bowl championship in 1997. The only problem was that Ed's son Maxwell, then two years old, thought his father actually was stuck in the locker until he was told otherwise. Other than that, Ed's rise to stardom in the advertising world was much quicker than his long climb up the ladder on the football field.

In the first of the two McDonald's commercials, Ed had pitched a two-for-one sale, and wondered aloud that if he gave the second sandwiches to his quarterback, maybe he would get more passes thrown his way, which in turn would make Ed famous as well. "Probably not," was Ed's last line in the commercial. But in fact, he has become one of the most popular and visible players on a team that has won back-to-back Super Bowl titles.

When it came to recommending Ed for the McDonald's commercial, it was an easy call for Broncos media relations director Jim Saccomano.

***Ed stretches before a practice in Denver.
(AP/Wide World Photos)***

"He's a terrific guy who is the quintessential hard-worker type. He's a role model, and a family man. What company doesn't want to identify with that?" Saccomanno said. "In a lot of ways, he's every-man. We all like that persona. We like it when success comes to someone who's a nice guy and works hard."

Ed's product pitching took off during the 1998 season. A connection with a company called Public Label Brands led to Ed's name and picture on mustard jars, horseradish bottles and cereal boxes. Ed's Rocky Mountain Mustard is available in two flavors, spicy and creamy dijon, with a jalapeno flavor in the works. The most successful product has been the cereal, Ed's Endzone O's.

"I never thought my picture would be on a mustard bottle or a cereal box," he said. "I never would have imagined something like that if they didn't come to me with the idea. It's been really fun."

Ed scores a touchdown in the first quarter on a pass from quarterback Brian Griese. (AP/Wide World Photos)

Typical of his popularity, Ed also was elected as the 1998 Sprint Broncos Man Of The Year, which goes to players on each team for outstanding community involvement. Ed, along with teammates Terrell Davis, Vaughn Hebron and Howard Griffith, also were part of a television commercial for the NFL's "Feel The Power" campaign, which centered on players thanking fans for their support. Ed was more than happy to do so.

"Honestly, if you would have asked me five years ago if any of this stuff would have happened, I would have laughed at you," Ed said. "It's an amazing story. I was just fighting to stay in the NFL. Then I play on three Super Bowl champions. It's been a whirlwind. I don't want it to end. I'm in a unique position to influence kids in the community. It's not just an obligation. I consider it an opportunity. It's very rewarding to give something back."

Among Ed's charity involvements are the Ronald McDonald House, the Colorado Coalition For The Homeless, and A Grass Roots Experience. Next season, Ed will be the Broncos' spokesman for The United Way. After signing a seven-year contract extension in July, he hopes to stay in Denver and with the Broncos for the rest of his career.

"The Denver Broncos are a professional organization from top to bottom," Ed said. "From the owner, Pat Bowlen, to Mike Shanahan, everybody is dedicated to winning. They do it right. Everything is first-class. They will have to send me somewhere else, because I don't plan on going anywhere."

Ed McCaffrey Quick Facts

Full Name: Edward McCaffrey

Team: Denver Broncos

Position: Wide Receiver

Number: 87

Height, weight: 6-5, 215

Birthdate: August 17, 1968

Hometown: Waynesboro, Pennsylvania

Years in the league: 8

Acquired: Free agent from San Francisco

Drafted: Third round (83rd overall)

College: Stanford University

1998 Highlight: In Super Bowl XXXIII against Atlanta, McCaffrey caught five passes for 72 yards, all in the second half of the game.

Statistical highlight: In 1998, McCaffrey was selected for his first Pro Bowl.

Little-known fact: McCaffrey's brother, Billy, was an All-American at Vanderbilt at guard after being a member of Duke's NCAA championship basketball team in 1991.

Ed McCaffrey
Statistics

Career Receiving and Rushing

Year	Team	Rec.	Rec. Yds.	Rec. Avg.	TD
1991	NY Giants	16	146	9.1	0
1992	NY Giants	49	610	12.4	5
1993	NY Giants	27	335	12.4	2
1994	San Francisco	11	131	11.9	2
1995	Denver	39	477	12.2	2
1996	Denver	48	553	11.5	7
1997	Denver	45	590	13.1	8
1998	Denver	64	1,053	16.5	10
1999	Denver	26	396	15.2	6
Totals		**325**	**4,291**	**13.2**	**42**
Playoff Totals		**45**	**669**	**14.9**	**2**

Career Scoring

Year	Team	Rec. TD	Point
1991	NY Giants	0	0
1992	NY Giants	5	30
1993	NY Giants	2	12
1994	San Francisco	2	12
1995	Denver	2	14
1996	Denver	7	42
1997	Denver	8	48
1998	Denver	10	62
1999	Denver	6	36
Totals		**42**	**256**
Playoff Totals		**2**	**12**

1996 Game-by-Game Receiving

Date	Opp.	Rec.	Yds.	Avg.	TD
9/01/96	NYJets	4	61	15.3	1
9/08/96	@Sea	3	26	8.7	0
9/15/96	TB	2	21	10.5	0
9/29/96	@Cin	5	80	16.0	0
10/06/96	SD	5	58	11.6	1
10/20/96	Bal	7	76	10.9	3
10/27/96	KC	1	10	10.0	0
11/17/96	@NE	2	24	12.0	0
11/24/96	@Min	6	83	13.8	1
12/01/96	Sea	5	43	8.6	1
12/08/96	@GB	3	41	13.7	0
12/15/96	Oak	3	20	6.7	0
12/22/96	@SD	2	10	5.0	0
Totals		**48**	**553**	**11.5**	**7**

1997 Game-by-Game Receiving

Date	Opp.	Rec.	Yds.	Avg.	TD
8/31/97	KC	2	37	18.5	0
9/07/97	@Sea	8	93	11.6	2
9/14/97	StL	1	23	23.0	1
9/21/97	Cin	4	62	15.5	1
9/28/97	@Atl	4	48	12.0	0
10/06/97	NE	3	26	8.7	0
10/19/97	@Oak	3	61	20.3	1
10/26/97	@Buf	1	17	17.0	0
11/02/97	Sea	1	8	8.0	0
11/16/97	@KC	2	16	8.0	0
11/24/97	Oak	4	51	12.8	0
11/30/97	@SD	7	111	15.9	2
12/15/97	@SF	1	5	5.0	0
12/21/97	SD	4	32	8.0	1
Totals		**45**	**590**	**13.1**	**8**

1998 Game-by-Game Receiving

Date	Opp.	Rec.	Yds.	Avg.	TD
9/07/98	NE	7	97	13.9	0
9/13/98	Dal	5	117	23.4	0
9/20/98	@Oak	5	44	8.8	2
9/27/98	@Was	4	74	18.5	1
10/04/98	Phi	2	60	30.0	1
10/11/98	@Sea	1	5	5.0	0
10/25/98	Jac	3	92	30.7	1
11/01/98	@Cin	7	133	19.0	1
11/08/98	SD	9	133	14.8	1
11/16/98	@KC	1	19	19.0	0
11/29/98	@SD	5	74	14.8	2
12/06/98	KC	6	103	17.2	1
12/13/98	@NYGiants	3	24	8.0	0
12/21/98	@Mia	3	42	14.0	0
12/27/98	Sea	3	36	12.0	0
Totals		**64**	**1,053**	**16.5**	**10**

Pro Career Highlights

• The ninth-year pro signed with Denver as an unrestricted free agent in 1995.

• McCaffrey has played in 125 games (53 starts) over his eight-year career, catching 299 passes for 3,895 yards and 36 touchdowns.

• He has also played in 13 postseason games (eight starts) and caught 34 passes for 479 yards, winning World Championships with the Broncos (1997 and 1998) and 49ers (1994).

•McCaffrey is one of just 30 players in NFL history to win a Super Bowl with two different teams, and one of only 13 to win one in each conference

• He entered the NFL in 1991 as a fourth-round draft choice of the New York Giants (No. 83 overall) out of Stanford.

1998

•McCaffrey was selected to start in the Pro Bowl for the first time in his eight-year career.

•Named second-team All-NFL by the Associated Press and All-AFC by Football News.

•Started at wide receiver in 15 of the 16 games and enjoyed the finest statistical season of his career in all four receiving categories.

•McCaffrey tied for the AFC lead in receiving TDs (T6th NFL), tied for sixth in total TDs, ranked sixth in the AFC in receiving yards and tied for 15th in receptions, while his yards-per-catch avg. of 16.5 ranked sixth in the AFC (11th NFL).

1997

• McCaffrey started 15 of the 16 games at wide receiver and ranked fourth on the team in receptions, with 45 for 590 yards (13.1), a long of 35 yards and a career-best eight touchdowns, tied for fifth-most receiving touchdowns in the AFC.

• His first big performance of the 1997 season came at Seattle (9/7) in Week Two when he was matched up with rookie CB Shawn Springs and produced one of the biggest days of his career, catching eight passes for 93 yards and two touchdowns in Denver's 35-14 victory.

• In Super Bowl XXXII against Green Bay, McCaffrey caught two passes for a team-high 45 yards, including a 36-yarder in the third quarter on Denver's 13-play, 92-yard drive (the longest of the game) that put them ahead 24-17.

1996

• McCaffrey started 15 of the 16 regular season games at wide receiver opposite Anthony Miller and caught 48 passes for 553 yards (11.5) with a long of 39 yards and a career-high seven touchdowns

•McCaffrey established a career high and tied a Broncos franchise record with three touchdown receptions against Baltimore (10/20).

1995

•McCaffrey played in all 16 games and made four starts.

•He had, at the time, the second-most productive season of his career, catching 39 passes for 477 yards (12.2), with a long of 35 yards and two touchdowns.

•McCaffrey was acquired by the Broncos as an unrestricted free agent from the San Francisco 49ers on March 7.

Baseball Superstar Series Titles
Collect Them All!

___ Mark McGwire: Mac Attack!

___ #1 *Derek Jeter: The Yankee Kid*

___ #2 *Ken Griffey Jr.: The Home Run Kid*

___ #3 *Randy Johnson: Arizona Heat!*

___ #4 *Sammy Sosa: Slammin' Sammy*

___ #5 *Bernie Williams: Quiet Superstar*

___ #6 *Omar Vizquel: The Man with the Golden Glove*

___ #7 *Mo Vaughn: Angel on a Mission*

___ #8 *Pedro Martinez: Throwing Strikes*

___ #9 *Juan Gonzalez: Juan Gone!*

___ #10 *Tony Gwynn: Mr. Padre*

___ #11 *Kevin Brown: Kevin with a "K"*

___ #12 *Mike Piazza: Mike and the Mets*

___ #13 *Larry Walker: Canadian Rocky*

___ #14 *Nomar Garciaparra: High 5!*

___ #15 *Sandy and Roberto Alomar: Baseball Brothers*

___ #16 *Mark Grace: Winning with Grace*

___ #17 *Curt Schilling: Phillie Phire!*

___ #18 *Alex Rodriguez: A+ Shortstop*

___ #19 *Roger Clemens: Rocket!*

Only $4.95 per book!

ootball Superstar Series Titles
Collect Them All!

____ #1 *Ed McCaffrey: Catching a Star*

____ #3 *Peyton Manning: Passing Legacy*

____ #4 *Jake Plummer: Comeback Cardinal*

____ #5 *Mark Brunell: Super Southpaw*

____ #6 *Drew Bledsoe: Patriot Rifle*

____ #7 *Junior Seau: Overcoming the Odds*

____ #8 *Marshall Faulk: Rushing to Glory*

Only $4.95 per book!

Call Toll Free: 1-877-424-BOOK (2665) or visit us at www.sportspublishinginc.com

Basketball Superstar Series Titles
Collect Them All!

____ #1 *Kobe Bryant: The Hollywood Kid*

____ #2 *Keith Van Horn: Nothing But Net*

____ #3 *Antoine Walker: Kentucky Celtic*

____ #4 *Kevin Garnett: Scratching the Surface*

____ #5 *Tim Duncan: Slam Duncan*

____ #6 *Reggie Miller: From Downtown*

____ #7 *Jason Kidd: Rising Sun*

____ #8 *Vince Carter: Air Canada*

Only $4.95 per book!

Hockey Superstar Series Titles
Collect Them All!

____ #1 *John LeClair: Flying High*

____ #2 *Mike Richter: Gotham Goalie*

____ #3 *Paul Kariya: Maine Man*

____ #4 *Dominik Hasek: The Dominator*

____ #5 *Jaromir Jagr: Czechmate*

____ #6 *Martin Brodeur: Picture Perfect*

____ #8 *Ray Bourque: Bruins Legend*

Only $4.95 per book!